HUMMINGBIRDS
BETWEEN THE PAGES

21ST CENTURY ESSAYS

David Lazar and Patrick Madden, Series Editors

# HUMMINGBIRDS
# BETWEEN
# THE PAGES

*Chris Arthur*

MAD CREEK BOOKS, AN IMPRINT OF
THE OHIO STATE UNIVERSITY PRESS
COLUMBUS

Library of Congress Cataloging-in-Publication Data
Names: Arthur, C. J. (Christopher John), 1955– author.
Title: Hummingbirds between the pages / Chris Arthur.
Other titles: 21st century essays.
Description: Columbus : Mad Creek Books, an imprint of The Ohio State
     University Press, [2018] | Series: 21st century essays
Identifiers: LCCN 2018006471 | ISBN 9780814254844 (pbk. ; alk. paper)
     | ISBN 0814254845 (pbk. ; alk. paper)
Subjects: LCSH: English essays—Irish authors.
Classification: LCC PN6142 .A77 2018 | DDC 824/.914—dc23
LC record available at https://lccn.loc.gov/2018006471

Cover design by Nathan Putens
Text design by Juliet Williams and Deb Jul
Type set in Adobe Sabon LT Std

# CONTENTS

# INTRODUCTION

he first time I encountered hummingbirds I was eight years old. They entranced me so completely that I still remember them now, vividly, half a century later. It happened in London, not a place usually associated with these little tropical beauties. My visit to the UK's capital was daunting, verging on the overwhelming. It was the first time I'd been out of Ulster. The density of people, the city's endless streets of bustling humanity, the perpetual streams of traffic, roads and buildings clogging every view and stretching to the horizon—London blotted out the possibility of fields or forests; it even seemed to shrink the sky. The sheer size of the place came as a shock after the small scale I was used to from growing up in County Antrim.

The hummingbirds punctuated a rare moment of tranquility in that jarring week of rushing between famous sights, jostled everywhere by crowds. We were visiting London Zoo. A door in one of the aviaries led into what seemed like an indoor garden—a glasshouse planted out with exotic ferns and flowers. It was hot enough to suggest a jungle. At first it was just the temperature, humidity, and lushness of the vegetation that struck me. I was expecting more cages and when I saw none wondered if we'd inadvertently strayed out of the animal part of the zoo into some purely botanical display. Then, with a whispered whir of brilliant wings, a hummingbird flew so close to me it made me start. Soon another followed it and, to my delighted amazement, I realized we were in an area in which lots of hummingbirds were flying free. They hovered at nectar feeders and then shot away again, only to flit back moments later. By incredible good fortune we'd coincided with a quiet time. Despite the crowds of visitors thronging the zoo, it was only me, my brother, and our parents in that enchanted green oasis—the four of us alone with scores of iridescent hummingbirds. The place felt like a sanctum veined with streaks of resplendent flight that fractured our accustomed measures of motion and color, suggesting a radically redrawn scale. It went so far beyond what we were used to that it shimmered with the promise of numinous impossibilities.

After witnessing the constraints of creatures held in dismally cramped imprisonment, the freedom of this place was magical. The hummingbirds could fly all around us—into us, if they so desired—there were no barriers between people and birds. They were enclosed, of course—but their tininess, the space afforded by the glasshouse, and the fact that we were free to walk among them without constraint, to be in their cage-that-didn't-seem-a-cage, right beside them, gave an air of immediacy that was breathtaking.

I've always been interested in birds. But at eight years old my avian reference range was modest and parochial, defined by robins, sparrows, starlings, thrushes, blackbirds—Ireland's common species that we saw often in our suburban garden. To be suddenly surrounded by these exquisite rarities, to be close enough to observe in detail the astonishing grace and energy implicit in their every movement, to see the fantastic richness of their plumage, was a kind of epiphany. I was spellbound. I stood stock still and let their unexpected presence claim me. Not surprisingly, that moment pressed its weight of passing on my mind with sufficient force to forge a lasting memory. In fact, what I remember most from that first visit to London isn't Madame Tussauds, or the Changing of the Guard at Buckingham Palace, or Big Ben and the Houses of Parliament, or the Crown Jewels, or any of the other famous sights, but being surrounded—and left awed— by hummingbirds.

⚘

Years later, I happened to be reading Annie Dillard's *An American Childhood* and was profoundly struck when she described how settlers in Pennsylvania in the eighteenth century pressed hummingbirds, as if they were flowers, between the pages of heavy books and then enclosed them in letters to friends and family back home in Ulster or Scotland. In part, of course, it was simply Dillard's mention of Ulster that caught my eye. As someone born and brought up there, I know that Ulster is often seen by outsiders as dour and hard; a cheerless place lacking in warmth, or vibrancy, or color. I'd not endorse that stereotype, but at the same time I can well imagine how a hummingbird might strike an emigrant; why they'd want to send home tangible proof of the new world that they'd come to and the marvels it contained. The stunning iridescence of these birds, their rich arrays of sumptuous color, their unlikely littleness, the intricate perfection of their flight—it's easy to see how those who'd grown up with sparrows might take them as splinters of a miracle; fragments of another world irrupting into this one—tokens of something wonderful.

Pressing hummingbirds struck me as at once grotesque and entirely understandable. I readily sympathized with those Pennsylvanian settlers. Newly arrived in a foreign place and encountering things they'd never dreamt of, what could be more natural than wanting to send irrefutable evidence of their revelations to those who might disbelieve them?

And of course Dillard's vignette immediately called back to mind my first visit to London. I knew that my eight-year-old self would have seized any opportunity to take away some memento of those treasured moments in a glasshouse filled with such astonishing bounty.

_🌿_

Essentially, the pages that follow are about hummingbirds—not the literal feathered morsels that can be pressed like flowers in heavy books, but their metaphorical equivalents. These may not be iridescent, or chromatically sublime, they may not move with the graceful perfection of real hummingbirds, but all of them have stopped me in my tracks, glinting with the suggestion of meanings beyond the commonplace; they've left me as spellbound and wondering before them as my eight-year-old self was before those little feathered gems.

Some of my metaphorical hummingbirds are far too heavy ever to take flight—a railway crosstie, for example, or a bronze statuette of the Buddha. Some are abstract and invisible—time, death, and memory. Some hide in unlikely objects—seashells, an ugly clock, old photographs. Some are disguised as other birds—woodpigeons or blue tits, for example—or as other creatures altogether—butterflies and foxes. But all of them are hummingbird-like in the way they offer unexpected challenges to the mundane scales by which we measure things; they suggest new calibrations in terms of meaning, connection, and significance as surely as the London hummingbirds suggested a different scale for color. Like pressing hummingbirds, what I've written tries to catch and preserve and (via publication) mail far beyond Ulster some of the things that have flown through my days and left me feeling that I'm standing on the frontier of the ordinary being given glimpses of the extraordinary dimensions it contains. It's as if doors have been opened into a secret, unexpected glasshouse hidden in plain sight whose denizens mock our usual categories and confinements.

⟡

It's risky, I know, to use something as exquisite as a hummingbird as a point of comparison by which to explain the nature of a book. Beside them, words look heavy, clumsy, colorless. Instead of the intricate perfection of form and motion that's so evident in these aerodynamic jewels, sentences seem lumbering; even the most poetic of them can appear as plodding parodies of a hummingbird's poise and grace. Like pressing, writing can reduce things to a faded husk, something emptied of its life and beauty and smacking of the mortuary. I hope my words avoid this, but I certainly don't want to suggest that they possess the brilliancy of color or artistry of flight that real hummingbirds so effortlessly display; it's simply that the keepsakes I've pressed into form in words and assembled here are things that caught my attention as compellingly as those free-flying birds did on my first visit to London. Also, color and iridescence apart, in terms of their small scale, and the way in which they move—forwards, backwards, hovering, meandering, moving from one thing to another and then back again—hummingbirds offer a pleasing totem for writing that likes to dart and wander, rather than following some ruled line that's straight as the proverbial crow's flight.

Dillard's description of mailing pressed hummingbirds back to Ulster didn't make the impression that it did solely because it mentioned my homeland and reminded me of my London hummingbirds. As well as being an Ulsterman I'm an essayist, and what those eighteenth century Pennsylvanian settlers did struck a potent chord with what I'm attempting in my essays. Like them, I want to place between the pages of books things I find eye-catching; like pressing, writing tries to preserve in a communicable form things that seem sufficiently arresting to want to bring to the attention of others.

To admit to being an essayist is even riskier than comparing writing to something as beautiful as a hummingbird. Conventional publishing wisdom advises authors to avoid the term "essay." There's a preference for "creative nonfiction," "memoir," even "meditation"—anything that avoids the dreaded "e" word. Readers prefer—or are perceived by publishers to prefer—a book that consists of serial chapters, not freestanding essays. They want something that obeys the niceties of predictable progression, moving from beginning, to middle, to end, with everything neatly linked together, introduced, resolved, and concluded. But I'm reminded of the sentiment expressed by the nameless protagonist in the opening paragraph of Flann O'Brien's *At Swim-Two-Birds*:

> One beginning and one ending for a book was a thing I did not agree with. A good book may have three openings entirely dissimilar and interrelated only in the prescience of the author, or for that matter one hundred times as many endings.

I've arranged *Hummingbirds Between the Pages* so that, to my mind, its contents sit easily together. But there's no singular beginning of the kind that O'Brien's hero condemns. There's no compelling reason for readers to start at the first page and read consecutively to the final one. Each of the book's constituent essays is independently intelligible and can be considered on its own and in any order—though I like to think that, assembled together, the essays gather cumulative momentum, draw strength from one another, that their proximity sets off echoes and resonances, that their voices, speaking together, companionably reiterate and reinforce common concerns, and offer sets of creative variations on the themes addressed.

In an essay about essays, provocatively entitled "In Defense of Incoherence," E. J. Levy writes that "the form doesn't lend itself to mass market sales." But, she says, "that is precisely its charm and our pleasure in reading it." In her view, part of the appeal of this ancient but now ill-served genre lies in the fact that it provides a "respite from the clamor of commerce." In putting together collections, she urges essayists to resist the temptation of presenting their work in a way that obscures the individual independence of each piece, or gives the impression that essays can be subsumed beneath some organizing principle that pretends there's an overarching structure within which they unfold quite logically, one by one, following the expectations of linearity. "The first impulse that brought us to the essay form," Levy reminds us, is art. And art is "not about the market or clever formal conceits, or even publication, but about wonder."

I hope my hummingbirds will not be read as an attempt to foist on the inevitable plurality of a collection an organizing principle that tries to force them into neat singularity, following a step-by-step progression. This is something essays just don't do. I reached for hummingbirds instinctively, simply because my experience of them—like my experience of writing essays—is rooted in wonder.

DARWIN'S FOX

*W*hen I was growing up in Ireland, magpies had an evil reputation. In contrast to our liking for robins, blackbirds, thrushes, and other common birds, magpies were reviled. They were considered rogues, condemned as the criminal element of the avian world. Accordingly, despite their handsome plumage, any that trespassed in our garden were quickly shooed away. The bad press they received stemmed in part from their readiness to raid the nests of smaller birds, in part from their compulsive thieving. Said to be attracted to shiny objects, in the same way that moths are helplessly drawn to a light, stories abounded of magpies hoarding trinkets in their nests and of their flying off with rings and coins and cufflinks left by the unwary too close to open windows. Perhaps an element of our dislike was also rooted in pure superstition. We all knew the old rhyme:

> One for sorrow, two for joy, three for a girl, four for a
> boy, five for silver, six for gold, seven for a secret never to
> be told.

However unfounded the link may be between numbers of magpies and outcomes in human experience, the rhyme suggests they've long been regarded as birds of portent—if not, since sightings of single birds are commonest, of outright evil omen.

I've certainly seen magpies raiding nests and feeding on the eggs or chicks they've snatched from there. But their reputed stealing and hoarding of shiny objects isn't something I've witnessed myself. When I was a boy, the only magpie nest I climbed to, high in a thorn tree and hard to reach, was a disappointment. I was hoping for a clutch of eggs and a trove of rings and coins and other treasures. But the nest, a beautifully made structure with a protective roof of twigs and a deep cup delicately smoothed and cushioned, was completely empty. Arrayed against the innocence suggested by this one nest free of booty, there are sufficient reports of guilt to have embedded the magpie's thievery into the verbal fabric of its name. The figurative meaning of "magpie," according to the dictionary, is "one who hoards or steals trifles."

I still recall an uncle's view of one of my contemporaries at school, a boy given to airs and graces about the extent of his learning. My uncle, a seriously well-read individual, dismissed him as having no more that "a magpie intellect." By this he meant a mind of no real depth and of dubious integrity; a quick but untrustworthy intelligence puffed up with its own importance, unable to resist the lure of anything that glittered, and willing to pass off as his own, ideas filched from others. That slighting label struck me at the time—as no doubt it was meant to—as something scalpel-sharp in the way it cut down to size the pretensions of a pompous schoolboy who was tiresomely deluded about how much he knew. My uncle saw him as someone who strutted and pecked his way across a handful of books, a fast but superficial reader who picked out what was obvious and dressed it up as if it was profound. He sought to dazzle others with a few glitzy baubles disguised as gold mined from deeper strata than he'd ever ventured to.

"A magpie intellect," said in my uncle's dismissive tones, is a phrase I've carried with me for decades. Until recently, it has acted as a kind of cautionary marker, a stake hammered into the boundaries of serious inquiry, warning that beyond lie quicksands—the realm of the showoff's shallow pick-and-mix mentality that my uncle so despised. Now I'm not so sure. I've come to suspect that all our knowledge, however specialized and weighty it may appear, has about it something of the magpie's bauble. Certainly when it comes to the way in which I read, I know what sticks in mind is often just whatever gleams with sufficient luster to excite my interest, or pique my curiosity, rather than because it's possessed of any great intrinsic import. I follow the glint and sparkle of what appeals as much as any magpie, even if I pay lip service to the discipline of a more systematic, step-by-step approach.

That's all by way of preface or prolegomenon, a magpie apology to introduce and excuse the bauble that I want to share. It's something that caught the light when I was reading Charles Darwin's account of the voyage of the *Beagle*. Its five sentences glittered with all the potency of a lure. As soon as I came to them the magpie in my mind's eye was captivated. It swooped and carried them off to add to the little cache of oddments hoarded in the untidy nest of memory.

Here's what Darwin wrote:

6th December 1834: In the evening we reached the island of San Pedro, where we found the *Beagle* at anchor. In doubling the point, two of the officers landed to take a round of angles with the theodolite. A fox (*Canis fulvipes*) of a kind said to be peculiar to the island and very rare in it, and which is a new species, was sitting on the rocks. He was so intently absorbed in watching the work of the officers that I was able, by quietly walking up behind, to knock him on the head with my geological hammer. This fox, more curious or more scientific, but less wise than the generality of his brethren, is now mounted in the museum of the Zoological Society.

Why did this passage catch my magpie-eye? What quality made it glitter so enticingly? Why did it seem like something to take away from the rest of Darwin's text, something to hoard separately so that it could be repeatedly reexamined? Was it simply the vividness of the violence, or its sheer unexpectedness—the shock of seeing a geological hammer wielded to lethal effect? Or was it that my picture of Darwin received such a blow that it left me reeling—the staid, scholarly naturalist that I'd always imagined from seeing photographs of Darwin in his later years suddenly revealed as an opportunistic killer? Perhaps such factors played a part, but I think what gave this little incident its irresistible allure, what made it beckon like a kind of talisman, is at once more interesting and harder to describe.

⚘

Some incidents—and Darwin's killing of the fox is one of them—seem to carry more than just the weight of their own unfolding. It's as if, within their straightforward occurrence, there's another stratum of significance. The raw elements of what happens point to something else. To me, Darwin and the fox hint at a far greater drama than the simple scene played out on San Pedro Island. That scene stands proxy for, is emblematic of, something on a far larger scale. What Darwin wrote about killing the fox with his geological hammer caught my magpie-eye not so much because of this incident's intrinsic violence, or its unexpectedness, but because it seemed imbued with clues about the wider nature of existence. It shone with the allure of something marked with a kind of secret tattoo whose intricate whorls trace around and make more visible the contours that determine the topography of our lives. It's not as if Darwin and his fox teach me anything new about the world, revealing aspects of existence I've never seen before. It's more that they make clear something I already know but which I often lose sight of nonetheless; they emphasize truths that, for all their obviousness, are easily forgotten.

Like everyone, I'm held in a complex web of circumstances, an intricate grid of interlocking causes and effects. An enormous network of interdependencies is woven around each of us, around every moment. If we stop to examine even the most mundane of our days, we'll find that they spiral back into a dense mesh of antecedent factors and forward into futures veined with a profusion of outcomes. Any moment offers a portal into the tapestry of time and chance and consequence. And yet we often plot our whereabouts according to cartographies of such commonplace, constrained projection that it's hard to grasp the scale of things, or recognize the interplay of choice and contingency, or see the intricacy of connection out of which history is woven. In their brief encounter, Darwin and his fox seem to burnish one minute link, a single stitch in the fabric of space-time. The incident possesses a kind of incandescence. Its glow illuminates not just the thread of its own happening but something of what's embroidered all around it, out of which it has emerged. It casts light on the intricate delicacy of the interconnections that run between things and generate the fine detail of what happens. How could I resist so bright a fragment, made lambent with its repertoire of meanings?

It's hard to decide if what happens, the way our lives unfold, is something locked into the iron of causal imperatives whose rule is absolute, or decided on the whim of chance and accident. Consider, on the one hand, how unlikely it was for a fox on a Chilean island to be slain by a blow to the head with a geological hammer wielded by a naturalist from England. How slight the probability seems of Darwin being in that exact spot at that exact time, coincident with the presence of this rare creature, and being able to surprise it. Think of the centuries—the eons—that lie behind each player in this fatal encounter. The backstory leading to the moment of their interaction is rooted in—is part of—a saga of fantastic duration and complexity.

In order to result in Darwin and this particular fox, numerous ancestors had to fall into a certain pattern, pair by pair, juggling through each generation the life-force of their species. Within the crucible of loins were bred countless babies, countless fox cubs, each one sucking on its mother's teats, each one growing into adulthood to mate and breed and die, the species-seed passed on, until eventually it issued in one fox and one man meeting at one moment in one place on San Pedro Island.

Think of the symphonies of cells—and of the atoms within them—that had to be conducted over thousands of years through all the creatures, human and pre-human, fox and pre-fox, which make up the music of this astonishing life-score. Think of the circumstances that had to interlock to guide so many factors into place, so that this was the music that was sounded, played out in the precise tonal quality of the actual—rather than some variation on the theme, or some different music altogether in which the minuscule trill of Darwin and the fox would be absent.

If a seabird had faltered from exhaustion, attracting the fox to easy prey; if Darwin had taken a different route as he explored the island; if a storm had made it impossible to land; if the *Beagle*'s crew had been laid low with dysentery; if he'd sneezed as he swung his geological hammer, this moment would never have happened. And it's not as if its happening was dependent solely on a chain of circumstances running through one day. Rather, December 6, 1834—like any day—was part of an unfurling that stretches back to the beginning of time itself, any part of which, if altered, might have led to other outcomes crystallizing into actuality instead of Darwin's dispatching of the fox.

But, on the other hand, think of how each circumstance in the chains of events that locked fox and Darwin into place, mooring their encounter firmly to the quayside of what happened, was obedient to a multitude of laws—laws that cut through randomness with the promise of predictability, making choice and chance seem more like unavoidable consequences than anything approaching the haphazardness of free will or accident. Viewed thus, the music of the way things are seems more to follow the only score there is, rather than being a set of riffs or variations drawn out of countless possibilities.

꙰

For reasons I don't fully understand, what Darwin says about killing the fox goes further than simply recording his slaying of this unfortunate creature. His account points to the colossal shifting network of causes and effects from whose interactions the material of what passes is made up. That in itself attracts me to it. But the incident is given further luster by the way it shimmers with the aura of what might so easily not have been. Its proximity to never having happened, the ease with which things might have played out differently, seems ingrained in it; it's as if it's colored with whatever hue contingency comes painted in. The slimness of the chance of its occurrence bestows upon it a kind of electricity, an added voltage. It's as if the hoar frost of its improbability marks things with an extra sparkle that lures the eye, beckoning it into far wider panoramas than those encompassed by one fox and its assassin on a remote Patagonian island.

When I think about the fox's killing, I sometimes muse about what might have happened if a larger, stealthier predator had crept up behind Darwin and dispatched him—dealing him a sudden deathblow while he was as preoccupied with the fox as the fox was with the surveyors. If, on December 6, 1834, it had been Darwin's brain, not the fox's, that encountered a fatal impact, how would the texture of history then have unfolded? How much would have been altered?

So much of what we take for granted now about the nature of life stems from ideas conjured in the brain of this young man. In 1834 Darwin was twenty-five. *Origin of Species* would not be published for another quarter of a century. But already the raw material for his great theory was gathering momentum with the data that the *Beagle*'s voyage provided in such abundance. Given the impact of his thinking, it's easy to imagine something of the scale of consequence had it been snuffed out. But who knows how much hinges on far less epochal individuals, ideas, and events? What if the fox, sensing Darwin's murderous intent, had run off seconds before he could swing his geological hammer? Or what if the fox had never been there and in its stead Darwin had found a butterfly, or a single magpie attracted by the theodolite's shine and sparkle as the sunlight struck its lenses?

Or, looking further back along the timeline of the threads that suture Darwin and the fox together, how might the warp and weft of circumstance have been woven if Darwin's father had been too poor to subsidize his son's lifestyle? Or if, in the distant past, a sharpened flint or saber tooth or shaft of sunlight falling on a rock pool had been blunted, distracted, clouded—altered—would history as we know it only have been tweaked or massively rewritten? We are blind to whether circumstances bear with them no more than minor potential for change, or if their occurrence holds poised within it a tide of implications that would cascade through the mosaic of what happens, rearranging the tiles of history into altogether different patterns.

꒜

Despite my uncle's disapproval all those years ago, as I've grown older I've warmed to the idea of a "magpie intellect." Far from the contempt with which he used it, I now embrace the phrase and apply it to myself and others—but in an altogether different sense from the one that he imposed upon it. Of course this may be because I've grown intellectually lax, with age bringing a falling off of standards so that my mind has simply lost whatever youthful rigor it once possessed. But—unsurprisingly—I prefer a different interpretation.

Whatever course we navigate through time, however brilliant our intellects may be, none of us is here for long enough to do much more than notice whatever falls most brightly on our consciousness. If we lived for centuries perhaps we could plod through our days more systematically, collect what's dull alongside what shines and sparkles. If Darwin hadn't had a magpie intellect he'd surely never have amassed the quantity of data that he needed to give his theory weight. Of course that theory—acting like a magnet on iron filings—swept them into line in a way that offered focus, coherence, and overarching sense. But without the collector's urge to gather and hoard all the separate pieces, the tiny shiny filings of individual foxes, barnacles and butterflies, birds and beetles, all the diverse creatures that caught his eye, any theory would have been unanchored to specifics and, as such, too abstract to gel or to convince. Few of us possess the insight of a Darwin—or his appetite for sheer hard work—and our interest may be tuned to catch very different things from the creatures that caught his, but I think we're all obedient to a magpie's-eye imperative that makes us seek out whatever shines for us most brightly. And this makes me unrepentant about fixating on this brief passage in Darwin's writings where he records his killing of the fox.

It appeared to me as the fox appeared to Darwin. Both bear upon them, if we stop to look, fingerprints that can tell us much about the nature of things.

It seems ironic that someone who understood so much about the ancientness of lineage behind each living thing, who knew the eons-long journey involved in making a fox's skull from the shifting ore of life, should have been the person who smashed his hammer down on the skull of this particular animal. And whether it's apt or odd that the species whose first discovered member was slain in this manner came to be known as Darwin's fox (*Lycalopex fulvipes*), it is surely just plain sad that it's become such a critically endangered species. It's thought that there are no more than 250 individuals left alive on Chiloé—the largest island in the archipelago of which San Pedro is a part—with little more than 70 on the mainland. It seems unlikely that this creature (which in fact belongs to the dog family rather than being a true fox) will survive much longer.

Just as I can't help wondering what might have been if something had shifted slightly in the timelines that coincided in 1834 to bring Darwin and his fox together, so I wonder what tides and currents of circumstance combined to edge *Lycalopex fulvipes* to the very brink of extinction. The things that bear us through the moments that we occupy often carry their significance invisibly. We cannot always tell, for instance, as we walk along our daily routes, whether stopping to tie a shoelace will make no difference to us or be the cause of our missing or meeting a potential life partner, or escaping or perishing in a terrorist attack. As would be the case for any creature, it would be fascinating to see a map of the gridlock of causes and effects that refined Darwin's fox out of the crude life-oil that first moved upon the planet, and to know what shoelace-tying equivalents resulted in its reaching the precarious position it now occupies.

꒜

For a short while in 1825, when he was a student in Edinburgh, Darwin lived in lodgings at 11 Lothian Street. When I was a student there a century and a half later, I lived only a couple of minutes away in Brighton Street, just around the corner. I find it strange to think of my footsteps falling on the same ground as Darwin's, and to realize that the cargo of ideas forming in a brain that once took in these same familiar streets would eventually, via print's geological hammer, strike the nineteenth century's consciousness. Darwin's blow would waken it from years of slumber, induced by a kind of theological narcotic. But the awakening he set in motion has been more than a little painful. As he paced the streets of Edinburgh, as my steps crossed where his had been before me, what was happening on the island of San Pedro? At what point were the foxes there locked into the trajectory that would take them toward extinction? And if Darwin had stopped to tie a shoelace one afternoon in Lothian Street, might everything that followed from that point on have taken a different course from what we now regard as history?

What became of all the magpie assemblage of pickings Darwin amassed during the voyage of the *Beagle*? In 1836 he presented a large collection of birds and mammals, including the San Pedro fox, to the Zoological Society of London (ZSL). But the Society no longer has these specimens. Their museum's collection was dispersed in the 1850s and, says Michael Palmer, the current ZSL archivist, "no list survives of where things went." Many specimens were sent to the British Museum—now the Natural History Museum—but the bulk of the collection, as Wilfred Blunt records in *The Ark in the Park,* "passed by purchase to provincial museums." One of these museums was in Ireland, at Queen's College Galway (now the National University of Ireland, Galway). Among the specimens bought on the instructions of Galway's Board of Direction were four that had been presented to the ZSL by Darwin. The specimens are a grison (a kind of weasel), a cavy or guinea pig, a variety of cuckoo, and an Azara's fox.

All of them had been collected by Darwin in South America in the course of his journeyings with the *Beagle*.

When I was in Galway last summer, I made a point of going to the university's Zoology Museum. It was a strange sensation to stand in front of the case where the Darwin specimens are displayed and to realize these are four trinkets taken from the great magpie hoard collected during the *Beagle*'s five-year voyage. Were they, like the San Pedro fox (of whose whereabouts I'm uncertain), slain by Darwin's geological hammer? Or shot? Or trapped? The rather tattered-looking specimens stare back at the viewer with their glass eyes, revealing nothing.

Just as "magpie" can mean "one who hoards or steals trifles," so the word "fox" also has embedded in it a meaning that's derived from our view of this animal's character. Used in a figurative sense, the noun "fox" can refer to "anyone notorious for cunning"; used as a verb, it can mean "to baffle, cheat, deceive, to act cunningly." The hammer blow delivered to our thinking by *Origin of Species* killed off some puerile beliefs as certainly as Darwin slew the fox on the island of San Pedro. His great book opened our eyes to how extraordinary life is, and to the intricacy and ancientness of connection linking one creature to another. But for all that it illumines, for all the explanatory power of his ideas about evolution and natural selection, there's surely a pleasing sense, almost of poetic justice, that we're still foxed by the nature of existence. As Darwin put it in a letter he wrote to Asa Gray in 1860: "I feel most deeply that this whole subject is too profound for the human intellect. A dog might as well speculate on the mind of Newton." As we hug our magpie baubles close, we need to take care not to mistake what it is they offer.

# HOW MANY WORDS DO
# YOU NEED TO DESCRIBE
# A WOODPIGEON?

*B*eing a writer, I suppose it's not surprising that I'm intrigued by the relationship between language and the natural world, or that I try to craft as close a fit as possible between my sentences and whatever it is I'm using them to word into being on the page. I've always liked the advice given by Japan's great master of haiku poetry, Matsuo Basho (1644–1694): "Let not a hair's breadth separate your mind from what you write." I know how hard it is to close that hair's breadth, but I also appreciate what a rich and flexible resource the English language is for effecting precisely this kind of closure and precision. Yet, even though I sometimes feel I've succeeded in saying more or less exactly what I have in mind, I know that there's a massive disparity between the actuality of the natural world and how we express our experience of it. In fact, the way we talk—and write—about nature tends to happen at a level of such simplification, so far removed from its sumptuous complexities, that it can seem as if we're talking about something else entirely.

Aristotle famously said that philosophy begins with wonder. I believe that responsible attitudes to the natural world have a similar point of origin. My worry is that the way in which we routinely apply language to that world may be a contributory factor leading to the mindset that allows us to wreak such damage on our environment. Verbal simplifications, and the superficial perceptions—or rather misperceptions—they foster, undermine the sense of wonder on which respect for nature is founded.

⚜

In case this all sounds too vague and abstract, let me tie these generalizations down to a specific example. It's tempting to go for something rare, beautiful, and endangered—a snow leopard, perhaps, or a quetzal—but I think the point is better made by something more mundane. So, let's take the woodpigeon that landed the other morning on the lawn just outside my window. Watching it strut and peck its way across the grass helped to crystallize the realization of how impoverished the verbal strategies are that we normally call into play and how often they make what's extraordinary seem ordinary.

Woodpigeons are common birds, of course, pests in the eyes of many farmers and gardeners. From such perspectives they're not deserving of any special use of language. Surely all that needs to be said in order to describe the moment is something like: "*There's a woodpigeon on the lawn.*" What's wrong with leaving it at that? At one level, nothing whatsoever—it provides a workable enough account in rough-and-ready terms of what happened at a certain time and place. My concern is that we too seldom recognize such statements for what they are: radical attenuations, disguised abbreviations, excerpts telling so little of the story that they only provide a massively diluted taste of the world's flavors.

In J. A. Baker's *The Peregrine,* a book which shows how language and nature can be brought into a far more potent alignment than we normally allow, the author observes that "the hardest thing of all to see is what is really there."

That comment came back to me as I tried to find a way of catching in words what was involved when the woodpigeon landed on my lawn. On reflection, the phrases I'd normally use to describe it all seemed designed to hide, rather than to see—still less to celebrate—what was really there.

The more I thought about it, all the words I normally rely on seemed badly flawed. Letting that commonsense statement *"There's a woodpigeon on the lawn"* stand as representative of our ordinary diction, it was as if it encountered four waves of assault. Each wave eroded its credibility. But the impact of these waves wasn't merely destructive; they also broke into a more encompassing vision, sweeping me towards what is, I hope, a less blinkered account than the one offered by our usual modes of discourse.

꙳

The first wave—the simplest and most gentle of them—formed around the question of color. It may seem easy enough to sketch a picture of a pigeon's plumage. If I were to attempt it, I'd start with the slate-grey head and striking white collar that doesn't quite completely ring the neck; the black shading on the tail; the plum-colored breast. A professional ornithologist's description of *Columba palumbus* relies on similar vocabulary. Here's what R. S. R. Fitter says in his popular guide to British birds:

> Head, neck and black-tipped tail blue-grey, with green, purple and prominent white patches at side of neck; mantle and wings grey-brown, with prominent white wing-patch; breast purplish-brown, much paler on belly.

But when you stop and really look at the bird as it pecks its way across the lawn, only a couple of feet away through the glass of the window, and when you scrutinize the words available to describe its colors, they seem approximations at best. "Green," for example, comes in a multiplicity of subtle-

ties and shades—which one fits the patch of verdant iridescence, shading into purple, on the bird's white-ringed neck?
What exactly is "grey-brown"? What variety of the fruit does
"plum-colored" seek to bring into play? If you'd never seen
a woodpigeon with your own eyes, how close would any
of these words bring you to an apprehension of the colors
it displays? The truth is, our words can't grasp with much
authority the chromatic spectacle presented by a woodpigeon. What they offer conveys only hints and suggestions, a
washed-out version of what's there.

Artists know better than writers how elusive color is, how
multifaceted, how changeable in different light, and how difficult to capture—but the point is put particularly well by a
writer imagining an artist's world. In Tracy Chevalier's *Girl
with a Pearl Earring,* a novel which weaves fact and fiction
together in fascinating ways, Johannes Vermeer is shown asking Griet, the maid who models for him, about the color of
the clouds in the sky over Delft. Her initial response, that
they are simply white, gives way to a far more nuanced and
considered answer when she's pressed by the artist to look
more closely:

> "There is some blue in them," I said after studying them
> for a few minutes. "And yellow as well. And there is some
> green!" I became so excited I actually pointed. I had been
> looking at clouds all my life, but I felt as if I saw them for
> the first time that moment.

Like Griet, we are often surprised when we stop to look at
something familiar and realize that we've never really seen it
properly before.

Coincidentally, a few days after watching the woodpigeon
on my lawn, I was at an exhibition of work by Scottish artist
Samuel J. Peploe (1871–1935). Beside a series of his still-life
studies a quote was given from one of Peploe's letters:

There is so much in mere objects, flowers, leaves, jugs, what not—colours, forms, relation—I can never see the mystery coming to an end.

In other words, no single study—no matter how skillfully drawn—can completely capture or exhaust what's there before the artist's eye. Though a woodpigeon sits uneasily under the label of "mere object," I think Peploe's point about the mystery never coming to an end is quite applicable to it. Not only do its colors challenge the vocabulary to catch more than a kind of conventionalized shadow of their hue, but as the bird moves across the lawn questions of form and relation also occur. How differently it appears when standing breast-high amidst grass and daisies, and when perched preening in a nearby tree; when it's sitting with its feathers fluffed out and when it's flying; when it's caught in a burst of sunshine or seen under gray clouds heavy with the imminence of rain.

⚘

Saying "*There's a woodpigeon on the lawn*" seems increasingly like a clumsy swipe with a crude verbal net that fails to catch more than a few downy feathers of its quarry. When the net comes back near-empty, when color, form, and relation start to act like wedges, splitting the log-like lumber of our ordinary vocabulary into an array of variations and possibilities, the second wave begins to form. This one erodes the adequacy of "*There's a woodpigeon on the lawn*" by picturing the multiplicity of things that are contained within— held back by—such a misleadingly simple sentence.

Behind the neat verbal stonework of the bare word "woodpigeon," erected like a dam wall upon the thing it names, there's a tonnage of unspoken water that only trickles hints of its existence through the close-fitting blocks of our vocabulary. There are the intricacies of its anatomy and physiology; the hidden scaffolding of bone and muscle. Each organ nestling in its warm, corporeal nest will have color, texture, flavor, scent—all as difficult to catch in words as it is to give a chromatic transcript of the plumage.

What is the weight of a sun-dried pigeon's skull, what sound would the wind make if it blew through the emptied eye sockets? How smooth would the brain's bone-casing feel to the tongue; for how long would it hold some residual tang of life-salt? "Woodpigeon" does little to convey the blood that pumps through this plump, feathered body, or to remind us of the flesh and bones beneath the skin, or the way light falls upon a pigeon's eye. It suggests nothing of how its pink feet might feel against the hand, or what odors might issue with the breathy coo-cooing of the bird as it softly, insistently, ululates its dreamily repetitive call.

Such rich complications easily proliferate even at the level of unaided perception. When we move to a microscopic perspective, "woodpigeon" and its associated words strain even more to hold the weight that they are trying to convey. Consider the cells and molecules and atoms that give substance to the bird, the warm intricacies of its biochemistry that fire each of its movements. As we imagine the delicate balance of processes and structures that are revealed as soon as we gaze upon it with the enhanced eye of scientific scrutiny, describing the woodpigeon is transformed from a difficult, but not impossible, verbal challenge into something that seems to defy words altogether—or to demand more and more complex combinations of them. I picture words streaming towards the bird in jumbled, desperate profusion, scores of sentences formed to try to catch it. Each one is instead deflected, pulled into orbit around something about which a great deal can be said, but in the end it remains mysterious, ineffable, enchanted. It shrugs off every attempt to shackle it.

⟶

The third wave forms when, in thinking beyond the immediate visible presence of the bird on the lawn, time is allowed into the equation. This individual woodpigeon then appears not just as a fully fledged adult occupying one particular moment, but as a life-form bearing with it a history of beginning, development, and dissolution. Here on the grass, just a few feet away, is a momentary presence, a point on a trajectory that arcs from egg-hatched genesis to the nestling helplessness of a "squab"—that curious word for a pigeon (or rook) chick—to its fledging, first flight, and on to its mating, death, and decomposition. Though they are integral to the bird's existence, the word "woodpigeon" holds no whiteshelled egg or white-boned skeleton within the calipers of its neatly linked consonants and vowels.

Words rarely hold much of the quantum of time that fuels and plays out in things. "Woodpigeon" in itself contains no clue about the duration of the thing so named; we learn from experience that it lasts longer than a butterfly, is less ancient than a boulder. But on their own, "woodpigeon," "butterfly," and "boulder" are mute about the spans of time each one encompasses.

The fourth wave forms when we step from the river of individual time—the pigeon's lifespan from egg through squab to adult bird and whatever death awaits it—into the ocean of species-time, in which every individual is only the tiniest ripple. When this wave of deep time washes across simple statements like *"There's a woodpigeon on the lawn,"* the bird becomes a temporal chasm. Falling into it, we drop through the centuries, plummeting down and down on a kind of woodpigeon slide—individual succeeding individual; life after life of egg laying, hatching, fledging, flying, mating, and dying, until the familiar pigeon form unravels into its ancient precursors as we reach the depth of time suggested by fossils like *archaeopteryx*. These ancient pre-birds in their turn give way to less distinct shapes, and then to vast stretches of time in which there was no life at all as we near the naked singularity, the so-called Big Bang, that point of inception some fourteen billion years distant, from which everything began. One of the tendrils from that ancient genesis stretches all the way from it to the moment when a woodpigeon landed on the lawn just outside my window. What words can catch more than a whisper of such stupendous lineaments of time, or decode more than a tiny fraction of their shifting expression? What they carry through the eons isn't something with the kind of fixity that simple labels like "woodpigeon" can catch. Their cargo is rather a shifting flux of changes as one form becomes another in evolution's majestic kaleidoscope of creatures.

↵

I picture these four eroding waves washing against the frail dam wall of "woodpigeon" until it's overwhelmed. The word collapses and its constituent letters are left littering the mind like flotsam, part of the explosive aftermath of the realization that our ordinary vocabulary holds so much more than we normally take from it. In a parallel motif of complication, one concerned with intricacies of language rarely acknowledged in its workaday application, it's worth remembering that each "w" and "o" and "d"—and all the rest—has a story, an evolution. Each letter is sunk like a peg into the history of the great cognitive revolution that allowed us to erect our circus tents of language as we let sounds and written symbols stand proxy for the things around us. Each of the ten letters of "woodpigeon" holds within it something of the saga of human literacy; our burgeoning insight into things as we moved—as if from egg to squab to adult—from the utterance of unwritten sounds to pictures, and then to hieroglyphic, phonetic, and alphabetic scripts. Take "o," for instance, occurring thrice in "woodpigeon." It's thought to have come to us—via Greek and Roman—from an ancient

Phoenician sign that began as a pictograph for the eye. When we look upon the world, how much of what our eye picks out is fed to it by the words we've woven? How far could we see without the lens of language? But if we always pare our language down to shorthand simplifications, can the eye look out upon the world with the requisite quotient of wonder? How can we hope to see what's really there and treat it in a fitting manner if we use words that blindfold rather than enlighten?

Of course my woodpigeon is just one example. Far from being unique, or even unusual, it stands rather as a kind of representative totem for the way in which every denizen of the natural world, like beautiful but deadly jellyfish, comes trailing filaments connected to a massive voltage. Touch one and we're shocked awake, find our eyes opened to perspectives normally left unspoken. How many words do you need to describe a woodpigeon? A wren? A worm? An oak tree? A frog? A trout? A dandelion or wasp or butterfly? All the words we have could be pressed into play without quite catching the intricate, ancient, and amazing textures of existence that nature presents to us in such profusion.

Think what we've created with the twenty-six letters of our alphabet! Yet, for all our fluency, for all the thousands upon tens of thousands of words we've minted, I still have a sense of casting their net and coming up empty—or of catching something so immense it simply ruptures every fiber in the net so that when we draw it in all that it holds is the ruin of itself and a few tantalizingly suggestive scales or feathers. From such oddments we fashion the fictions that we lean on. A comment made by one of the protagonists in Barbara Kingsolver's epic novel *The Poisonwood Bible* comes to mind here: "Illusions mistaken for truth are the pavement under our feet. They are what we call civilization." There are some illusions that support us well enough, but there are others—those that present nature as two-dimensional, ordinary, expendable—that we urgently need to challenge.

I know the practical, day-to-day function of words is to allow us to navigate our way through reality, rather than attempt to replicate it, and of course in one sense and for most occasions statements like *"There's a woodpigeon on the lawn"* perfectly suffice. Common sense demands their shorthand. But if we always filter out the incredible backstory and only focus on what's immediately apparent, if we fail to see what it's joined with, what it's anchored to, then perhaps the routes we plot lack sufficient metal of truth upon their surfaces to be reliable lifeways, however comfortable the pavements they offer us to walk on may be.

I'm not sure how best to negotiate the relationship between *"There's a woodpigeon on the lawn,"* something straightforward and singular which lands and flies away again as I'm writing, and the pigeon that carries with it so heavy a load it doesn't so much fly as plummet through all our conventional descriptions, taking us into the astonishing strata of deep time and microscopic structure. But it is surely perilous to allow either perspective to eclipse the other. Yet, as things stand, that is precisely what we tend to do—ignoring the fact that the bird on the lawn carries with it the potential to take us into depths that are more numinous than navigable; where wonder cries out to be wired into any words we utter. As John Muir famously remarked (in his 1911 book *My First Summer in the Sierra*): "When we try to pick out anything by itself, we find it hitched to everything else in the Universe." The value of "nature writing" is that it helps to counterbalance our tendency to unhitch, isolate, and simplify. Of course we need ordinary discourse to cut its swathes of simplification through the world, to pick out straightforward threads that we can follow, guidelines that let us get from A to B unhindered by complication in the countless commonsense transactions of our everyday existence. But we also need the warp and weft of words woven in a different register to help us see what's really there and to appreciate something of the astonishing connectivity that so entranced John Muir.

Sometimes I think our words act like a kind of verbal snow. They lay down a muffling monochrome canvas upon the world so that we can trace out on it the straightforward stories that we tell each other. But underneath every "*Once upon a time*" and "*There's a woodpigeon on the lawn*," odysseys of incredible color and labyrinthine complexity are unfolding all the time. On the drifts of ordinary diction fallen on the world, my woodpigeon can strut and peck and fly away, the prominent white bars showing on its wings. I can describe the moment in a handful of words and almost believe I've caught it. But when I think what "*There's a woodpigeon on the lawn*" actually points to, I know I could exhaust my wordstore completely without ever catching more than a fraction of what's really there.

# THE WALKING BUDDHA
# BECKONS

f course it doesn't.

It is completely still, completely silent; as incapable of gesture as of speech. Though finely wrought to mimic the figure of a man in miniature, this piece of metal, ghosted to the shape of something living, is frozen and inert. For all the sculptor's artistry in making a simulacrum of human form, the metal remains mute. This small, well-crafted bronze can no more tell its story than a stone could recite a poem. Beyond the few immediate impressions it lays upon the senses, the metal remains dumb. It yields to perception only a bare list of superficial features: cold, hard, dense, heavy, unperfumed, silent.

Yet, despite this, its muteness can be made to sing. That, after all, is what the artist was about when, more than a century ago, he forged elements from the earth—copper, tin—into this particular shape and tuned it according to a Buddhist score. What songs does the walking Buddha sing? I've come to think of him as having a repertoire that's set in two entirely different keys. The first is the approved one. Tuned to the official note, it's for those melodies sanctioned by tradition. The songs are formal; they give orthodox renderings of Buddhist teaching. The second key is informal, if not illicit. It hums along with, and distracts from, what the walking Buddha is meant to convey. It's not my principal interest here, but looking briefly at the music written in the officially approved key will help provide a picture of the statuette and set the scene for the song I really want to listen to.

Though to casual scrutiny they're invisible—inaudible—there's a swarm of symbols neatly clustered in the metal, each one in its appointed place. These symbols are like notes in a chord that sounds out Buddhist teaching. To take a couple of examples, the stylized swollen point atop the figure's head, the *ushnisha,* is meant to recall the Buddha's wisdom—too much for an ordinary head to contain without this domed cranial extension. The flame emerging from it represents the radiance of his spiritual energy. The elongated earlobes (stretched by years of wearing heavy gold earrings) remind us of the Buddha's royal birth. The *ushnisha,* flame, and elongated earlobes are the most obvious of the *lakshanas*—magical marks whose presence on a body supposedly indicate a state of enlightenment within. Traditionally, there are thirty-two *lakshanas,* though often only a few are shown. It would be tedious to run through them all. Suffice it to say that the *lakshanas* are believed to be like naturally occurring tattoos that appear as a result of spiritual advancement. Each of these little markers—thirty-two variations on an underlying theme—reiterates the idea of perfection and flags up the difference between enlightened and unenlightened beings.

The walking Buddha's left hand is raised, palm forward, thumb and forefinger touching. This is commonly taken as a gesture of peace, though technically it signifies an appeal to reason, or the giving of a teaching. Held thus in the so-called *vitarka mudra,* it taps into the rich repertoire of hand gestures—*mudras*—which convey a range of meanings. With just a little alteration—if, say, thumb and forefinger weren't touching—the hand gesture's message would change; instead of indicating an appeal to reason it would become a sign of fearlessness (the famous *abhaya mudra*). Like verbal language, the language of *mudras* can convey meaning via the subtlest changes of inflexion. Underlying all of them, the eight-petalled lotus flower etched into the palm of the walking Buddha's raised left hand recalls the Eightfold Path—the philosophy of Buddhism condensed into an easily memorized octet of teachings.

So, for those who can see beyond the confining anonymities of its metal chrysalis, this fifteen-inch figurine soon smiles and points and sings, hatching a whole spectrum of Buddhist ideas from the bronze. But however much this may be the walking Buddha's official message, what he's meant to say, it's what's sung in his repertoire's other, less formal key that touches me most deeply.

☙

Though it would be interesting to know exactly where, when, and by whom this statuette was crafted, such details would be difficult—if not impossible—to establish. What's certain is that it's a nineteenth-century bronze from Thailand. Clearly it's been influenced by—and is part of a continuing expression of—the famous Sukhothai style. "Sukhothai" means "the dawn of happiness" and refers both to an ancient capital city and the civilization associated with it. The Sukhothai period, dating from the thirteenth to the fifteenth centuries, is often seen as Thailand's Golden Age. This was the country's first Buddhist kingdom and marked Thais' freedom from their Khmer rulers. It sparked a great artistic-spiritual efflorescence. The style of sculpture produced by artists at this time constitutes one of the pinnacles of Buddhist art, and the image of the walking Buddha is one of the most striking innovations of the Sukhothai aesthetic. Previously, he was always shown standing, sitting, or reclining.

I'd love to be able to trace the history of this walking Buddha, from its point of inception—when copper and tin were smelted together—right up to the moment it beckoned to me, but for all the richness of its symbolism it's impossible to reconstruct more than a fraction of the statuette's itinerary. Its metal can't be made to yield the notes that would detail all the hands that have held it, all the eyes that have beheld it, all the places in which it's been in its long journey from nineteenth-century Thailand to twentieth-century Scotland (I found it in Edinburgh in 1983). Like so many of the things around us, the walking Buddha points to connections of symphonic complexity whose music is lost to all but imagination's retrieval of a few hauntingly suggestive notes.

My interest does not lie in listening to the official melodies of this statuette's iconography, or in trying to reconstruct year by year its long walk through time until the moment when it entered the little orbit of my attention. Instead, I want to listen to the song it sings to my ears only, sotto voce, alongside its role as publicly recognized Buddhist symbol. I hope these softer notes, unsanctioned by tradition, sung in the undertone of personal memory, will explain something of the significance this object has come to have for me. They show how it offers a portal into that dense entanglement of past and present, known and unknown, potential and realized, between whose poles the threads of who we become are woven.

⚘

The walking Buddha is about to take a step.

Of course it isn't really; but that's exactly how it looks. The artist has depicted the Buddha mid-stride. The left foot is flat down, taking the body's weight, but the right one is raised, its toes are pushing off the ground and there's a centimeter of clear space between the heel and the flat surface on which the Buddha walks. A sense of movement is masterfully conveyed, not just by this raised right foot, but by the whole body-posture of the figure, and the way the Buddha's loose robes seem to billow gracefully behind him. It's a measure both of the skill with which the bronze is wrought and of the strength of our tendency to animate objects with a life they don't possess, that in trying to describe this statuette, "he" is the word I reach for automatically. I have to make myself say "it." To suggest loose robes and billowing in bronze, to transmute "it" into "he," to instill such a sense of gathered grace and calm into this walking figure, to create an aura of focused discipline without any hint of inhumanity, to render it elegant without being arrogant, serene without being cold, betokens a high order of artistry indeed. No wonder Sukhothai bronzes are held in such esteem.

Yet, for all the spiritual and aesthetic qualities invested in this statuette, for all its apparently effortless refinement, when this walking Buddha beckons he summons me to something earthy rather than sublime.

꽃

The walking Buddha is barefoot.

But the tiny feet he always makes me think of are clad in yellow moccasins. These soft suede moccasins were so appealing I was tempted to buy them, even though, at the time, I had no children of my own. Clearly designed for a tiny human's virginal first shodding, the moccasins were objects possessed of a high order of sensual appeal. Though pleasing to the eye, they cried out most insistently to touch; they were the kind of things you just wanted to reach out for, to handle and to have. They were one of several beautiful designs of handmade children's shoes displayed on a stall at a craft and antiques fair held in Edinburgh's Assembly Rooms, a majestic eighteenth-century building in the heart of Scotland's capital city.

Before I saw them, I'd never have believed I could have been so susceptible to tiny shoes. I've said they had an intrinsic allure, and yes, I think they did. But I suspect that more than any qualities they possessed themselves, their impact on me was due to the way in which they irresistibly spoke of babies, children—the promise of new life and its kindling. I might not have stopped to look at them at all if I'd been going round the stalls alone. But I was with my girlfriend and we were newly together. Seeing them in her company gave these beautifully crafted children's shoes a special magnetism—the same kind that jewelers' windows exert on lovers as they walk past hand in hand. Potent as a pheromone, the shoes, like rings, exuded the lure of possible commitment, procreation, the unfolding of a life together.

꧁

"Shoemaker" seems too poor a word by far to convey the skill that went into the making of these exquisite children's shoes. "Cobbler" is even further from the mark, yet both terms shuffle clumsily into mind, dragging with them all the wrong connotations. I picture an old man, wizened and gruff, bad-temperedly tapping nails into crudely cut soles in some squalid den that reeks of leather. He makes his wares unsmilingly, his craft lit by no fire of vision beyond grudging practicality and profit. Half cast from dimly remembered fairy tales, half from a real-life cobbler's workshop that I was fearful of going into as a child, I know this picture is mere stereotype. But it serves to underscore how different from it was the person responsible for making the yellow suede moccasins that captivated me. More artist than artisan, there was nothing of the cobbler-as-troll about Sally Damson. In terms of fairy tale typologies, she was closer to the elfin, the enchantress.

I've remembered her name for thirty years (though I've changed it here, of course), but her features have slid away over time, becoming as indistinct as the fine detail of the shoes she crafted. I don't remember much about her now except for her artistry in suede and leather, the fact that she was young, dark-haired, attractive, and—most of all—that she signaled to me with breathtaking frankness that she was—what? I struggle for the right words here and fail to find them, so end up falling back on rough-hewn, if not crude approximations: "interested," "more than willing," "up for it." None of these tired formulae of attraction catch the strength, still less the sincerity—or the sheer unexpectedness—of the warmly wanton invitation she so unambiguously gave me.

My girlfriend, neither fanciful nor overly possessive, was at first incredulous—and then outraged—that anyone would send such openly seductive signals to her partner when she was walking with him hand in hand. At her urging, we moved on.

⚘

Beside Sally Damson's stall, an antique dealer had set up his display—assorted bric-a-brac spilled out across a trestle table. If we'd not stopped to look at the shoes, I'd not have spotted the walking Buddha amidst this cluttered array of old china, glassware, jewelry, and paintings. But as I studied the exquisite suede moccasins, and the girl who'd made them, the Buddha figure at the next stall caught my eye, even though it was obscured by an ornately framed oil painting propped up against it. When I examined the figure properly, it immediately became apparent how fine a piece it was. I negotiated a price and bought it.

The walking Buddha has been with me ever since that day in Edinburgh. It has stood in the various rooms in the various countries I've lived in over three decades. Like some kind of tutelary spirit, it has witnessed love and marriage, children and bereavement, illness and rude health. It has seen the routine pleasures and frustrations of a goodly chunk of my adult life. Its silent gaze has fallen on me awake, asleep, alone, with friends and family. To talk of it "witnessing," "seeing," "gazing" is of course to commit a series of misnomers—but it indicates again how easy it is to personalize this lifeless lump of beautifully crafted metal.

It's inappropriate, I know, in view of Buddhist teaching about nonattachment, but the walking Buddha is one of the few possessions that I value—to the extent that if I'm traveling or away on holiday I'll often hide it. This is irrational, I know; few thieves would want it. Why do I value it so much? It's an intrinsically appealing piece of course—a beautifully cast example of the elegantly serene spirituality typical of Sukhothai sculpture. It's a tangible reminder of a man, a philosophy, a religion that I hold in high esteem. But—just like the suede moccasins—much of the walking Buddha's appeal comes not from anything it possesses in itself but from what it suggests, what it points to, what it beckons towards—and for me this statuette's beckoning leads in directions not intended by its makers.

Thanks to Sally Damson, it stands for paths not taken, routes not followed, forks in the way that might have led to different outcomes. But when the walking Buddha beckons and I follow, he doesn't just take me back to a girl making bedroom-eyes at me, still less to any orthodox reading of his symbolism. Rather, when I walk beside him now I see scores of alternatives, possibilities, turns off the roads I've followed. The *vitarka mudra* becomes less an appeal to reason than a gesture that reminds me of the fragile contingencies out of which our lives are woven. Our choosing of one way rather than another as we negotiate each day's tangled nexus of possibilities seems at once utterly tenuous and provisional, yet also cast in something as inflexible as bronze.

ॐ

I never saw Sally Damson again, and it's highly unlikely I ever will. I no more know what paths her footsteps took than I know what feet were shod with the beautiful shoes she made. I've often wondered since what might have happened *if*. Would it have been just a momentary carnal diversion, or a lifeline leading from that moment into a quite different unfolding of the future? Were the advances she made rooted only in the raw voltage of a passing lust, or did they reach further into the mysterious field of attraction's electricity, a field through which we often find it hard to plot a way? Is it possible they may even have been drawing on the hidden aquifers of love, whose imperatives it can be as perilous to obey as to ignore?

Whatever the answer to such questions, I know that if I'd taken that path, others would have closed, just as others would have opened. The whole mesh of entrances and exits with which we're surrounded might have been completely rearranged; the gridiron of actual and possible reworked into different patterns altogether. Whichever paths we follow are close-shadowed by those we don't. To use a famous Buddhist formula: "When this is, that comes to be; with the arising of this, that arises. When this is not, that does not come to be; with the cessation of this, that ceases."

The second time I visited Edinburgh's Assembly Rooms—years later—was to hear the Dalai Lama speak on a rare visit to Scotland. Sitting in the packed audience listening to his message of peace made me think of my walking Buddha's peace *mudra*. But it also reminded me of a grim fact I'd discovered about the Assembly Rooms' history. During the First World War they were taken over by the military and used as the principal recruiting office for the east of Scotland. Sitting there all those years later, my life having taken the twists and turns it had, it was strange to think of the scores of young men who had come to this place between 1914 and 1918 and gone from it to their deaths. The interlocking mesh of choice and consequence, of action and reaction, the complex web of interdependence through which we have to navigate our way, is both humbling and terrifying. Can we bring into any intelligible alignment the lives of those young recruits, and the figure of an elfin shoesmith; the smile of a saffron-robed monk and a war in which so many died; my purchase of the walking Buddha and a recruiting sergeant's beckoning; the notion of enlightenment and the raw electricity of attraction?

_⟡_

The walking Buddha beckons and I follow.

I've learned to see through his camouflage of silent stillness. This fifteen-inch figurine soon smiles and points and sings, hatches from his bronze all sorts of memories, associations, and imaginings. Yes, he sometimes brings Buddhist teachings into mind. But, in the main, for me, he walks outside any named philosophy; sings from the heart, not from some set of sanctioned doctrines. The melody is haunting, elemental, elegiac. He sings of the mysteries of time and transience and death, of paths taken and not taken, of love and loss and longing.

I hope it's not idolatrous, but I've come to see this little statuette as a kind of icon of the complex patterns made as we each tread out our lives upon this earth, and of the possibility—albeit remote, albeit difficult—of finding ways through the perplexing labyrinths of being that might allow us at least a measure of the walking Buddha's poise and grace.

# SLEEPERS

Note: *American readers may be unaccustomed to using the word
"sleeper" for a piece of timber (or other material) used to support
rails. I hope they will forgive me for not changing this to "tie" or
"crosstie." In the context of this essay, these terms would have the
wrong resonance.*

nlike many people today, I grew up with fires.
There was no central heating in my parents'
house. An anthracite stove burned day and night in
the kitchen. It provided a hob and oven for cooking, and hot
water for baths. It also lent a trace of background warmth to
all the rooms. This was easy to miss, especially in winter, but
was nonetheless an essential part of the signature of home. It
was only on those rare occasions when the stove was allowed
to go out that its role in providing ambient warmth throughout the house was appreciated. Before we went on holiday,
the fire at its metal heart was allowed to die. Coming back,
as soon as we opened the front door, the house felt saturated
with an unaccustomed iciness. It only lifted once the stove
had been relit and was burning steadily enough to provide
the core of warmth we were so used to. Its absence made
the house seem not our own. It was my mother, mostly, who
tended the stove's enclosed fire of anthracite embers, though
we all knew how to rake and empty the ashpan and pour in
fresh fuel from the hod. We occasionally relieved her of these
chores, but in truth she preferred to trust her own sure hand.

The room we sat in was heated by an open fire. The fireplace was set in a tiled hearth that was framed by a mahogany mantelpiece. The coal fire that burned here was only lit on winter evenings, or in the afternoon on special occasions—if guests were coming, or at Christmas. Until he became too old to manage the heavy buckets of coal and ash, tending this fire was mostly my father's preserve—though we all knew how to clean and set it, and occasionally took a turn. Although it was a coal fire, getting it to light was heavily dependent upon wood. Firelighters—those paraffin-soaked tablets of white, slow-burning wax—were viewed with contempt. My father saw them as a kind of cheating, employed only by the lazy or inept. He prided himself in being able to set a fire with crumpled newspaper, kindling he'd chopped himself, and coal expertly arranged on this carefully constructed pyre, then getting it to light with the strike of just one match.

If, unusually, a fire faltered and went out, it was taken as a reflection of the fire-setter's ability, however much it might have been due to poor coal, damp kindling, or a soot-fall from the chimney smothering the initial flames. A failed fire cast a pall about the house that was deeper than the temporary absence of heat, or the nuisance of resetting, could account for. It was as if an adverse judgment had been passed on the setter's mastery of an elemental skill. The unspoken mix of disappointment and disapproval that accompanied unsuccessful fires made it feel as if you hadn't measured up against a venerable tradition; that you couldn't be relied on and had somehow let the side down. Fires were an important part of family life; there was a lot more tied up in them than just providing warmth.

⁓

I don't think my father ever delivered anything as self-conscious as a lesson. But as a small boy I witnessed fire-making so often that I soon absorbed its essential processes via that invisible osmosis by which so much passes from one generation to another. As well as learning how to lay a latticework of sticks on top of a layer of crumpled paper, and how to arrange pieces of coal of the right size upon the acrated platform thus constructed, I dutifully absorbed the view that firelighters were wrong. Even today, although I know there's no basis for this judgment, I look askance at those who use them, almost as if they were guilty of some petty crime.

Buying bundles of ready-cut kindling was also frowned on. Like using firelighters, such kindling was seen as symptomatic of the kind of laxity that suggested little moral fiber. My father viewed such purchases as a dereliction of duty— the cutting of essential corners; a deceitful taking of the easy, lazy way. To buy kindling or firelighters made someone suspect in his eyes, as if recourse to convenience betrayed an inner flaw.

At the time, I simply absorbed such opinions automatically. It didn't occur to me to question them. It was years before I realized that as well as the basic practicalities of fire-making I was imbibing a set of values that had nothing to do with chopping wood and arranging paper, sticks, and coal together so that they'd ignite and burn. It's as if, moored invisibly alongside the simple vessels of such mundane tasks, there was in their harbor of hands-on learning a well camouflaged battleship, heavy with armaments and assumptions. It fired its propaganda, unnoticed, directly into hearts and minds.

It was, I'm sure, in this kind of stealthy, osmotic way, rather than through overt sermonizing, that I grew up believing—as matter-of-factly as that firelighters and ready-cut kindling were suspect—that Ulster was British; that Catholics were, if not the enemy, at least possessed of dubious sympathies and allegiances; that Southern Ireland (which we called Eire) was an alien nation, hostile to the Presbyterianism in which I was raised; that the Royal Ulster Constabulary was the upholder of law and order, protector of our essential freedoms; that London could be trusted to support us, whereas Dublin meant subservience to Rome. The naivety of such views, their blinkered mix of ignorance and innocence, astounds me now. But at the time they had the imprimatur of identity; they were simply part of the mix of features defining who we were.

⁓ℛ

The kindling my father used began as railway sleepers. Every now and then he had a supply of them delivered. We lived in Lisburn, a town not far from Belfast, and our house was only a short walk from Lisburn station, one of the stops on the main Belfast to Dublin line. I'm not sure when concrete sleepers came to be favored over wooden ones. Perhaps the process of replacement had already started when I was a boy. Whether that, surplus, or damage caused by routine maintenance work explained it, Northern Ireland Railways always had sleepers for sale at knock-down prices. They arrived in a flatbed lorry. The driver and his mate unloaded the massive, creosoted beams by hand, stacking them neatly in our garage against one wall, with that made-to-look-easy nonchalance that is the fluency of repeated practice. When we tried to shift them it was a different matter. Our struggles were like a clumsy parody of their deft, balletic maneuverings.

To get from a whole sleeper to pieces of wood suitable for kindling is a laborious process. The first step was to saw each sleeper into shorter lengths. My father used a deep-toothed bow saw, sometimes single-handedly, sometimes allowing me to act as partner once he'd got the saw fixed firmly in the furrow of its cut. Sawing reduced the full-size sleepers—eight feet or longer—to blocks of wood that were the right length for splitting. Dad never favored axes and, to my disappointment, we didn't own one. He preferred wedges and a sledgehammer for the initial splitting, followed by a hatchet for the finer work.

Looking back, I'm astonished at the amount of sheer hard work he invited. There was no financial necessity for this. He was a high-ranking civil servant and could easily have afforded to buy ready-cut kindling, rather than taking on such heavy labor. That he preferred to start with sleepers was in part, I think, simply because he enjoyed the process of rendering them down. But it also reflected habits of thrift and self-reliance that stemmed from growing up in a family with five children and little enough to support them. Why throw away good money on wood to burn when sleepers could be had for next to nothing?

I can still hear pitch-perfect in my memory the sounds involved in making kindling. The heavy thud and echo of whole sleepers dropped lengthways on a concrete floor, gently enough not to crack it but their weight still ensuring a heavily resonating wallop of impact, even when the driver and his mate were careful not to let them fall for more than a few inches. The different tones as the other sleepers were added on top of the first one so laid down, like monstrous, loose piano keys piled on the ground, each one adding its rough-hewn note to the jangling chords they played together. The rub-and-cut noise of the bow saw's teeth made a kind of tuneless monotone as they were drawn through the wood, a yammering of two repeated near-identical notes. The thunk of a wedge as it was driven into a sleeper's end, and that ear-shimmering aural glint of metal clinking heavily on metal as the sledgehammer's head slammed hard against the wedge, driving it into the wood, levering it apart. The somehow angular sound, like curt, metallic wind chimes—discordant, muted—as the wedge split through the full length of the sawn sleeper, fell clear of the wood, and hit the concrete floor. The dull tap-tap of the hatchet looking for its mark and then the tearing split and crack of wood as the blade found the weakness in the grain and wrenched the thick stakes open, cleaving them asunder. The littler echoes of the same refrain as these thick stakes were split a second and third time. The shallow percussive shuffle of the thin sticks—finally judged ready for the fire—as they were bundled together and piled in a wooden box.

I wonder now just what I learned as I watched these giant lengths of timber being sawn into chunks, split and then chopped into sticks—reduced from heavy-duty beams, as thick as a man's body and strong enough to support rails and trains, to something easily snapped in your hands. Of course I learned the obvious lessons about how to wield wedges, sledgehammers, and hatchets, the advisability of wearing goggles, how to deal with splinters, but spliced into this syllabus of basic skills there was another, covert curriculum. Like learning to mistrust firelighters and shop-bought kindling, a cluster of other judgments—most of them unnoticed for years—passed through the permeable membrane that separates a small boy from his father. Alongside the formal learning that goes on at school, the bulk of the images and impressions that are loaded into memory and supply life's ballast come from sources that are pedagogically unsanctioned but deeply formative in the influence they exert. They act like sleepers which bear the track of conscious schooling, doing much to direct the paths it takes. Who knows exactly what a child absorbs when working beside a parent chopping wood, or how the points of reference that will provide the mind's echo chambers are formed from the things we happen to encounter as we are growing up?

The way in which mundane objects are transmuted into touchstones, how everyday experiences fill a reservoir with symbols—such things are hard to map. But I know that chopping kindling and making fires left an indelible impression on my life. They also seem to tap into something deeper than their ordinariness suggests. When I think about it now, picturing the way we sat around our fire on winter evenings, I have a sense of shadowy archetypes, as if the ghosts of our forebears who first struck sparks from flint were sitting invisibly with us, witnessing how their campfire repertoire had been refined. A family group gathered at a hearth surely connects with ancient strata of the human story. It is in such moments of intimate familial exchange that the sleepers and the rails are laid that carry us on our life-journeys.

My father worked in the Ministry of Finance at Stormont, the seat of Northern Ireland's then Protestant-dominated government. Sectarianism was institutionalized. The religious apartheid that ran through every social structure was scarcely noticed. It wore the camouflage of simply being the way things were; it was what everyone was used to. Discrimination was rife. Unsurprisingly, discontentment was building. But as we chopped wood in our garage we were oblivious to the fact that the country was poised like a chunk of sleeper just before the hammer hits the wedge.

Every weekday morning shortly after eight, Dad left the house to catch the train to Belfast. My brother and I often ran up the road to meet him when he got home again just after six, his suit smelling of trains, the leather briefcase under his arm bulging with the papers he'd work at in the evening once we were in bed. I used to wonder if his weekend wood-chopping ever saw him splitting one of the sleepers that had supported a section of the track he'd traveled on to work. I'm not sure why, but the thought of him doing this appealed to me; perhaps it bestowed an aura of independence, even rebellion—a throwing off of the routine that dominated his days.

Although, as with almost everything he did, the rendering down of sleepers into kindling was done methodically and neatly, it's not possible to split wood with the same precision or uniformity that a civil servant brings to paperwork. There's an inherent unpredictability in the task. How a sleeper saws and splits depends on variables of knot and grain and seasoning; the extent to which the ground it's lain on has been dry or damp. Did making kindling represent a therapeutic change in tempo, a healthy counterbalance to his weekday world? His job required the following of strict protocols, an accurate tallying in words and numbers; he was relied on to help maintain the rails of governance. Perhaps the sledge-hammer, wedge, and hatchet afforded a relaxing change of gear; allowed into his life a pinch of controlled violence; the spice of mayhem kept within reasonable bounds. Or perhaps, as a fair-minded man, he recognized the unfairness of the system he was caught in—helped administer—and the breaking up of sleepers represented a repressed desire to smash the injustices on which the rails of Ulster society had been laid.

⚜

As a Protestant, my father read *The Newsletter.* Established in 1737, it's one of the oldest continuously published newspapers in the world. Had he been a Catholic, he'd have read *The Irish News.* In this, as in so much else, Ulster's two tribes had their favored habits, part of a catechism of little markers of identity and allegiance. To a native of the place it's never necessary to ask directly whether someone is a Protestant or a Catholic—or, in the local patois, a Prod or Teague. This is evident from a multitude of signs—the newspaper you read, the sport and team you follow, your school, the whiskey that you drink, the brand of bread you buy.

Old copies of *The Newsletter* were stacked in a tile-floored walk-in cupboard off the kitchen, next to the rest of the paraphernalia for making fires—the coal and ash buckets, and a small box filled with kindling from the garage. A ton or more of coal was stored in an outhouse. The bucket was filled from there and held only enough to set one fire and replenish the supply of coal held in the scuttle by the hearth.

Once the ash and cinders from the previous day's fire had been cleared, the first step in setting a new one was to crumple up sheets of newspaper into rough balls and set them on the heavy iron grate that fitted neatly into the fireplace, providing the platform for all our fires. The paper acted as tinder that would light immediately, as soon as a match was applied. The paper would then set light to the kindling placed on top of it and that, in turn, would ignite the less readily combustible coal, small pieces of which were carefully arranged on the sticks. As Ulster's Troubles took hold, *The Newsletter* was full of accounts of bombings, shootings, riots, intimidation, burning out. It was often hard not to be drawn into some of the reports again as details of violence close to home, or some terrible picture of a familiar place, caught your eye. Fire-setting became an opportunity to go through the news again, at a different pace, and to think abut what was happening. I remember setting one fire with crumpled paper filled with pictures of burnt-out buildings in a street in Belfast that I'd walked down only days before. Using this as tinder had a muddled sense of rightness and irony about it, almost as if it was part of some ill-considered ritual that served no one well. For however much we loathed the violence and wanted no part in it, was it not the outlooks nurtured at family hearths all over Ulster that had sparked the conflagration that now threatened them?

⚘

Beside the buckets of coal and ash in the walk-in kitchen cupboard there was a third bucket, heavier than the others. It was filled with slack—a kind of black gravel made of small pieces of coal. With water added, it makes a slow-burning mortar that holds a fire together and stops it burning through too much fuel. Knowing when to add it, how much to put on, judging the right degree of dampness—all this was part of the syllabus of practical skills in fire-making that I learned from years of observation and imitation. Expertise in using slack makes for a longer-lasting, hotter fire; carelessness in its preparation or application can put a fire out, or reduce it to a scarcely warming smolder, the flames choked by lack of air.

In Seamus Heaney's final collection, *Human Chain* (2010), there's a wonderful poem simply entitled "Slack."

Heaney's faultless choice of words about what he calls these "weighty grounds of coal" vividly reawakens memories of the hearthside that was such a feature of my childhood. In one verse Heaney points to

The cindery skull
Formed when its tarry
Coral cooled

Staring into the coal fire as a child, it often seemed as if the red tunnels in the embers were eye sockets in some fantastic skull, or that the glowing cinders were a kind of enchanted reef, drawing the gaze into the promise of their depths. The shapes were always more interesting after slack had been added. It hardened into a crusty carapace that cracked and fissured, creating its own fiery topography of miniature hillocks, dells, and valleys. I spent longer gazing at these shifting landscapes in the hearth than I did at TV. Looking at the changing features of the fire prompted a plethora of daydreams and imaginings. I'm not sure how much of the self is woven in such moments, or how we could ever measure such invisible processes, but I have a strong sense that a core part of who I am was tempered at that fireside.

Reading Heaney now is a very different experience from reading him when I sat by the fire at my parents' house in County Antrim. My first encounters with his work were tentative—almost furtive. They were accompanied by mixed feelings of breaking free and betrayal. As a Catholic with nationalist sympathies, Heaney wasn't exactly approved reading for someone in the Protestant community. The eminence achieved by the poet did eventually make for a measure of recognition, if not acceptance. But this had yet to happen when I was in my teens reading *Death of a Naturalist, Wintering Out,* and *North.* Then, the pleasure of savoring good poetry, and the sense of looking beyond the approved canon, edging towards some degree of literary independence, was underlain by a feeling of something close to treachery. It was as if my choice of reading meant deserting my own clan in favor of a turncoat embracing of the other side. Though he never criticized me directly, I could see that, to my father, reading Heaney's books was comparable to using firelighters and shop-bought kindling.

_ଥ

Partly because of their name, and partly because the sound of trains in the near-distance was such a regular accompaniment to falling asleep in childhood, I came to associate sleepers with actual slumber. As I lay in bed I imagined those nighttime trains, whose sounds were so strangely soothing, stitching their seams of soporific rhythm across the Ulster countryside as they rumbled and clanked their way between that litany of local stations whose names I whispered to myself as I pictured the lighted carriages passing through them: Hilden, Lambeg, Derriaghy, Dunmurray, Finaghy, Balmoral, Adelaide. The sleepers beneath the track, like the sleepers bunked together in our garage, seemed like so many bodies stretched out at their ease, snoring gently, so fast asleep that even the shuddering weight of trains didn't wake them. Perhaps this association of wooden sleepers with real sleepers was also forged by my occasional dozing by the fire, and by the powerful smell of creosote that emanated from the wood. It seemed like a kind of chloroform, strong enough to put you under.

As the Troubles took hold and I started to look for images that might fit the horrors that were emerging all around us, it's not surprising that sleepers came to mind, given how much they featured in my childhood. So I came to think of these heavy beams of wood as totems of intransigence and intolerance. They offered a way of picturing how inflexibly divisive attitudes had been bedded into the track of all our lives. It sometimes seemed as if the whole country was asleep, lulled into a kind of stupor by its history, and sleepwalking towards disaster. Like the background warmth provided by our anthracite stove, people had got used to their partisan perspectives, the automatic favoring of one side's outlook over the other's. When these adversarial assumptions were challenged, it felt like something integral to their identity had been taken away. Henry David Thoreau suggests (in *Walden*) that "moral reform is the effort to throw off sleep." The last several decades in Ulster have been an effort to throw off the sleep of sectarianism and bigotry. There have been encouraging signs of wakefulness (and poetry has played a creditable role in this). There seems more willingness now to allow difference without disparagement; there's more readiness to tolerate disagreement without embracing enmity. Whether the peace will hold will, of course, depend on politicians, teachers, and religious leaders. But more crucial to success than any of them will be the countless little transactions that occur between parent and child, the conversations at family hearthsides, as this generation lays down for the next whatever sleepers are going to support the rails of Ulster's future.

# HOW'S THE ENEMY?

*A*bout ninety minutes' walk from where I'm sitting writing this essay, there's a curious feature of the landscape called "the Rock and Spindle." I'm in St Andrews, whose university—founded in 1411—is the oldest in Scotland. The town is also famous as the home of golf. Walk from here in the opposite direction to the Rock and Spindle, and in only twenty minutes you'll reach the Royal and Ancient Club. If a six-hundred-year-old university and a golf club that traces its founding back to 1754 are not enough to establish the town's historical credentials, St Andrews also boasts an impressive ruined cathedral, the original structure of which dates from the twelfth century. But all these venerable human institutions are dwarfed by the age of the Rock and Spindle. It's some 300 million years old.

St Andrews has two main beaches. The West Sands—two miles long—is by far the larger and better known, made famous by the opening sequence of the film *Chariots of Fire.* It's here that Eric Liddell and the rest of the 1922 British Olympic team are shown training, running in their old-fashioned white shorts and singlets along the water's edge.

The smaller East Sands stretches from the harbor to the foot of Kinkell Braes, at which point you can join the thread of a narrow footpath that shadows the shore's nips and tucks like a nerve, leading to Boarhills, Kingsbarns, Crail, Anstruther, Pittenweem, and Fife's other coastal villages, some of which have a history as long and interesting as St Andrews. Start at Kinkell Braes and in less than a mile the path will bring you to the Rock and Spindle. It's not signposted, but you'll know you've reached it well enough—it's an unmistakable landmark.

‸

The Rock and Spindle stands alone in a small bay. It's an upright column of rock, perhaps thirty feet high, with a kind of swollen circular base, the flattened face of which is marked with curious radial striations suggestive of a giant spinning wheel, hence the name. It has a distinctly phallic air. Were it in India rather than Scotland, one would be forgiven for thinking it might be some sort of gigantic Shiva lingam, one of those frankly penile pillars of devotion to the great Hindu god that dot the Indian countryside. Such explicitly sensual religiousness, homage to a deity perceived as both erotic and ascetic, would seem outlandish here. The colorful exuberance of the Hindu pantheon is a world away from the strictures of John Knox—who preached in St Andrews; Hinduism's ability to accommodate, if not absorb, a diversity of views is alien to the brutal sectarian antagonisms of Scottish religious history. There are brass markers set into some of the town's cobbled streets, indicating where, in the sixteenth century, Protestant martyrs were burned at the stake for heresy. But despite the austerely Calvinist outlook cultivated hereabouts since the Reformation, it would be an improbably chaste mind, I think, that—as the Rock and Spindle comes into view—would not have enter it some sense, however fleeting or denied, of an erect male member, its hard tumescence rising from the spindle's swollen bulb.

Whatever its sexually symbolic potential may be, the Rock and Spindle is no lingam cast by human hands, but a naturally occurring feature. It's a volcanic plug, marking out in stone where a vent once ran hot and liquid, spouting the fiery ejaculate of the earth's magma. The roaring throat of the volcano that erupted here in the Lower Carboniferous has slowly been weathered away until this single tracheal thread of basanite—a variety of basalt—has been left like a final frozen scream of fury cooling over the eons. Volcanic ash and debris would once have sheathed this spurting vent. But its camouflaging cone has long since been eroded away to nothing, leaving behind this single finger of congealed stone to point at itself, and mark where the membrane of the now quietened earth was once riven by eruption. It stands isolated and faintly absurd in the ragged remains of what was once a crater but has now become just part of the landscape, littered with sand and rocks and sea.

⚘

I've not walked to the Rock and Spindle for perhaps a year. It came to mind, improbably enough, when I was thinking of a favorite expression used by my friend and teacher Arnold Benington. The expression had nothing to do with volcanoes, still less with Shiva lingams, but its persistence in my mind over many years makes it seem kin to this stubbornly enduring basalt plug. Like the Rock and Spindle's obvious singularity, its lonely upthrust drawing the eye of every walker to its form, Arnold's *"How's the Enemy?"* also had an air of difference about it; it didn't sit flush with the surface of everyday conversation, but rather jutted out of the usual metaling with which we pave the pathways of our talk. It always drew attention to itself, made listeners stumble, think that they'd misheard. Moreover, just as the Rock and Spindle's faintly ridiculous shape, its proximity to the ribald if not grotesque, belies the weight of its history and the interest of its story, so beneath Arnold's strange locu-

tion lay depths of significance unsuspected on first hearing—
when one's immediate inclination was to mock what seemed
a quaint archaism, rather than meditate on what it might
portend.

⚘

To begin with, Arnold was always "Sir," or "Mr. Benington." He was my biology teacher at Friends' School Lisburn.
"Friends," as its name suggests, is a Quaker school; Lisburn a
County Antrim town (granted city status in 2002) some eight
miles from Belfast. I lived there until I was eighteen. Arnold
was an active and committed Quaker. My agnosticism—if
the swathe of shifting uncertainties that came to charac-
terize my outlook warrants such a term—was a source of
considerable concern to him. An educator rather than an
evangelist, he never tried to pull me into the same niche
of Christian believing he occupied with such secure assur-
ance. Instead, he sought only to increase my depth of learning about the plants and animals around me, confident that
faith is born from knowledge of the natural world, rather
than through any kind of proselytizing coercion. He seemed
to see in nature incontrovertible evidence for a benevolent
creator. He was an all-round naturalist, interested in wild-
flowers, insects, birds, and trees—life in all its myriad diversity of forms—but raptors were his special passion. Their
fierce beauty entranced and lured him. Incredibly to me, he
saw no contradiction between a loving God and the violent
death routinely meted out by these merciless avian preda-
tors. For me, such bloodiness raised questions. I found it
impossible to reconcile the butchery of a sparrowhawk kill
with the unfailing compassion with which Arnold credited
his God. Often its prey is not dead when the hawk starts to
eat it, hacking and slashing with its hooked beak, hungrily
devouring the shreds of living meat. Such a brutal communion seemed to me no likely harbinger of any overarching
benevolence.

Arnold was one of those rare teachers who can pass on the fire of their interest, skillfully feeding enough material to keep it burning brightly without blanketing the embers with a smothering weight of information. He was expert at fostering that sense of novelty, exploration, enjoyment, and discovery which keeps an interest vital. He was inspiring too in the out-of-school activities he encouraged—making a butterfly garden in a neglected corner of the school grounds, organizing bird-watching trips (some as far afield as Iceland), running a natural history society and taxidermy club. I didn't know it at the time, but was unsurprised when I discovered later that in the midst of Ulster's Troubles, in addition to all he did at school, Arnold had been involved in reconciliation work between the country's warring faiths. He made visits to a school in one of Belfast's most notorious Catholic enclaves, quietly forging links of understanding and affectionate regard with the other tribe, of whom we knew as little as they knew of us. For years, Ulster society operated a kind of religious apartheid that was almost invisible to outsiders. Protestants and Catholics lived, worked, and were educated apart. Their mutual estrangement—and frequent demonization—provided the poisoned wellspring which fed the violence that so disfigured Northern Ireland's history.

As I grew older and Arnold became a friend, "Sir" or "Mr. Benington" slowly gave way to using his Christian name. Given the age difference between us—fifty-two years—and the respect in which I held him, it was not an easy transition. I found it hard to take those first few steps into the spoken familiarity of "Arnold."

_y̆

Despite the time we spent together, much of it "in the field," as he termed it; despite our many conversations; although I can picture his face precisely, bring back to mind without effort his gestures, the exact timbre of his voice, though he's someone I held in high esteem and listened to both in and outside the classroom, I can't remember now verbatim anything he *said*—beyond two odd, isolated phrases. I suppose talk wears a kind of camouflage when it comes to recalling it, so that memory is unable to pick it out—it simply merges with the spoken landscape of the past and becomes more or less invisible beyond approximation. The wash of words between us is so much a part of us, so constant and commonplace an accompaniment to the moments we inhabit, that expecting it to be remembered in any detail would be as unreasonable as expecting memory to grasp the air that surrounds us. In any case, a word-for-word preservation of our discourse would soon overload the mind and risk clogging the operation of its other functions.

Conversation is, I think, as liable to erosion as volcanic ash; in the end, all that time's weathering leaves intact are a few isolated columns of singular expression. Their ability to perdure, their resistance to erosion, seems rarely if ever linked to any intrinsic significance. On the contrary, many of these verbal rock-and-spindles seem markedly trivial. For instance, out of everything one uncle said to me over all the years I knew him, only the residue of a single whimsical vocable remains—"*boys-a-boys*," his gentle exclamation of wonderment or surprise, interspersed with a kind of tutting shaking of the head, whenever he was listening to some exciting piece of news. Likewise the wraithlike wordy revenant to which a much loved neighbor's talk has now been reduced, consists of his oft repeated "*wouldn't ye know.*" What was once a wholly insignificant phrase, a verbal tic peppering his intelligent and amusing diction, has swollen since his death, grown almost monstrous, all but eclipsing what it once merely punctuated. In a similar manner "*Lorblessus!,*" my grandmother's contraction of "Lord bless us"—exclaimed with the genteel reserve of her generation where mine might come out with "Jesus Christ!" or worse—has become a kind of grotesque idol of crude idiom beneath the shadow of whose recall the delicate substance of what she said has been sacrificed. The gross aural physiognomy of "*Lorblessus*" has all but obliterated the finer features of her talk. No doubt it is the promise of durability that it offers which confers upon writing some of its allure; inscribed upon the page we can invest our thoughts and feelings with a basalt-like permanence quite different from the transience of the unwritten occurrence of our spoken words.

Whenever I think of Arnold now, the two strange verbal plugs that stand upright in memory's weathered crater are: "*Tight lines!*" and "*How's the Enemy?*" However unimportant—ridiculous—they sound, this is what catches on the hooks of recollection. As the mind's ear sweeps back across the vanished vistas of our talk together, all the words that we exchanged, it's these odd pillars that break the flat surface of forgetfulness, rising out of the anonymous dust of thousands of forgotten sentences.

"*Tight lines!*" was the cheery greeting Arnold called out to any fishermen we passed. One wood we visited frequently to watch sparrowhawks was bordered by a lake, popular with local anglers. Standing in their green thigh-waders, patiently casting their lines into the waters, most of them—especially the younger ones—were bemused by this tersely phrased expression of good luck, shouted out as we went by without any other comment. I can still recall the expression of one angler, no older than I was. He looked at Arnold as if he was certainly mad, possibly dangerous. The cry of "*Tight lines!*" engendered fearful incomprehension. I can understand his apprehension—though I didn't then. Arnold was a striking figure—keen eyed, as fierce looking as one of the raptors he adored, and with a shock of white hair emphasizing the craggy, character-laden features of his weather-beaten face. He had something of the air of an Old Testament prophet; his aura of passionate engagement with the natural world carried an edge of something almost threatening, certainly to be wary of. To find such a figure suddenly bearing down on you by a lonely Ulster lakeside, not far from where sectarian atrocity had recently been perpetrated, would be worrying enough, even without his mouthing of apparent gibberish. It's no wonder the boy angler was unnerved. I was reminded of *"Tight lines!"* recently when I was reading John Gimlette's *Theatre of Fish* (2005), a marvelous account of his journeys through Newfoundland and Labrador. Gimlette records the traditional greeting locals used to shout to Newfoundland sealers as they set sail for their annual harvest. Not *"Tight lines!"* but *"Bloody decks!"* Had Arnold shouted out this more alarming Newfoundland expression of good hunting, I doubt whether the boy could have looked any more puzzled or alarmed.

⚘

*"How's the Enemy?"* was Arnold's customary way of asking what time it was when we were "in the field." Or, more precisely, how long we had left before, reluctantly, we had to call it a day and head back into town. We both lived in Lisburn's suburbs then, near the railway station, a pleasant enough locale but entirely inferior, in Arnold's estimation, to the precious moments he could spend in the countryside, glorying in its natural wonders.

The first time he asked me, *"How's the Enemy?"* I'd no idea what he meant. Contemporaries I've tried it out on are likewise left bamboozled by this expression. Some dictionaries give *"How goes the Enemy?"* as a colloquialism for "What time is it?" and suggest it was a popular way of asking the time in the nineteenth and early twentieth centuries (improbably derived from a catchphrase in Frederick Reynolds's 1789 play, *The Dramatist*). It's evidently one of those sayings whose currency for one generation isn't carried over to the next or, if it is, its transition must be localized and uncertain. Perhaps there are some parts of the English-speaking world today where *"How's the Enemy?"* would still be recognized as legal tender, but for me it was as archaic as a farthing or gold sovereign. After my initial incomprehension, I quickly grew accustomed to the phrase and thought no more about it; it was just one of Arnold's verbal mannerisms. It was only much later—the Enemy having advanced further against me, felling Arnold as it came (he died in 1982)—that I started to think about the implications embedded in this odd locution. Gradually, his peculiar question took on a depth of resonance I never suspected in those affectionately remembered days together "in the field."

⁂

Should time really be regarded as our Enemy (the capitalization was always implicit in the manner of Arnold's asking)? Despite his casually casting it as foe each time he asked what time it was, I suspect that had he stopped to consider the matter, he'd soon have parlayed with his old Enemy and brought it into the sunny purview of his optimistic outlook. The natural world—as he saw it—provided abundantly persuasive proof of the God he believed in. Time is the element underpinning—allowing—our experience of that world. It is the canvas enabling the seasons to be painted, the stuff out of which are forged the hooks of minutes, hours, and days on which life hangs its colorful apparel. Time is the medium that brokers the hatching of a hawk's egg high in a swaying spruce tree, allows the delicate mechanisms of momentum that see the fluffy chick fledge into adult raptor, each unfolding nuance of development pegged and knotted by the cord of time, the umbilical drip feed of nanoseconds swelling to encompass not only the life of every individual bird, but the existence of this bloodline as it traces out its evolution and continuance from *archaeopteryx* and before, threading through the eons.

Arnold read reinforcement of his faith out of whatever script the world presented. Time provides the blank pages on which are written all the stories that caught his attention. As such, he would have somehow accommodated it within his welcoming theology. I don't mean to suggest by this any naivety or dishonesty in the way he viewed the world. It's not as if he turned a blind eye to the violence that abounds in nature. He didn't hurry over or ignore the pages showing blood and death. No more was he blind to the dark side of our humanness; he'd looked at Belfast's bigotry up close, witnessed the tragedies it birthed. It's more that he possessed an ability to see benevolent design even in ugly places—or perhaps he was afflicted (blessed?) with a kind of color blindness when it came to horror, so that its terrible opacity, the fact that no light shines through it, went unseen.

⚘

I often wish I could read things the way he did, but whilst Arnold's outlook inclined towards the "healthy minded," mine is more geared to a "sick souled" mentality—to use the divisions of William James's great typology. This Jamesian dichotomy divides us into those who affirm, and those who question, life's essential goodness. However much he referred to it as "the Enemy," time too would have succumbed to the positive theistic hue that stained his understanding of existence in such robustly cheerful Christian colors. Perhaps, had his upbringing encountered a more plural and contested scene, something that went beyond Ulster's cramped religious duopoly, the bright primary colors of his faith might have been chipped and streaked, muddied with a whole spectrum of less certain, more subtle shades. Put the cyclical complexities of a Hindu worldview beside the rock-and-spindle certainties of Christian doctrine—a linear trajectory through time for every life, begun at birth, ended at death, judged thereafter—and the ripples we leave in time's waters might suggest an altogether different mapping. Can we be sure the narrow path we follow through the days is something plainly linear? How can we know the trajectory we're set on isn't covertly, intricately looped?

*How's the Enemy?* There are so many ways in which we can pace out its condition, measure how it leans its intangible weight against us, how its life-giving, death-dealing embrace is contoured into stranglehold or caress. If you set out from where I'm writing this, leaving at noon and walking until six, following Fife's coastal path from the end of the East Sands, it would take you way beyond the Rock and Spindle—perhaps as far as Crail or even Anstruther. It took that time—six hours—to burn Patrick Campbell at the stake in 1528. The spot where he died in St Andrews is marked by a monogram of his initials set into the cobblestones outside St Salvator's Chapel in North Street. *How's the Enemy?* It allows the time for execution, for agony and ecstasy. It lets 300 million years pass between the forming of the volcanic plug at the Rock and Spindle and our perception of it today. It gives the minutes needed for a sparrowhawk chick to peck its way out of its egg, the decades required to reach maturity by the tree that bears its nest; the choking minutes gasped by those herded into Nazi gas chambers. *How's the Enemy?* Sometimes it appears gargantuan, draped in the 4.6 billion years that have elapsed since the world was written on its fabric; or we can cleave it into comfortable dimensions that are easy enough to handle—like the ten minutes taken to read from the first word of this essay to here. Set side by side, the measures grate and jar, rip the canvas of any picture that tries to place time within the neatly calibrated frame of benign purpose. Could Arnold's theodicy really have coped with seeing the conflicting expressions that writhe and jolt and leer across the face of his old Enemy?

Each moment that we live moves us simultaneously further from and closer to enormities of time in which we don't exist. The Enemy is at once the embrace that holds everything in its effortless containment—both delicate and awesome in the encompassment it effects—and the unstoppable leak in every life, every object; the conduit of universal loss. No wonder the eighteenth-century Irish thinker Bishop George Berkeley was moved to remark (echoing St. Augustine's famous perplexity) that when trying to understand time he found himself "embrangled in inextricable difficulties." There are no easy tight lines of philosophical enlightenment when we come to grapple with it.

_ℒ_

Some day soon I'll walk to the Rock and Spindle again, my mind an embranglement of sparrowhawks and slaughter, gods and martyrs, enmity and friendship, remembered faces, forgotten conversations, and the totems of a few odd phrases. If, as I sometimes do, I follow a route that takes me past the cluster of houses on the quayside of St Andrews Harbour, I'll derive a moment's wry amusement from the fact that I'll pass Shiva, Lord of Destruction and Creation, before reaching the East Sands. In a ground-floor window—no more than a stone's throw from the walls of the cathedral—a large brass statue of the dancing Shiva sits on the inner sill. How horrified the monks would have been to see this, to their eyes a pagan idol, here in the heartland of their faith; how disapproving Knox and his ilk would have been at this exuberant expression of divinity! This form of the god—the so-called Shiva Nataraja, or Shiva as Lord of the Dance—is an eloquent expression of time and birth and death and "that gleam in the midst of a long night," as Poincaré dubs the marvel of our sentience. Both an aesthetic and symbolic masterpiece, the Shiva Nataraja is now widely regarded as one of the triumphs of Hindu art, blending in a single image a wealth of religious vision with an essential simplicity of form. Its aesthetic merits have not gone unnoticed in the West, where no less an authority than Rodin has praised its beauty. Titus Burckhardt suggests that it is perhaps "the most prefect fruit of Hindu art"; its metaphysical potency has moved that great commentator on Eastern art and philosophy, Heinrich Zimmer, to write some of his most lyrical passages in explication of what the image means.

The Nataraja shows Shiva as an androgynous figure, neither male nor female, dancing life into and out of existence within a ring of flames, his feet trampling the demon of ignorance, his four arms laden with icons of becoming, extinction, continuance, and the intricate interconnections that flow between them. In this complex diagram of time and space, of life and death and the riddle of existence, there is a consummately realized portrait of the Enemy who has reduced billions of our conversations to nothingness and provided the echo chamber of history in which all our talk reverberates. Shiva's *prabhamandala*—the ring of flames within which s/he is shown dancing—and the naked flame held in one of the deity's four hands, ignite a collision of fiery images in my mind. The volcanic light flickering upon an ancient landscape; the campfires kindled in our ancestral caves; stakes lit here in this small coastal town; the countless funeral pyres far off along the Shiva-haunted Ganges, where the newborn and the dead are not seen as beginning and end but as points in an arc that wheels through eons. Can we find any warmth of meaning at such flames? Do they illumine more than their, in the end, incomprehensible incandescence?

When I reach the Rock and Spindle, I'll put my hand upon the ancient stone surface as reverently as if it were a lingam I believed in. *"How's the Enemy?"* I'll whisper affectionately, frustratedly, as if greeting an old and sometimes irksome friend who never tires of posing "inextricable (yet entrancing) difficulties." I know the hard stone column will remain fixed and cold and utterly unresponsive, but it will feel as if the very atoms jangle beneath my touch in a dance in which it's hard to know what's fire, what's ice, and whether it's a god, or demon, or just the echo of our own lonely steps across incomprehensible distances, that partners our brief pirouette into oblivion.

GLASS

It was a small blue bird that first impressed the reality of death upon my daughter Lucy's consciousness. We were living in rural Wales at the time and it was a perfect spring morning—cloudless blue sky, sun, warmth, lots of birdsong. The weather was as ill-matched to what happened as the key player was unsuited to its role. Stage directions for something as epochal as one's first encounter with death would be unlikely to cast so insignificant a creature as the star. Instead, they might read: "DEATH SCENE: tearful family members around hospital bed," or "FUNERAL: mourners clumped around open grave, raindrops beading on huddled umbrellas." But the way things actually unfolded on that perfect spring morning was completely different from such well-worn cameos of mortality. Yet, for all its understated nature, I still vividly remember what happened, years after the event.

Lucy was only three. I can't remember what we were doing, or why we were inside on such a beautiful morning, but hearing a noise in the bedroom (the soft flutter of wings, as it turned out), we went to investigate. A blue tit had flown in through the half-opened window. Normally these are birds of seemingly perpetual movement—always flitting, bobbing, darting—but this one was uncharacteristically still, perched on the rim of a vase by the bed, dazed by the unfamiliar surroundings in which it found itself. We could admire it at close quarters, see its pretty presence far more clearly than usual. Blue tits are exquisitely plumaged little birds. The head, wings, and tail are richly daubed with eye-catching blue. Paired with the yellow breast, greenish back, and white face-patches cut through with blue eye-stripes, they look like the embodiment of a specification that reads "cute." Their size— small enough to perch on a grass stem without breaking it— makes them entirely unthreatening, almost toylike; Lucy and I were both entranced.

The bird seemed to return our stare. Then it slowly gathered its wits. Alarmed by our proximity, it made to escape— but its flight took it at speed straight into the closed half of the window, through which the green sanctuary of the garden beckoned.

The impact when it hit the glass was gentle enough, a softly cushioned thud. But this muted syllable was enough to convey immediately that there could be no continuance beyond it. The sound communicated with wordless and unwelcome eloquence the sure knowledge of something fragile smashed beyond hope of mending. We were witnesses to the exact moment of the bird's annihilation. The little body fell on the carpet with no more noise than a leaf makes when it falls from a branch and settles in the undergrowth. We waited for a moment, willing it to move; knowing it would not. Then we went over to examine it more closely.

To begin with, trying to catch how the moment struck us, I wrote this:

> What was so shocking was the suddenness of the transformation from creature to cadaver; the way we'd witnessed so abrupt a metamorphosis—a small life cuffed into instantaneous extinction.

But I recalled Mark Twain: "Use the right word and not its second cousin." "Shocking" is only distantly related to what played out on that spring morning. To use it might be in keeping with situations where death horrifies with the pain it inflicts, or with its bloody violence. But it doesn't fit our seeing a little bird dashing itself to death against a window, however unexpected the collision. Lucy and I were certainly struck by what we'd witnessed, she—naturally—much more so. This was something arresting. It caused us to stop and think. But "shocking" risks exaggeration. The word has too high-blown a resonance to fit. Using it would obscure the essence of this moment—how it showed momentous things nestling at the heart of humdrum normality.

It's impossible to know what, if anything, registered in the blue tit's perception on the very verge of impact, just before it struck the glass. I can't help wondering if there would have been a split second of awareness that something was wrong, a sense of incomprehension, maybe terror, at finding the air turned solid. It's just as likely, I know, that encounter and annihilation were so exactly coterminous, impact and extinction dovetailing together with perfect synchronicity, that there would have been no awareness of anything awry. But it was the glass, rather than the bird itself that, for me, created the moment's potency.

The blue tit's death seemed not just to announce the particular circumstances of its accident, how one individual's demise occurred. Rather, it pointed to the fact that the hard transparency of death can occlude any life, materializing anywhere, at any moment, to fill the space we occupy with its lethal presence. The annihilation of this feathered morsel underscored something every adult knows and every child soon learns—namely, that what looks like life's safe continuance minute by minute, day by day, isn't guaranteed. As surely as the window blocked the blue tit's airspace, so our way through time will one day be sealed and stopped, passage refused beyond whatever moment we happen to have reached when the glass of closure hits us.

Death that spring morning was frightening, not because it came clad in lurid symbols of violence or funereal gloom, but because it was so completely without features other than its unavoidable there-ness; its nonnegotiable occurrence; its utter finality. Existence and nonexistence are two sides of our coin of being—and it can be flipped with little or no warning. On one face of a moment a bird, a life. A nanosecond later, on the other face, there's just a body.

⚘

Written accounts sometimes make things more vivid, more exciting, than they warrant. It's tempting to embroider, particularly with something as negligible as a small bird's swift eclipse. I've tried to resist the theatrics of exaggeration; tried not to make mountains out of molehills. But an opposite tendency is, in fact, as common a failing. We routinely scale down the mountains that are an integral part of our everyday experience. The truth is that vertiginous summits and precipices litter the topography of terrain we've come to see as mundane and unremarkable. All around us are the Himalayas of being and nonbeing. The mystery of beginnings and endings is threaded through the skein of life on which, so momentarily, blue tits and humans and myriads of other creatures shimmer their precarious way between the systole of birth and the diastole of death. Revealing the peaks of this mountain range, erupting right there in the midst of a commonplace spring morning, was what gave the blue tit's death its unexpected gravity.

꒰ᵛ

I picked the blue tit up, held it in my hand; felt that strange communion of the quick and the dead, so intimately entangled with each other. Lucy and I pored over its stilled perfection for a while, voyeurs exploring as we never could have done while it was alive the detail of this little flying machine. I gently stretched out both wings, held the lolling head straight again, felt the warmth rapidly fading from the body's core. Lucy was at the same moment keen, yet reluctant, to touch it; it was as if she'd been presented with a lovely toy that, before her eyes, had been inexplicably besmirched. We admired the form and color of a design that I knew had been sculpted over eons. The chip and flake of millions of individual moments of existence has molded every feather, every bone, in the long journey from single-celled organisms to the complexities of *Archaeopteryx* and other precursors and prototypes. I thought about the slow emergence from the Earth's primeval substance of the lovely intricacy we name "blue tit" (*Parus caeruleus*), how it had flowered into being; how this one individual had borne the blossom of its bloodline—until the moment that it hit the glass.

We tread a precarious path along the uncertain spans we're allocated, precipices on either side, a narrow, scary route. All around us, just beyond the curtain of custom and routine, looms the unknown. And one day, inevitably, we fall; our onward progress encounters the glass on which life's grip can gain no purchase. In its presence we can no longer be. The mind's flight will be grounded and we'll be wiped from the scene as surely as bugs from a windshield.

Glass may seem as inappropriate a symbol for death as a blue tit is, but I think it has much to recommend it. Keyed to the register of ice, it seems more fitting than some of our more obvious icons. Its annihilating translucence razors through us. Indexed to blankness, nullity, and absence, the transparency of glass surely represents death's colors as well as any draping with the traditional livery of black.

_✕_

Having marveled at it, and mourned its passing, we took the blue tit's body out to the garden and buried it in a flower-bed underneath a gingko sapling. Lucy shaped the soil over it into a little mound and marked the grave with a piece of slate stuck upright like a tiny headstone. Thereafter, the occasional dead bird found in the garden was buried beside the blue tit. For a while, "underneath the gingko" became a kind of family euphemism for death. I'd like to think that her encounter with the blue tit and all these other little harbingers of finitude—robins, sparrows, blackbirds—will help armor Lucy's heart with the resilience it will need to weather life's larger losses. I hope each of the tiny graves she excavated by trowel, assisted sometimes by her younger sister, will gently make the ungentle point that death isn't something rare or distant, something safely locked into the domain of the old, or of those who live far away. It's always crouched beside us, part of the familiar moments we inhabit; it's present in perfect spring mornings as surely as it is in the wintered corners of illness, aging, and catastrophe in far-off places. The wing-beats of our hearts are already preset on a collision course; no one can avoid the glass ahead.

# (UN)SENTIMENTAL
# TIMEKEEPING

*A*esthetically, the clock that sits on my desk has nothing to recommend it. To describe it as ugly would only be a slight exaggeration; at the very least it's plain. Its circular white face is marked with large Arabic numerals. Neither they nor the hands that point to them have been designed with any attempt at subtlety or grace. Two black lines run around the full circle of the face's circumference. They're only millimeters apart, with sixty little crossties laid between them, marking out the minutes. Each fifth one, on the hour, is emphasized by being marked more thickly. It's as if a child's picture of a train track has been drawn around the face's rim, giving the illusion that time's trains run on a scale and at a tempo obedient to our purposes.

Because it's cased in metal, not plastic, the clock is surprisingly heavy for its size. The weight is added to by the thick glass that fronts the face. If you unscrew two metal nuts on the back, placed on either side of the control for setting the alarm, almost the whole back comes off—a saucer-sized disc—to reveal the mechanism and battery, both encased in transparent plastic. They take up only a small part of the space inside the clock. There would be room for at least five more mechanisms and batteries beside them. The inner chamber's pointless profligacy with space further emphasizes the sense of something shoddily designed and put together.

~~~

Why do I have this frankly unappealing object sitting on my desk, where I'll see it every day? If I say it's because it has sentimental value I know this is likely to trigger an unsympathetic response. Indeed the weight of disapproval now attached to "sentimental" is enough to render it an unseaworthy verbal craft; setting sail in it can spell doom. Yet its genealogy is perfectly respectable. It can trace a direct lineage back to the Latin for "to feel." It seems curious to criminalize such a basic trait of our nature, yet that's often the tenor that now accompanies it. "Sentimental" has come to be understood as an indulging or wallowing in emotion rather than an honest feeling of it. Seen in this light, "sentiment" is invariably prefaced by "mere" and cast in the role of something weak-willed, almost sickly, that threatens to undermine our rationality. Being sentimental is seen as the affectation of emotion rather than its genuine unforced occurrence. Admitting to it risks sparking accusations of insincerity or self-indulgence. When someone is "sentimentally attached" to something, when an object has "sentimental value" for them, this is often said in a tone of disparagement, as if they should know better. The implication is that they've turned away from clear thinking, lost touch with common sense, embraced something that occupies much the same level of foolishness as superstition. Let me hasten to stress, then, that when I say the clock holds sentimental value for me I mean this in a different sense to the one that's usually associated with this expression.

⤳

The room in the nursing home where my mother died overlooked the town's railway station. It was close enough not
just to see the trains, but also to hear the platform announcements. "The train approaching platform 2 will be the 9:28
to Belfast." "The next train from platform 1 will be the
10:15 to Dublin, calling at Portadown, Newry, Dundalk, and
Drogheda." These announcements, the knowledge of trains
leaving and arriving, and of passengers traveling to different
destinations all over Ireland, threw into stark relief the fact
that the residents of the nursing home were embarked on very
different journeys. "The train now standing at room 2 is the
8:53 for Parkinson's, pneumonia, stroke, and heart attack."
"The next arrival at room 15 will be for cancer and Alzheim-
er's, calling at stations no one recognizes, with names no one
can remember, and for a destination from which no one will
return." What my mother and many of the others wanted was
a comfortable overnight service, a sleeper train that would
whisk them away with no further stops at any of those trying
stations of decrepitude where they'd already been delayed too
long; an express service out of life without their even knowing it had happened.

I was living in Scotland when my mother's life was drawing to a close. The easiest way to make the journey back
to Ireland was by ferry and train. My frequent sea crossings, plus the proximity of the station to the nursing home,
the way in which all our conversations were underlain by
the sound of trains coming and going, meant that this whole
period of my life took on a sense of being in transit; it
moved to the rhythm of setting out and coming back again.
The clock was a focal point in her room. As never before,
we were conscious of time passing, the imminent departures
that we faced, and the uncertainty at each parting of whether
we would see each other again. Steeped in that atmosphere,
and with its circumference marked by the little cross-hatched

railway track of minutes, it's not surprising that the clock took on a sense of journeying and distance, of boats and trains. For me, it still carries strong hints of the sea. In fact it often seems more like a ship's chronometer or compass than a simple alarm clock.

There's something elemental in a ferry crossing, something that raises questions that are often pushed aside once we're safely back on land. It's as if the experience of departure and arrival, of being exposed to the elements of sea and sky, of being in a kind of liminal state—a period of transition between one place and another—sounds notes that temporarily tune our psyches to a more reflective pitch. Crossing and recrossing that narrow stretch of sea between Ireland and Scotland to visit my mother in her final years seemed to set off a kind of metronome. It kept time to a rhythm that was different from those I was used to. One of the things its beat made me think of was all the people who, over the centuries, must have crossed here between the ports of Cairnryan and Larne. The journey will have been made from whenever humans first tenanted the land on either side. Crossing the sea at this point of repeated human passage kindled a sense of something ancient and enduring alongside the transience of individual lives.

Our minds are not calibrated to catch duration in more than thimble-sized containers. Minutes edging into hours, days, weeks, months, years offer scales that we can comprehend. Measuring the time it takes a ferry to leave its moorings and then dock safely, or how long we've sat together talking in a room, or when the next train is due, or even the length of an individual's whole lifespan are all thinkable, they fall within our compass. It's harder to see ourselves as particles of the earth's long history, as witnesses to millions of years of life's evolution, as denizens of a universe that's been in existence for some fourteen billion years. As I repeatedly made that same passage, a sense of history mingled with a sense of mystery as I imagined the gathered tribe of those who had made this voyage before me, who will make it long after I am gone. I thought of the crafts they have used, and the patterns that this cluster of life-stories trace out upon the earth, and the fact that we all disappear, leaving no perceptible trace of our presence on the waves that have borne us. The raw amplitude of planetary time—time on a massive, dwarfing scale—edged into mind on these crossings as the context in which all our little voyages are set.

❦

Anthony Powell once said that "growing old is like being increasingly penalized for a crime you haven't committed." The last two years of my mother's life were like an illustration of Powell's dictum. To begin with, she read, watched TV, talked with visitors. Slowly, each of these small comforts failed and she was left marooned in the cul-de-sac of her own incapacity. Age, and Parkinson's disease, and several minor strokes ravaged her body. Her mind remained alert throughout, allowing her the cruel savor of being able to witness her own ineluctable downward spiral.

She had notional membership of a local church but was never a believer and didn't attend services, even in her able-bodied days. The ministers and elders dutifully visited her. Mostly she welcomed the distraction, but one of these churchmen insisted on heavy-handed evangelism. She viewed his attention as a kind of faux pas, a breach of etiquette bordering on boorishness, but was too polite to tell him. I raged on her behalf but she forbade me from saying anything—that, too, she would have considered a lapse in manners, a drift toward the kind of behavior she deplored.

The clock was bought at her request. As her eyesight worsened and as arthritis and Parkinson's disease made her hands clumsy, the small traveling clock she'd always relied on became another source of frustration. The face was too small for her to make out the time with any certainty; the controls were too delicate for her swollen, shaking fingers to set or cancel the alarm. She asked for a new clock, saying that she didn't care what it looked like, so long as it was big enough to see clearly and that she could operate the controls with ease.

⚜

An object is usually said to have sentimental value if it's something closely associated with a person, place, or time of which we have fond memories. Such an object is highly valued by whoever treasures it, but rarely possesses any value of its own. The best example I can think of is my father's walking stick. Although I've no practical use for it, I'd hate to lose it—simply because it reminds me so strongly of him. Even now, years after his death, whenever I grip the handle it summons him back. I can hear his footsteps and the tap of the stick's ferrule on the ground, picture him walking beside me and listen to his voice again. But I know this scratched and battered walking stick would be worthless to anyone else.

In trying to explain why I keep the clock sitting on my desk, saying it has sentimental value doesn't therefore quite convey the reason. It carries no fond memories for me. Yes, it reminds me of my mother—but at a time in her life I'd rather not recall. To say I keep it as a memento mori might be closer to the truth, except that it sounds too macabre—as if the clock was a skull sitting bleakly beside me, a crudely theatrical reminder of mortality. Instead, I've come to think of it as helping me to see things as they are. This ill-loved, lumpish object functions as a kind of corrective lens, a counterweight to those mundane calibrations by which time is routinely measured out in hours and minutes, weeks and days. The clock is set to a more elemental scale—it's a kind of temporal compass that helps me keep in sight the true north of our finitude and all the uncertainties that attend it.

⚜

This is the clock that sat in the room overlooking the station. For two years it was within earshot of the passing trains and the echoing announcements of arrivals and departures. As the hands moved around its face the trains came and went, bearing with them their varied human cargoes, those unmet strangers whose lives were also ticking past, each going about their business in those tantalizingly secret worlds of other people that orbit so closely to our own. As the minutes passed, as the clock's hands silently semaphored the phases of each day and night, my mother's breathing sounded in that room, changing rhythm as she slept or wakened. As the metronome of the battery kept the hands in perfect time, her biological clock was faltering. Blood cells moved around her body, pulsing through her veins, but her pumping heart was nearing the moment when it would stop. This is the clock she looked at—discreetly—if a minister's visit seemed interminable, or when hungry evangelism grated on her sensibilities. Her glance fell on it repeatedly through the long nights of restless sleeplessness when she wished the hours away. This is the clock she looked at on stormy winter days when she knew I was on a ferry, coming to see her or going away again. She wondered how long the weather would delay things and worried that the vessel might founder. This is the clock she must have looked at the very last time she wondered what the time was. This is the clock that showed the minute of her death, whose hands moved between the second in that room when she existed and the second when she didn't. In their transit around those twelve crudely formed numerals the hands must have traversed in one of their revolutions that mysterious space between the last moment she was alive and the first moment she was not. Now, it acts like a marker buoy reminding me of her presence and her absence, a time capsule left behind that resonates with a sense of her last days.

For me, the clock does much more than simply tell the time. It reminds me of ferry journeys, of stormy seas and skies, of the fact that we are all embarked on a life-cross-ing. It makes me recognize that hours are not just neat divisions of a day, each one holding sixty minutes, but that they are—as the old Scottish saying has it—"time's shafts" and that "one comes winged with death." The clock doesn't just tell me what time of day or night it is, but reminds me of what of course I already know, yet too often lose sight of—that my store of days and nights is limited and fleeting and will end. As much an aide-mémoire for finitude as a practical chronometer, I like to think that it helps me not to waste time, that whether its alarm is set or not it provides a kind of permanent wake-up call, letting me keep track of the days and learning to value them more appropriately than if I relied solely on the usual quotidian reckonings by which we plot time's passing. Given that this (un)sentimentally valued clock is a purveyor of hard, unpalatable truths, there is perhaps a certain appropriateness in the plainness of its appearance.

Sometimes I think the empty space inside the clock, instead of merely being evidence of shoddy design, is in fact an apt symbol for the way in which mundane objects can contain so much more than they appear to. I picture the clock's empty innards filled with a great store of the compacted moments that have played out around it as it sat in that nursing home room within earshot of the station. This invisible reservoir holds transcripts of all the conversations that took place there—the chats with family and friends, the minister's unwanted efforts at an unseemly deathbed conversion, the many kindnesses of nurses. It holds pitch-perfect all the platform announcements from the station, the noise of passing trains, the sound of rain against the windows and wind crashing through the trees in winter storms. I like to think that a manifest of the clock's hidden cargo would also list fugitive traces of my mother's thoughts and dreams and memories, the way she pictured my journeys, looked forward to visits, worried about rough sea crossings. The clock seems heavy with her unspoken feelings, what occupied her mind as she sat alone, the time slowly passing in that room over-looking the station that was the last place she occupied on earth.

Is it ridiculous to imagine this plain clock's emptiness being pregnant with such bounty? Perhaps such animation of an inert object is unwarranted—but I'd prefer to see it as a recognition of the fact that the ordinary things around us can convey a wealth of stories, that they carry a weight of sug-gestion and association that goes far beyond their quotidian function. Far from succumbing to sentimentality, by listen-ing carefully to the testimony of such mute witnesses we can attune our ears to the wavelengths in which some of exis-tence's most haunting notes are sounded.

ᴥ

I'm rarely in Ireland now. But when I am, I try to find time to walk past the nursing home and look up at the window of what used to be my mother's room. Whenever I do that I have a sense of ferry crossings, of people in transit, of the fact that as I stand there ships are plying between Scotland and Ireland, following the same routes they've taken for centuries, bearing their passengers on their journeys. It's strange to think that the clock sitting on my desk hundreds of miles away, still mark-ing time in another country, was once here, within earshot of the station. But stranger than that thought is the realization that when its hands moved to a particular position, her heart took its final beat. I go to the station too—just to watch a few trains come and go and listen to the platform announce-ments calling out the names of stations so well known they feel like chanted prayers learned by rote in childhood. In the tinny, echoing tone of the loudspeakers a voice marked with a heavy Ulster accent announces:

> The next train from Platform 2 will be the 10:08 to Belfast Central, calling at: Hilden, Lambeg, Derriaghy, Dunmurry, Finaghy, Balmoral, Adelaide, Great Victoria Street, City Hospital, Botanic, due to arrive in Belfast Central at 10:40.

I imagine the same voice announcing my mother's name and reciting the stops of her life-journey—conception, birth, childhood, marriage, children, grieving for parents, husband, sisters, then old age and death. And I'm struck both by the familiarity of life's stations, the well-trodden routes we follow, and yet the utter strangeness of the voyage we're embarked on.

# BEFORE I KNOCKED

## I

LA-7   FLOWER BORDERED WALKS AND DRIVES, ELYSIAN PARK, LOS ANGELES, CALIFORNIA

A-61363

*T*he title that's printed on the narrow white frame of this picture postcard is: **"Flower Bordered Walks and Drives, Elysian Park, Los Angeles, California."** To a contemporary eye, what's immediately apparent is a sense of datedness. The poor quality of color and resolution acts like a fingerprint of out-of-date technology. Pictures like this haven't been produced for years. This is an old postcard, verging on the antique. I'm not sure when the photograph was taken. The card looks similar in style to one that's marked "Mailed in 1910" in a selection of Elysian Park postcards displayed on www.image-archaeology. com, a website whose name alone points to a rich stratum of inquiry for anyone interested in recovering the fabric of the recent past.

Whatever year the photograph was taken, I know this postcard was mailed in 1931. Inside the black circle of the postmark is printed: "Calif. Arcade Sta. 1 Jun 29 1PM 1931." It's addressed to "Miss Herron, 15 Bedford Street, Belfast, Ireland." Like the address, the message on the card is written with a thick-nibbed fountain pen. The blue-black ink has begun to fade. It says: "Having a much enjoyable holiday here. This is a lovely spot wish you could see it. Kindest Regards, F. W. Adams." This eighty-seven-year-old message only carries a single one-cent stamp, but a yellowed space beside it suggests that, originally, a second stamp accompanied it.

The postcard was given to me by a friend in Ireland who knows my liking for such shards of history. She found it among papers she was going through after her father's death. "Miss Herron" was a distant, only hazily remembered relative; who "F. W. Adams" was, nobody now remembers. I'm fascinated by this little piece of card sent across the Atlantic years before I was born. This isn't because of what's written on it. Its variation on the hackneyed theme of "Having a lovely time, wish you were here" isn't interesting at all. The postcard appeals to me for reasons that have little to do with what it says.

Part of the appeal lies in the way it acts as a tiny uncurtained window giving a tantalizing glimpse of other lives. It's like a spyhole that offers a peek into someone else's room. Looking at it reminds me of nighttime train journeys when the carriage passes close by lighted houses and, for a moment, cameo scenes of their occupants are vividly displayed. Despite their ordinariness, these scenes are sometimes so striking in their brief illumination that they can seem like icons depicting how other people live. Of course the postcard sparks a raft of questions. Who was F. W. Adams? What was the relationship between him, or her, and Miss Herron? What did Miss Herron think when the card arrived and she recognized the handwriting? Did it spark a smile of recognition? Make her frown? Was she pleased that F. W. Adams was having a "much enjoyable holiday" or disapproving of such an expensive foreign jaunt? And what stands behind that oddly formal "F. W." of the signature? Was it Frank Wallace? Frances Wendy? Frederika Wilma? Was withholding a name just the convention of 1931 postcard writing, or might opting for initials reveal where F. W. Adams stood on a contour map of class, gender, nationality, or age? This little splinter of communication gets under the skin of the imagination and prompts a whole ream of possibilities. The clues it gives are sparse, but they spark countless scenarios of human interaction.

Another reason I find old postcards like this one appealing is because they offer such precise coordinates of when and where. In doing so, they almost seem like pieces of petrified time. What was once a now is caught in the teeth of this minute card-trap, the moment preserved in the amber of its ink. This postcard is a tangible fragment of June 29, 1931, at 1:00 p.m. Holding it brings powerfully to mind the lives that were being lived at that vanished moment alongside those of Miss Herron and F. W. Adams. The card's smallness, the fact that it represents so tiny a part of the great buzz of humanity, seems to summon an awareness of the belittling cornucopia of lives happening around the two it names. And I realize, as I scrutinize it for further clues, that in the maelstrom of lives and events of which it's such a minute remnant, the threads were being woven that would eventually lead to me.

I'm particularly drawn to this postcard because I can connect it with my father's life. June 29, 1931—my father is twenty-six, working as a civil servant. He's living in Belfast, not far from Miss Herron's Bedford Street address. It's almost certain he'll have walked past her door on more than one occasion since her house is in the same street as a theater he frequented as a young man. Did their paths ever cross? Might they have exchanged a glance? How strange to think of a look passing between them, neither knowing anything about the other, and how each of their lives continued from that moment in all the intricate particularity that created the histories they embodied. In eight years from the now preserved in this postcard, Dad will leave his job to fight in World War II. He won't get married for another eighteen years. In 1931 he's not even met my mother. She's only fourteen when F. W. Adams was visiting Elysian Park. What, I wonder, was she doing, the girl who would become my mother, at the precise moment that F. W. Adams licked the stamps and put the postcard into a mailbox in California?

I know she's living on a farm in the County Antrim country-side not many miles from Belfast. It's likely that she too will have walked down Bedford Street—her mother had friends who lived near there. In fact they might easily have passed by Miss Herron's door—perhaps even glimpsed the tall, dark-haired young man walking by who was to become her husband. When I look back at—or imagine—these encounters now, decades later, I'm filled with a sense of the precariousness of individual being. How easy it would be for any of us never to have existed.

I'm pleased to have the convenience of electronic communication. But somehow texts and emails don't have the same appeal as something that was there, in that place, at that time; something that was held in the hands of those named on it. The postcard has the authenticity of presence. It acts as a tangible token of a vanished time, a remnant of lives now over. It summons them back to mind in a way an email couldn't. I realize that the postcard's obsolete, just junk—it's long served whatever purpose F. W. Adams may have had in sending it. The writer of the card and its recipient would doubtless have been astonished to find people eavesdropping on their business all these years later. Listen! You can almost hear Miss Herron tut-tutting at the ill-bred nature of such spying. Yet I'm reluctant to heed her and throw the postcard out. It's poised to cross the uncertain border that runs between the mundane and the historical. I suppose any artifact becomes interesting if it's kept for long enough. I don't want to disturb the slow metamorphosis of this little splinter as it works its way out of the ordinary and into the realm of the revelatory. Soon it might warrant a place in a museum. In any case, the Elysian Park postcard has recently acquired additional value because of how it relates to two other images. Put together, they form a kind of triptych whose interconnections fascinate me.

## II

"Herod's Gate framing two strong men standing face to face! Mosque of Omar Behind." That's the caption written on the back of this small black and white photograph. The writing has been traced out first in pencil before being gone over again in ink. The ink writing has been carefully done, but has left that first penciled draft like a ghostly presence peeping out behind each letter. The photo shows two men in military uniform standing beneath what looks like a massive stone archway (not all of it is visible). Beyond them, across some dusty wasteland pocked with a scattering of stones, a domed building dominates the scene. There's no date on the photograph, but I'd guess it was taken in the early 1940s, nine or ten years after Miss Herron received her postcard.

*Herod's Gate*
*framing two*
*strong men*
*standing face*
*to face!*

*Mosque of Omar*
*beyond.*

JERUSALEM

One of the "two strong men" pictured is my father. I also recognize his style of handwriting in the "JERUSALEM" that's been added in block capitals, in biro, on the back of the photo. He's standing with his arms folded, looking relaxed in his knee-length khaki military shorts, short-sleeved shirt, and peaked officer's cap. He wears a holster on his belt. I'm not sure of the identity of the similarly attired figure beside him, whose face is turned away, but I'm pretty sure it's Felix Hague, an old friend of Dad's from Belfast who was in the same platoon. The fountain-pen writing is probably Felix's too. Whoever wrote the caption on the back, I warm to their self-deprecating exclamation mark, suggesting that "strong men" was a piece of gentle mockery rather than evidence of too much self-regard.

When I look at the photo now, it's as if a current has broken free from my father's history, overrun the channel of time-past, and flowed invisibly into my waters. It ripples through them with the tug and flex of his presence. I wonder what he and Felix are thinking, what they're saying, at the precise moment the camera's shutter clicked and this immobilized instance began its long journey down the years to me. They look as if they were unaware of the photographer's presence; it seems a natural, unforced shot that just catches part of the ordinary flow of time, rather than attempting to irrigate it with the deliberation of a self-conscious pose specially assumed for the camera.

It's strange to see a picture of my father before his life-map was triangulated by marriage, children, and career. Here he is, a young man far from home, embroiled in a war that had the world in turmoil, but in which he didn't have to fight. Unlike the rest of Britain, there was no conscription in Northern Ireland. Those who joined up did so out of choice, not compulsion. Would he have enlisted if he'd known that, only a month or two after this photo was taken, his right leg would be shattered by shrapnel and never recover completely, so that he'd limp for the rest of his life?

If he hadn't enlisted, if he'd spent the war at home in Belfast, would that have changed things so much that I might never have existed? I'm intrigued by the countless things that could have happened so that his life wouldn't have set into the course I know. There seems to be a fantastic improbability about its familiar patterns ever being woven. It's daunting to think of all the things that had to happen— and could so easily not have happened—for his life to lead to my life and for both our spans of days to unfold in the way that constitutes our history. There is such a tangle of turnings, relationships, and events that could so easily have been otherwise.

Was his standing at Herod's Gate, at that precise moment, young and uninjured, an integral and essential part of the pattern, or could this detail have been changed—even cancelled—without altering anything more than the irrelevance of its own occurrence? Or would changing it by even the merest whisker of degree (say he'd uncrossed his arms) have led to a completely different unfolding; perhaps to one that resulted in death, not injury, a few months later, or to a radically altered triangulation; different wife, no children, a career

bearing no similarity to the one he followed? Such speculations have their icon in chaos theory's butterfly. Its poised
wings seem palpable in photographs like this; the weight of
hurricanes delivered or withheld are almost tangible in the
frozen scene at Herod's Gate.

The photo includes two figures who are easily missed at
first glance. If you look towards the Mosque of Omar (more
usually referred to now as the Dome of the Rock), there's an
open metal gate in the high wire fence running across the
rocky wasteland in the foreground. A dark-robed female figure is standing there. She's holding a child, who is looking
intently towards the two foreign soldiers. The costume of the
figure I assume is the child's mother (though it could as easily
be an older sister) is traditional, archetypal, almost timeless.
This, coupled with the weight of history implicit in Jerusalem, sparks a sense of Madonna and child, of pietà, of the life
of Jesus rippling out in waves of consequence that reached
across the world, touching successive centuries with its presence. Like my father, like most folk in Northern Ireland then,
I'm sure Miss Herron was a churchgoer. Think of the intricate web of events, the complicated networks of cause and
effect that link the life she lived in 15 Bedford Street with
the ideas and values forged in the desert country surveyed by
two strong men standing framed in Herod's Gate.

Photographs like this come laden with a potent sense of
paused stories; stories caught like waves just at the crest of
their breaking on the shore of what happens next. What tracery of outcomes will follow on from here? What patterns
veined through all the preceding centuries to lead to this particular unfolding, the precise set of circumstances pictured
here at Herod's Gate? Where did my father and Felix go after
they left the frame, as they walked on into the rest of their
lives? Each step they took provided another cameo scene that
might have been frozen by the camera, part of the mosaic of
the way things were. But each step also possessed the potential to take a different direction and so to have things unfold
in a way that would not lead to the present that I know.

How did the child held in its mother's (sister's) arms grow up? It's not clear from the photo whether it's a he or she, but I would guess a boy. It's even possible he's still alive. If he was five when the photo was taken, he'd be in his seventies now. I find it disconcerting to think of him being in the world right now, conscious, thinking, seeing, breathing—perhaps even remembering the moment pictured in the photo. Or the child may be long dead, no more trace remaining of that little close-held body staring towards the soldiers than some bone fragments interred in ground as dry and dusty as that in the photograph. Or maybe his or her descendents still tread Jerusalem's narrow streets; the child's blood and breath passed on, knitted into other flesh. I'm reminded of Roland Barthes's comment in *Camera Lucida*. Looking at one of André Kertész's photos—simply entitled "Ernest, Paris, 1931" and showing the boy in question standing in an old-fashioned schoolroom—Barthes, writing in 1980, comments, "It is possible that Ernest is still alive today, but where? how? What a novel!"

The fact that André Kertész's photograph dates from the same year as F. W. Adams's postcard from Elysian Park makes me imagine an improbable coincidence: that the shutter clicked on Ernest at the exact moment the postcard was being written. Of course I know this is unlikely, but the image conjures in a kind of visual shorthand a symbol of the rich simultaneity of occurrence that characterizes every moment. If it was possible to trace out the web of connections that link such disparate events as ink drying on a Californian postcard bound for Belfast and a little boy staring at a camera in Paris, would the patterns in such cartography show a landscape that was navigable to human-scaled meaning, or would it just depict a blizzard of happenstance, a wealth of brute occurrence?

There are certainly novels implicit in each of the figures pictured in the snapshot of Herod's Gate. The photograph is like a pothole in time, a crevasse in the ordinary passage of the days, disrupting their routine chronology with other senses of duration. Looking at it I have the feeling of missing my footing, falling into it, and being drawn into other times and lives. Yet I don't want to escape so much as trace out and try to understand the way in which the specifics of the stories glimpsed here ravel and unravel, knot their particularities into the wider human story of which they're such a tiny part, find out how their unfoldings might be plotted and where the interface is located between these facets of being and home territory I would recognize. How does this fragment of existence dovetail into mine? It's as if, glimpsed for a moment here, I can see a thread of connection between some of the tiles in time's mosaic, a kind of umbilical cord running between Belfast and Jerusalem, and Elysian Park, a hidden nerve that snakes its way through the lives that are connected to these moments.

## III

**Newcastle June 1954.** Thinking about it now, I'm not sure which surprises me more—the weight of cargo carried by this photograph, or the fact that, for so long, I didn't see it, but instead dismissed it as merely commonplace, a feather-weight image of the familiar that contained no more than it showed. Like the photo of Herod's Gate, it's in black and white. But in this image the war is over and the sand is on a beach in a popular coastal resort in Ireland, thousands of miles from the desert where my father fought.

The photograph shows a man in his forties with two younger women, sitting on a rug spread out on the sand. He's in shorts and has the sleeves of a white shirt neatly rolled up past his elbows. One of the women is in a swim-suit, the other's wearing a short-sleeved summer frock that's been pulled up to expose her legs to the sun. The women are both knitting. They're sitting with their backs against a wooden groyne. It resembles a giant railway crosstie crudely fixed into the sand with thick stakes hammered in on each side at intervals along its length. None of the trio in the photograph is looking at the camera. The man is looking down and to his right, as if at something in the sand beside him. The woman next to him is concentrating on her knit-ting. The other woman—wearing sunglasses—is looking to her left. "Newcastle June 1954" is in my father's handwrit-ing. I'd recognize it anywhere. The photo shows him with my mother and one of her sisters, Kay (wearing the swimsuit and dark glasses).

Dad's shorts are an old army pair he wore every summer for years—khaki issue for the desert, very likely the same ones he was wearing in the photograph taken in Jerusalem. On his right leg, clearly visible on the shin, is what looks like a kind of elongated dimple. This is the scar left by the shrap-nel wound he suffered when his unit was fighting in Egypt. The leg was badly damaged. He spent months recuperat-ing on board hospital ships and in hospitals in South Africa and England. The injury meant that his right leg was weaker than his left, and more susceptible to pain. It was obviously excruciating if he ever got it bumped. Often the area around the dimple was red and inflamed and the skin there looked thinner, tauter than elsewhere on his leg.

Nineteen fifty-four. Twenty-three years since F. W. Adams mailed the Elysian Park postcard to Miss Herron, fourteen or fifteen years since the photograph was taken at Herod's Gate, and only nine years since the war ended. I wonder if my father, his toes on the sand of Newcastle's sun-warmed beach, is remembering a hotter sun and redder, coarser desert sand and those comrades-in-arms who didn't make it back to Ireland. He looks thoughtful, but of course it's impossible to know what was in his mind the moment the shutter clicked. He might have been worrying about a dental appointment the next day, or remembering a strange dream from the night before, or wondering where they should have lunch.

The photographer was almost certainly Kay's husband, my Uncle Brian. Like Dad—and so many Ulstermen of their generation—he had joined up when the war came. Brian served in Italy and was awarded a Military Cross for repairing vital communication lines under heavy enemy fire during the assault on the Gothic Line in September 1944, the largest and most costly of Allied actions in the Italian campaign. Returned from distant, war-torn places to the quiet domesticity of wives and jobs and families, to sitting relaxed in the sun on Newcastle beach, were they content, these two recent volunteer soldiers? Is this what they dreamed of when they were in uniform, facing mortal danger, hundreds of miles away from Irish shores? Or do they miss the camaraderie and excitement of wartime? Have they found it hard to settle down?

The camera can deliver unsettling perspectives. I find it odd to look at my father, mother, and aunt pictured in "Newcastle, June 1954" and realize that they're all younger then than I am now, and also that, as I look at them, they've been dead for thirty years, nine years, and ten years, respectively. It's hard to keep these two threads of thought together in my head: their youth and their old age and decrepitude; their setting out on married life, and their coffined corpses and grieving families. It's peculiar to see them at this stage in their lives, when they had plans and dreams, desires, uncertainties, but didn't know how things would work out, whilst for me, looking at them now, the detail of what happened is well known. I'm reminded of a comment of Susan Sontag's in her brilliant meditation *On Photography*:

> To possess the world in the form of images is, precisely, to re-experience the unreality and remoteness of the real.

Looking at "Newcastle, June 1954" kindles a sense, not so much of unreality as of the complicated texture of the real, of how even familiar subjects can seem remote and strange.

It was the caption's date—its significance not taken in at first—that changed the way I looked at this photograph. Given when it was taken, my mother must be in the early stages of pregnancy. I'll be around eight weeks old. This means that, measured from crown of head to rump, I'll be about an inch and a quarter, or a little more—maybe forty millimeters at most—and will weigh around five grams. When I realized I was there, albeit unseen, the pregnancy too early to show, some stray lines from a Dylan Thomas poem came to mind:

> Before I knocked and flesh let enter,
> With liquid hands tapped on the womb

In "Newcastle, June 1954" you can still hear the echo of my knocking. It's so recent it seems to reverberate around the image and point to that forbidden territory of speculation into which we've all surely trespassed now and then—the nature of our parents' sexuality. Who has not at some point turned voyeur in their imagination and pictured possible scenarios for their own conception? Was it was a tender, passionate, careless, aggressive, or reluctant moment?

In June 1954, flesh had just opened its doors to me; I'd only moments ago stepped inside its warm embrace. "I who was liquid as the water" (to quote the next line of Dylan Thomas's poem) was starting to take shape. My eyes will still have been closed—they'll not open for another seventeen weeks—but my hands and feet will even then have been forming, my limbs starting to become recognizable. Connections in the brain would have begun their complex proliferation into the network that will make the person who, years later, will write these words and look back at this image of his unborn self.

John Berger has pointed to how the presence of words can impact on the way we see an image. On one page of his book *Ways of Seeing*, Van Gogh's painting "Wheatfield with Crows" is reproduced with only the painting's title and the artist's name and dates written beside it. On the next page, the same painting is shown—but this time with the caption: "This is the last picture that Van Gogh painted before he killed himself." Berger comments:

> It is hard to define exactly how the words have changed
> the image but undoubtedly they have.

Likewise with a photograph—words can lean their weight against the raw visual lineaments and bend them into different shapes. I know I'd see the Elysian Park postcard quite differently if it had no writing on the back, or if it had been written to an address in London; Herod's Gate would come into a different kind of focus if Felix's caption wasn't there; "Newcastle, June 1954" shorn of this date and the information that goes with it would make it easy to dismiss the photograph as just routine. There's a complex chemistry of influence at work between words and pictures whenever they're put together. "I'm in the photo" (albeit invisibly). It's hard to know exactly how the words of this realization affect the way I look at this picture of my parents and aunt on Newcastle beach, but it feels as if they change it profoundly. The photo seems to take on a gravity it didn't previously possess. It's as if the knowledge of my unseen presence was pencil writing, beckoning the ink of my interpretation to follow the lines it traces.

When do we begin? The instant of conception is often seen as pinpointing our genesis, constituting the moment from which we exist, before which we do not. It provides a kind of starting line from whose ruling across time our race begins, and in whose absence we would not have run at all, or run some different race. Yet it's not as if the flints of egg and sperm that knapped us have no antecedent story before they combined into our individual life-thread. Each is already ancient at the time of the collision that sparked new life into existence; each of them has an eons-long contrail, a complex train of connections in which each of us—F. W. Adams, Miss Herron, me, you—has a place.

How appropriate that my mother and her sister are *knitting*. Of course they're doing so for entirely practical reasons—making clothes for an expected baby. But there's a metaphysical richness in that activity which sits well with the underlying import of the photo. It's as if they're symbolizing the way in which the generations make something new out of a preexisting thread. Our human yarn is repeatedly cut and knit and twisted into the garments of particular people (the mother and child at Herod's Gate, my father, Felix Hague . . .). Life's rich spool of thread is spun out, individual by individual, flexed and formed into varying patterns that all share a common fabric but trace out a blizzard of different patterns on the countless frameworks of each allotted span.

Would I, as an unseen embryo that June day in 1954, have been aware of the loud clicking of knitting needles working their rhythmic, repetitive tattoo so close to where I lay, safely curled in the womb? Did the sound of the sea, the screeching of the seagulls, the sun's bright warmth penetrate that fleshy fastness? Or did the drumbeat of my mother's heart, the rushing of her blood, the gurgle of her gut provide a muffling protective, reining my awareness to the blinkered orbit of within—that ancestral home we all start from, the flesh-cave with its campfire warmth of blood, bearing who knows what paintings daubed on its ancient, membranous walls?

As I looked at "Newcastle, June 1954," prompted by my own invisible presence in the picture, my parents and aunt took on a new guise—not the fixed, familiar faces that I know so well, foundation stones of childhood. Rather, they seemed to shuffle through countless faces—identities—as, through them, I saw the long road that led to this pictured moment, and the long road that leads from it into my life and beyond. Sitting on their rug on the sand, backs against the groyne, what seemed pressingly evident was the fact that they were themselves once embryos curled in other wombs, as Miss Herron and F. W. Adams and my father and Felix and each Madonna, every child—everyone—has been, and that we are all also corpses in waiting. That realization of the obvious fractured the image, made it point towards beginnings, endings, and connections that are too massive to encompass, their scale outreaching what it's possible to embrace within the hold of sentences.

Sixty years after my parents and aunt sat on that beach, I'm sitting at a table writing, trying to convey in words some glimmer of what I see, what I feel when I look at "Newcastle, June 1954," and the Herod's Gate photograph, and the postcard of Elysian Park—three stray images, photo-shrapnel from the past that's embedded itself in my attention. It's autumn and the day is cold. I'm huddled in warm clothes, but around midday the sun comes out. Its brightness shines through the window and falls on the table where the postcard and photos are laid out beside me. I feel the sun's warmth upon my skin as, sixty years ago, I'd have felt it filtered through my mother's belly as it touched with feather-light delicacy the nascent fabric of my embryonic form. This blink of autumnal sunshine falls on the pictured blooms in Elysian Park and throws shadows across the stones of

Herod's Gate as it would have done—as it still does—in the actual places that are pictured. And it occurs to me that photographs and words have a functional similarity to groynes. Just as a groyne stops sand from being swept away, holds a beach in place against erosion by wind and tides, so we try to fix on the great strand of time that so momentarily hosts our presence a few sand-grain specifics of our lives. Despite our best efforts, these will—inevitably—be washed away.

Theorists of the spoken and written word—like Walter J. Ong and Jack Goody—have suggested that one of the cognitive consequences of the shift from orality to literacy is a change in religious consciousness. Once the idea of "God" gets written down, once what could only be felt or spoken could be isolated upon the page, fixed there in three letters joined to make a word, then it becomes possible to manipulate it in sentences and consider it from different angles. And that facilitates a range of speculation that simply wasn't possible before. The whole pace and rhythm of what can be thought about "God" changes when the word gets written down. Script opens up new possibilities of belief and unbelief, doubt and devotion. Having a visible verbal form by which such a concept may be handled means we can do different things with it than when it was solely a spoken or listened to sound, something that evaporated as soon as memory lost its grip upon it.

I'm not sure how well-founded such ideas are, but I sometimes wonder if the fixing of moments in photographs, like the fixing of sounds in writing, possesses a similarly revolutionary cognitive potential. It's only relatively recently, historically speaking, that our repertoire of seeing changed so significantly and we were able to catch and hold what passes in photographed form. Who knows what impact gazing at such haunting facsimiles of transience may have on our thought processes? We can all now routinely engage in image archaeology, explore the different visual strata of our lives and the lives of others, see time past held for close inspection and examine perfectly preserved fragments of its appearance long after the moments that generated them have gone. But for all the sophistication of our newfound visual literacy, the mystery of our being—its origin, its outcomes, and its end—remains outside the frame of any picture.

# BUTTERFLY SMOKE SIGNALS

*A* poster that was popular when I was a student featured a cartoon drawing of two American Indians. Lest the viewer be in any doubt about their provenance, so many familiar markers were included that the picture fairly dripped with cliché; it was as if it had been heavily stippled with droplets fallen from a cloud of passing stereotype. Set in a location that shouted out Wild West—arroyos, buttes, and canyons dotted with giant cactuses—there were clusters of wigwams in the middle distance. Beyond them, a wagon train was visible, and a herd of buffalo. On and around the two central figures, the artist had indulged in a littering of indigenous accoutrements: moccasins, bows and arrows, peace pipes, tomahawks, feather headdresses. One of the figures is drawn sitting beside a campfire with a blanket, poised to make smoke signals. His expression suggests extreme puzzlement. The other stands beside him, arms folded, looking stern. There's a small noticeboard affixed to a wooden stake that's hammered into the ground between them. It bears the words: "Examination in Progress." The speech bubble above the standing figure—clearly the examiner—says "Existentialism."

Why did we like this image? In part, it simply amused us to think of the absurdity of trying to convey a word like "existentialism," still less what it means, via the medium of smoke. In part, as regular exam-takers we were wryly sympathetic to the plight of someone faced with such a challenge—we'd all struggled with difficult questions. But at a deeper level the cartoon spoke to a realization that, as novice philosophers, we'd just come to; namely, that the process of communicating what's in our thoughts isn't the unproblematic thing we'd previously taken it to be. Instead, it's pregnant with philosophical conundrums. Our wording of the world, once seen as limited only by our inarticulacy or shyness, now appeared as something hedged with approximations, dubious assumptions, and the potential to mislead. The whole process of expression seemed laced with problems every bit as tricky as being tasked with communicating "existentialism" in smoke.

Had we really once believed that "the cat sat on the mat" caught what was there; that it was a literal, point-by-point description of what appeared before our eyes, rather than a complex construct relying on convention, artifice, abstraction, and omission? How could we have been so naive as to suppose that "I" or "justice" or "God" were ordinary descriptors rather than the tip of icebergs of enormous complication? Had we really been so innocent as to think that "the sky is blue" painted the same straightforward picture of plain fact for everyone?

Newly introduced to the philosophy of language, with its fracturing of old certainties, our virgin intellects had been easily seduced by the spare economy of Wittgenstein's dicta, those terse, Zen-like apothegms whose scalpel clarity promised to flense away confusion: "The world is all that is the case"; "The limits of my language mean the limits of my world"; "That whereof we cannot speak we must pass over in silence." Yet far from clarifying anything, such pared (and paring) down assertions often left us floundering in the arrogance of hollow mimicry. We liked the idea that "uttering a

word is the striking of a note on the keyboard of the imagination," but whether that keyboard was tuned to the same
pitch as the world around us was something we had come
increasingly to doubt. We thought, without in truth much
thinking, that "philosophy is a battle against the bewitchment of our intelligence by means of our language." The cartoon of the bemused smoke-signaler seemed like the kind of
picture that Wittgenstein himself might have brought into
play to illustrate such bewitchment. It showed how ideas are
often ill-served by the means of communication available to
express them—whether those means take the form of smoke
or words. Lost in that uneasy no-man's-land between what's
in the world, what's in our mind, and what can be signaled
about the interface between them, words often seemed as
unsatisfactory as smoke as a way of bestowing the labels
and weaving the meanings by which we might begin to parse
our experience into sense.

Back in my student days, this picture of the smoke-signaling
exam was often encountered stuck up with blu tak on the
walls of our rooms, part of the array of posters we mixed
together in that cocktail of allegiance, aspiration, postur-
ing, and pretense that announced to the world the shape we
wished our emergent identities to take. But I've not thought
about it, still less seen it, for close to forty years. What brought
it back to mind so unexpectedly, so vividly, was an evening
spent with butterflies.

I like the sound of that.

The idea that an evening spent with butterflies could act
as a mnemonic creates a pleasing image. It pictures distant
memories being brought back from the brink of forgetting's
oblivion by the quivering of butterflies' wings—as if what's
comatose, almost gone, could be resuscitated by their gentle defibrillation, the wings' opening and closing massaging
remembrance's pulse until it's able to restore the rhythm of

the past to present consciousness. Seeing it this way bestows a kind of magical dusting on things, as if the opening of an insect's wings offers an enchanted portal into time, giving access to the deep strata of remembering, in whose hidden seams all manner of fossilizing memories are embedded, the poster of the smoke-signaling exam just one among them.

Appealing though it is to say that what brought this image back to mind was an evening spent with butterflies, I know this is only a partial truth. Left unqualified it will mislead, however pretty the picture that it paints. Yes, an evening spent with butterflies lies at the root of the matter. But what sparked the memory of the smoke-signaling exam wasn't the butterflies themselves—the allure of their vibrancy and color meant that at the moment of encountering them I was fully immersed in the immediacy of their presence; perception, rather than recollection, dominated. It was only later, when I tried to put one aspect of the evening into words, that I realized what I wanted to say about it posed as hard a challenge as trying to signal "existentialism" in smoke.

꙰

Given the gap between experience and expression, it's easy to exaggerate the inadequacy of words. I don't want to give the impression that the evening spent with butterflies was some kind of mysterious event, something so swathed in ineffability that it defied every attempt at verbal apprehension. On the contrary, many aspects of it were entirely unproblematic in terms of finding words to fit the contours of what happened—or at least to fit them *reasonably*. Words are never a perfect fit, of course. They can't trace out exactly the precise curvature of what transpires; there's always a space between things and their linguistic shadows. But such inevitable shortcomings apart, there's much that can be said that's quite straightforward. What led up to the evening in question, for example, is easily enough outlined.

In an effort to attract more visitors and boost its flagging revenues, a botanical garden near where I live decided to convert an orchid house into an area where tropical butterflies could be displayed, flying freely. Pupae were bought in every week from a specialist entomological supplier—with the hope that these purchased hatchings would soon be supplemented, or even replaced, when the butterflies started to breed in situ. Temperature and humidity were carefully controlled, ripe fruit and nectar sponges were placed strategically, food plants suitable for larvae were provided. The butterfly species were selected for their size, color, and robustness in captivity—tailed green jays, blue morphos, king swallowtails, giant owl butterflies, and others. In addition, one moth species was included—the spectacular Atlas moth (*Attacus atlas*) with a wingspan of around twenty-five millimeters (10 inches). The native habitats of the species chosen ranged from Mexico, Central, and South America to Southeast Asia, New Guinea, and Australia. No endangered species were included. The suppliers sourced their pupae from captive breeding programs in butterfly farms in the Philippines, Thailand, and Costa Rica.

A few days before the "tropical butterfly experience" opened its doors to the public, the director of the botanical garden invited those who had supported this new venture to an early evening reception "to meet the butterflies." It was when it came to describing one element of this occasion that the poster of the smoke-signaling exam came back forcefully to mind.

That such an occasion should prompt the recall of this image may not seem particularly surprising. After all, who could hope to catch in words the incredible beauty of these exotic insects? Such a task can easily seem like a kind of nightmare exam scenario, at least as challenging as the one faced by the student smoke-signaler. I picture myself in an examination hall seated at a desk with a pencil and paper in front of me, an expression of intense puzzlement on my face.

I have a single question to tackle: "Describe the appearance of the blue morpho butterfly (*Morpho peleides*)." Under such circumstances, it's easy to see why I might recall the banjaxed American Indian faced with conveying "existentialism" via puffs of smoke.

At rest, motionless and folded, the wings of *Morpho peleides* would be hard enough to describe. To say that they're brown with large eyespots offers only the roughest approximation; it gives no more than the most impoverished reflection of the subtle intricacy of hue and pattern that marks the undersides of these magnificent insects. But when the morphos fly and the upper surface of their wings become visible, language seems even more helpless. All our color words are pallid when it comes to conveying the breathtaking shades that are semaphored with each wing-beat. Knowing that every hand-sized flash of bright metallic blue isn't due to pigmentation—the effect comes from iridescence—does nothing to augment the wraith of words that is all a verbal description can muster. The millions of tiny scales on a morpho's wings distort the light; their layers create refractive ripples that cause us to see wavelengths in the blue-violet spectrum. Changing the angle of the wings—or the stance of the viewer looking at them—provides a glittering variety of sheen and tone. It's a bit like seeing rainbow colors in an oil-streaked puddle—only with a morpho it's as if a special kind of azure rainbow has fallen into the water and saturated it with blue, rather than there being only a dilute smear of color on the surface. If words acted like the scales on a butterfly's wings, bending the light of meaning so that the wavelengths allowed our utterances to fit like gloves around each shape we seek to chart, then I might catch the beauty of a morpho in a sentence. But words rely on the fixed pigments of definition and convention so that describing a morpho's resplendent blue leaves me feeling even more at a loss than someone trying to convey "existentialism" via smoke.

Much of the impact of these tropical butterflies comes from their fantastic colors—and color is notoriously difficult to convey in words. But I don't think the bringing back to mind of the poster featuring the puzzled smoke-signaler was occasioned simply by my tripping up again on the inadequacy of language for properly expressing blue or red or green. That's too familiar a deficiency to raise an image from so long ago. To occasion its unearthing required something less commonplace, less expected. What warranted its return wasn't just being faced with the challenge of netting the butterflies in words, but in trying to describe an element I observed in the interaction of butterflies and people. It was something that flashed out as eye-catchingly as a morpho's magnetic blue, but was nothing as straightforward as a color.

Again, there's lots about the evening that I could describe—I was about to say "without difficulty," but I mean with no more than the usual difficulty that attends any composition. I could, for example, work at finding the right words to create a lifelike sketch of the eagerness of several individuals to photograph the butterflies—their frustration with lenses steaming up in the humid atmosphere, the way the insects rarely settled long enough for a close-up portrait shot, occasioning ungainly dances of pursuit as, be-slung with camera equipment, the photographers clumsily pursued their fluttering quarry. Were I to focus on this aspect of the evening, I'd be tempted to remark on the way in which some of these individuals seemed more interested in reviewing the secondary world of what they'd captured on their camera screens than in what was actually happening in the primary world all around them. Or, forgetting the photographers, I might try to catch the occasional wave of muted aggression in the polite, well-mannered crowd as people subtly jockeyed for position to give them the best view of the specimens in an overcrowded space, or I might note how the pupae cabinet acted as a kind of magnet, drawing people to its window to watch the magic of eclosion happening before their eyes, or I could try to sketch the variety of reaction—ranging from fascination to terror—when the butterflies occasionally alighted for a moment on people's hands or faces.

Likewise, there's lots about the evening that falls into the category of what might be called the routinely indescribable. People's faces, for example, are as hard to depict in words as the colorful heraldry of a butterfly's wings. It's also impossible to draw in words with any sense of satisfactory likeness a picture of someone's voice with the exact cartography of cadence, pitch, and intonation charted so that it traces all the contours of accent and inflexion, volume and phrasing. Moreover, although the hubbub of conversation in a crowd could be recorded and noted word for word, this would soon show how much of our talk relies on nonverbal aspects of communication which entirely elude such transcription. Shorn of the repertoire of body language that adds such volumes to them, unaccompanied words give only the sketchiest impression of a conversation. But it wasn't anything to do with people's faces or voices that made me reach for my net of words and recognize again its woeful inadequacy. The elusive element that interests me, what struck me most about that evening spent with butterflies, is something that threads its way between the describable and the indescribable, the mundane and mysterious. I'm not sure how much of it my smoke-signal words can capture.

ॐ

There, happening before our eyes in glorious butterfly Technicolor, were life's fundamental processes. For us, birth and aging, procreation and death are far less visible. The metamorphoses we go through are not nearly as evident as they are with butterflies, because they take longer to unfold—and because we sequester so much in privacies that shield key stages from public view. We may hear the hum of life's engine all around us, feel its vibrations thrum through us, sometimes glimpse the thrust of a naked piston, but in the main what drives us is covered over; we see little of the essential inner workings and spend much of our time preoccupied with peripheral things that mask life's elemental aspects. At the evening reception to meet the butterflies it was as if the engine cover had been lifted to show all the working parts engaged in the raw processes of being. The butterflies emerged from their pupae, momentarily crumpled from being packaged in these little exo-wombs. Soon, fluid pumped through their wings and the creases billowed out into perfect little sails, they flew, fed, and mated, laid their eggs, and died. The eggs hatched into larvae which in turn pupated and so the life cycle turned. There was no disguising the fact that initial perfection of form and color was a quickly passing thing and that the wings would soon fade and tatter. Their metamorphoses happened as we watched (speeded up, of course, by the bought-in pupae). The size and striking color of these tropical insects made it impossible to ignore them—their exotic brightness acted as a highlighter drawn across life's page. They emphasized a single, recurring word: "transience."

Vladimir Nabokov—famous for Lolita, Pnin, Pale Fire, and other works—was also a keen entomologist and for a time was employed as curator of lepidoptera at Harvard's Museum of Comparative Zoology. He once described morpho butterflies as "shimmering light-blue mirrors." (Magnum photographer Marc Riboud's striking shot of Nabokov shows the author standing beside a case that holds nine mounted specimens of these resplendent shimmering mirrors.) Nabokov's description came back to mind as I struggled for a way of putting into words the impact of the butterflies at the botanical garden's evening reception. All of them, not just the morphos, acted as mirrors—mirrors in which we didn't just see straightforward reflections of ourselves, but rather images of our mortality. Despite the differences between our life cycle and a butterfly's, when we gaze at them, witness time's passing written so boldly into their various stages, what is reflected back is our own story as much as theirs. It's as if the insects constitute—in a miniaturized form that's easy for the mind to encompass—a symbol of time's passage, the fleetingness of bodily perfection, the momentary nature of individual being, how beauty and brevity are inextricably intertwined. It's almost as if these eye-catching specimens offered a condensed and speeded-up version of our passage through time, emphasizing how quickly it is gone. Amidst the hubbub of inconsequential conversation, they acted out a potent reminder of the non-negotiable realities on which all of us are impaled; the way in which we're all plummeting down a gradient of time and loss toward death.

Of course it's hard to read from someone else's expression, from their mien and stance, how they are reacting to the butterflies; perhaps I was alone in reading them thus. But I got the strong impression that others too were seeing them as mirrors of mortality, little fluttering pennants of transience; live bunting that at once celebrated and mourned time's passing. The fact that many of the people who came to meet the butterflies that evening were elderly—several walking with the aid of sticks, two in wheelchairs—made their proximity to these flawless life-gems, perfect in the moments after hatching, particularly poignant. The contrast between newly minted morphos and old men and women who were as worn and tattered as butterflies nearing the end of their lives gave added luster to the sheen the butterflies possessed as mirrors of mortality.

꒰ꔚ

It's tempting to think of butterflies as something delicate and fragile. After all, individual specimens succumb easily to damage; they are not long-lived, not robust enough to survive harsh weather. They fall prey to birds and wasps and boys, possess no fangs or horns or venom, and are built on such a small scale that most other creatures dwarf them. But quite apart from the remarkable feats of migration undertaken by some species (monarchs, painted ladies, clouded yellows), the lifelines they are part of are sufficiently ancient that they must be tough. Watching the exotic butterflies flitting among the people, I was reminded of something a respected British entomologist once said about a more homely species—the small tortoiseshell (*Algais urticae*), one of the commonest butterflies in Europe. Small tortoiseshells hibernate and are often found tucked away in that strange stasis in sheltered nooks in houses. According to L. Hugh Newman, writing in his *The Complete British Butterflies in Color,* they

> almost certainly sought winter shelter in caves before man came to share them, and when our ancestors began to build houses the small tortoiseshell followed us there.

Think of the eons-long line of tortoiseshells stretching back to our cave-dwelling past and beyond it. That line is laced and knotted into repeated sequences of egg-larva-chrysalis-imago, the quartet of forms that sutures this species to its niche. The billions of individuals since the thread of tortoiseshells first was spun constitute a capillary that reaches back to the heart of their distant beginning. As each wing opens and closes it's as if we can hear an echo of this ancient pulse. Tortoiseshells engrave the filigree of their presence across time, their thread entwined with ours. Imagine all the individuals since humanity first began whose eyes have alighted on one of these butterflies. Such moments of perception must pepper time. If we could access each one of them, uncover every instance of person-tortoiseshell interaction, if we could see what was triggered in the numerous minds touched by the presence of these butterflies, would we come any nearer to an understanding of either species? If we could read out this section of the manifest of time's cargo—compile a register of interaction between *Homo sapiens* and *Algais urticae*—would it provide more than repeated instances of incidental perception, of a coming together that offers no indices of significance beyond circumstance and accident? And, looking forward, if tortoiseshells and humans coexist for the same length of time into the future as they have in the past, what point in time would that take us to? And if we could arrive there, at that vantage point in a far-distant present that will be built on a foundation of millions of vanished individuals, ourselves among them, would we understand our brief existence any more than we're able to right now, at this very instant? Would the thread of *Algais urticae* at that point seem as mysterious, as finally unaccountable, as it does today, or would some detail not yet discovered resolve it into new frames of understanding?

Beyond the stages of their life cycle—egg, larva, pupa, imago—the quadrant of being danced out by the countless species of butterflies there have been, is there some wider story, a story that might be told at a pace and in a manner that would bestow some sense of sense on the brute facts of their and our existence in all its bemusing ancientness and seemingly accidental occurrence? Is any message semaphored by the blinking on and off of the human-tortoiseshell connection over millennia as the butterfly's movement, form, and color were laid upon people's perception? Or is their repeated quadrant of being, the four steps they've used to walk through the eons, all that there is? Are there any grounds—beyond our thirst for meaning—for supposing that these insects that delight us with their beauty constitute a set of ciphers whose code, if we could only learn to break it, might give us clues about our own provenance and purpose? Or is there nothing to decipher beyond the rubric of cells and atoms, no reason for the amplitude of space-time beyond whatever our stumbling calculations can reveal about its scale and duration? Perhaps the reason I remembered the poster of the smoke-signaling exam wasn't only because of the difficulty of wording into satisfactory form what I felt on the evening when I met the butterflies, but because of an underlying feeling that the butterflies themselves might act like smoke signals, bearing messages we don't yet understand, coming from a distant fire we cannot see but whose smoke still stings our eyes.

Or do such speculations edge too close to trying to smuggle past the critical intellect some version of the long-discredited argument from design? Are the questions that they pose a kind of covert theologizing that attempts to smuggle within the little mules of butterflies cues that supposedly point to deity? Of course, like any element of the natural world, butterflies can be read in different ways, accorded different values. For my own part, I can see no obvious theistic pointers in them—but that does not mean that they cannot speak of meanings far beyond the compass of the ordinary. What those meanings might be remains tantalizingly elusive—so much so that, in the end, I see butterflies as being like exotic, unpronounceable words whose meaning is as strange as their sound. And as yet there is nowhere we can look up what it is they're saying to us—or even if it is to us their million-year-old message is addressed.

⟍ᶌ

Picturing pupae posted across the world to maintain stock levels at the botanic garden's tropical butterfly experience creates a powerful image of potential in transit. It's as if fabulous collections of living fireworks, held momentarily dormant in their pods, are packaged up in dull containers and sent to their destinations alongside all the usual mundane detritus that constitutes the mail. Would senders or receivers of invoices or advertisements or letters ever suspect that alongside these dry husks of paper are fantastic miniature barques bearing fuses already lit that will issue in the colorful explosions of green tailed jays, blue morphos, and all the other species? The boxes and padded envelopes that mute these resplendent glories, hold them safe as they journey, give no hint from their bland exteriors of the treasures they contain.

This image of pupae in transit prompts me to draw a parallel with language and to see words as strings of pupae. Like those of lepidoptera, the chrysalises of written language can be posted across considerable distances. But unlike their insect parallels, which don't survive for long (an Atlas moth pupa won't last for more than a month at most), word-pupae remain viable for centuries. Meanings can still emerge from them, strong and vibrant, years after they were formed. I pack my larval meanings into the seeming fixity of vocabulary's verbal cases. Thus contained, I hope the passage between mind and mind can be safely negotiated. The word-pupae stir as a reading eye moves across the page, but the imagoes that emerge from them are not always those that I intended. Meaning fluctuates with use; how one person reads a line will not necessarily result in the same patterns of understanding that another person takes away from the exact same word combination. Each verbal eclosion adds variations to a theme rather than offering up the uniformity of unvarying replication.

There is likewise variation in how we read the world. The cues it gives us prompt a range of interpretations. Of course there are swathes of broad agreement: we don't much differ when it comes to understanding what counts as day, what counts as night; we agree about what's hot, what's cold; the way water, mud, and stone feel different underfoot; what gives us pleasure and what gives us pain. But as we each engage our history, personality, and perception with the moments that we live through, as the intimate fabric of who we are makes contact with whatever the world offers us, as the substance of our person touches the elements of our experience, the result is uniquely particular—and, taken en masse, such individuality issues in a rich diversity.

The crowd of people who were invited to the evening reception to meet the butterflies will each have read that event in their own particular way. Of course there will have been areas of common ground between us—how jarring the contrast was between the temperature and humidity inside and outside; the fact that the butterflies were so vividly colored; the taste of wine; the aroma of fruit and flowers. But however many overlaps there may have been in our experience, I'm sure the butterflies will have nudged and prompted very different catalogues of memory, association, and reflection from each individual who accepted the invitation to meet them. The insects acted as beautiful lures cast upon the surface of our present. They hooked from our depths a varied haul of responses.

⚘

The way the same thing may be read quite differently by different individuals can be symbolized by the Atlas moth. The botanical garden had several specimens of this giant species (*Attacus atlas*). Their sheer size meant that they kept catching the eye. But it was a dying or dead one on the ground that afforded the best opportunity to examine the markings closely. The adults only live for a matter of days. Their sole function is to breed. They do not eat—in fact they don't even have mouths.

Some say that this moth is named because its wing patterns are reminiscent of the markings on a map; others argue that "Atlas" comes from classical sources and that the name was given simply because of the moth's size, Atlas being the Titan condemned by Zeus to hold up the heavens. But of course these two possible derivations are not as separate as they might seem. Our use of "atlas" as the name for a book of maps stems from the fact that Mercator's book of maps, first published in 1575, had on its title page a picture of Atlas with the world on his back. How should we read the maps inscribed on the wings of this Titan moth—or on those of any other species? What do they tell us about our whereabouts, the relationship in which we stand to other creatures, where we've come from, where we're headed, the nature of our life-journey and the topographies we traverse? What keys should we consult to ensure that we decipher without error the code signs that are written into insects' wings?

What I find particularly interesting is that the Cantonese name for *Attacus atlas* translates into "snake's head moth." When I first heard this I was bemused—for there was nothing I could see about the Atlas that was remotely snakelike. It's only when you're pointed to the leading edge of the forewings and particularly their tips that the name makes sense. Sure enough, looking there reveals a startling resemblance to a snake's head—a resemblance so strong it's hard to see how it could be missed. I find it a mixture of surprising, pleasing, and chastening to know that I have often looked at the map-markings of an Atlas moth's wings but seen no trace whatsoever of the shape or pattern of a snake. It was something I'd been entirely blind to—as if I could only see the duck or rabbit in Wittgenstein's famous example of a drawing that can be read in both ways. Once pointed out, of course, once recognized, once the colors and lineaments are seen to fall together to make this pattern, it's hard to revert to non-snake's-head seeing. And so I'm left wondering whether—on a wider scale—my way of looking at the world may be missing interpretations that would be obvious if only they were pointed out. Depending on the stories we are told, the languages we learn, the traditions of outlook and value in which we're raised, so the world will appear clad in that livery. Being shown a different way of seeing something is a useful corrective to our tendency to assume our own singular correctness. The markings on the wings of an Atlas/ snake's head moth map a key feature of existence—namely how little it takes for the world's smoke signals to rearrange themselves into new alignments suggestive of readings we would never have suspected.

# WATCHWORDS

## I

W hen I rediscovered my father's pocket watch, years after first seeing it, it immediately made me think of a scene of prehistoric slaughter. I was surprised by both the strength and the unexpectedness of this linkage. The watch is quite ordinary looking. There's nothing in its appearance to account for bringing such a violent image to mind. The picture—one of Zdeněk Burian's illustrations in Josef Augusta's large-format book, *Prehistoric Man* (1960)—shows a group of Stone Age hunters brutally dispatching a mammoth.

Montaigne once observed:

> It is a thorny undertaking, and more so than it seems, to follow a movement so wandering as that of our mind, to penetrate the opaque depths of its innermost folds, to pick out and immobilize the innumerable flutterings that agitate it.

My ambition here is modest compared to the kind of meticulously detailed, if often rambling, mind-maps that Montaigne constructed over the course of his 107 essays. I want to examine the impact of finding my father's pocket watch and in so doing try to explain why this little timepiece came to be conjoined with Burian's picture. I may not need to penetrate the opaque depths of the mind's innermost folds to the same degree as Montaigne did, but it's still a thorny undertaking to unravel the "flutterings" that were set off by finding the watch in question and that led to it being fused together with a picture from a book that I've not looked at since childhood.

Explaining why the watch called such an unlikely image to mind necessitates a clear view of what Burian depicted, so let me start with a description of his painting. In the center of the scene, a mammoth flounders in a pit trap. It has evidently just crashed through the branches arranged carefully on the ground to camouflage a deep hole. It's uncertain whether this deliberately concealed hazard has been dug to purpose, or if it's an inspired making use of a natural feature of the landscape. Whatever its provenance, by covering it up and luring or frightening the mammoth into it, the creature's imminent death has been secured. Its massive head, trunk and tusks, and about half of its body are visible. The rest of the animal's immense bulk has disappeared, as if the earth had swallowed it. Around the immobilized mammoth swarm a group of human hunters, clad in animal furs, intent on finishing off their prey. The dispatch will be brutal given the very different size of quarry and killers. Two of the hunters have boulders raised above their heads and are poised to hurl them at the trapped behemoth. Others are stooping down to arm themselves with similar projectiles. At the mammoth's head, standing carefully clear of tusks and trunk, a tall figure prepares to swing a heavy club, which has a sharpened stone crudely lashed to one end. Another hunter has a bow and arrows and is making for a vantage point that will give him a clear shot at the animal's neck and eyes. One spearman has already thrown his weapon, another is about to. The mammoth is helpless—unable to raise itself more than partially from the pit.

Although the painting is reproduced in the sepia tints of duotone, and is a single static image rather than a moving film clip, Burian has managed to convey all the bloody violence of a hunt. The brutal denouement of the successful trapping of this gigantic creature is depicted in a way that suggests sound and smell and color; the frantic movement of the beast and men. You can hear the yells of the hunters, the trumpeting screams of the injured mammoth, the snapping crash as its weight plunged it through the branches camouflaging the pit. You can almost smell the blood and sweat and excrement. The terror—the excitement—of the moment is palpable.

## II

With that description of Burian's mammoth hunters in mind, the discrepancy between it and a pocket watch should be obvious. Yet it was this image that the watch retrieved from memory. Let me say something about the circumstances of finding the watch, and briefly describe it, before trying to explain this incongruous pictorial connection.

Before the finding that brought Burian's picture to mind, I'd only seen the watch once before, years ago, when I was a boy. I came into the room where my father was working at some papers. There, sitting on his opened desk, I noticed an unfamiliar pocket watch. Perhaps the papers were urgent things from work demanding his full attention, or maybe he was just tired, but when I picked the watch up and asked him about it my curiosity was met with uncharacteristic terseness. He told me it was a gift from his mother before he shipped out with the army unit that he'd volunteered to join at the outbreak of World War II, but he didn't elaborate beyond that and followed his summary account by holding his hand out for the watch. When I gave it to him he promptly stowed it away in the little desk drawer in which he kept his medals, cap badge, empty bullet cases, and other wartime tokens that so fascinated me, but about which I'd learned not to ask. He was obviously reluctant to talk about the watch and, in truth, I wasn't particularly interested in it back then—it lacked the allure of the more overtly military mementos. What was a pocket watch compared to his revolver holster, gasmask, or desert-issue water bottle?

I never remember him using the pocket watch. For all the years I knew him, he wore a wristwatch. Pocket watches belonged to another age. At some point—I don't know when—he must have put it into a box in his desk. Shortly after his death, when I was going through his things, I found the box—but only gave the contents a cursory inspection. The house needed to be cleared prior to being put on sale and there was little time to attend to details. My impression was of an untidy assemblage of odds and ends—old pens and pencils, rulers, glasses, a penknife, some copper coins, a few loose keys. Nothing in the box looked valuable, or particularly useful. It wasn't really worth keeping. But for all its unimportance, this cargo of oddments seemed sufficiently imbued with a sense of my father's presence to make me reluctant just to throw it away. Dealing with the material residue that someone leaves behind often involves a kind of phased disposal. In the immediate aftermath of losing Dad, I didn't feel able just to cast aside things that, gradually, lost the power bestowed on them by close association. Only when they took on the mantle of what they really were— junk—did it become possible to dispose of them without feeling guilty.

When I got home, the house clearance completed, I put the box away and forgot about it. It sat untouched for years. Then, looking for a mislaid memory stick which, in the way of small objects urgently needed, seemed to have vanished into thin air, my search reached that desperate phase of looking in places I knew it really couldn't be. It was at this point that I found the box again and looked through its contents more carefully. Among the pens and pencils I felt the smooth body of the watch, disconcertingly rotund amidst their linearity. It was like finding a bird's egg in a twiggy nest, your fingers closing on something with a quite different texture from everything around it.

## III

A description of the pocket watch won't explain why it woke from memory Burian's picture of the mammoth hunters, but it would seem odd not to give some indication of what it looks like, especially since "pocket watch" can so easily suggest something ornate and valuable, a beautifully worked piece of gold jewelry. Let me say at once that this pocket watch is not like that. It's made of stainless steel, not precious metal. The face, numerals, and hands are simply worked, without flourish or embellishment; the whole design is determinedly without frills. This is a functional watch rather than a decorative one. Yet, for all its plainness, it's clearly something of high quality. "Swiss Made" is written below the little circle around which sweeps the second hand. "Vertex" is printed more prominently on the main face. The Arabic numerals—12, 3, 6, and 9—are in white on a band of grey color, about five millimeters wide, which runs around the circumference. At the edge of this grey band are marked out the sixty divisions that cut every hour into its constituent minutes. The winding mechanism above the 12 is a straightforward pull and turn design: turn for winding; pull out and turn for adjusting the position of the hands. A small metal hoop loops round the winder, encircling it with a ring that allows a chain to be affixed. The face is covered with plain glass that's slightly curved. The watch measures fifteen centimeters around the circumference, with a diameter of four centimeters—just a little smaller than a mammoth's eye. It's remarkably slim for a pocket watch. It would fit snugly in the breast pocket of a well-cut jacket and scarcely make a bulge. Its smoothness, shininess, slimness, and weight unambiguously announce that here's a finely worked artifact—something appealing to the hand. Far from being in mint condition, it possesses the patina of use that essential tools and gadgets carry with them, a sense of frequent handling.

On the casing at the back, engraved in small letters, there's an inscription: "M to W 1939." The M is for "Mother," the W for "Willie"—which is how my father was known to parents and siblings. It always sounded odd to hear him thus referred to. To us he was just "Dad," and to friends and neighbors his "William" was invariably shortened not to "Willie" but to "Bill."

## IV

How did the watch lead me to a pit trap? Yes, it made me recall Burian's powerful picture, but it would more accurately describe its impact if I said that the watch *itself* concealed a pit trap and that picking it up I had a sense of falling through flimsy branches into a deep shaft hidden just beneath them. It was this that brought Burian's painting back to mind: a feeling of sudden falling, of having been ambushed by the unexpected, of finding that the temporal ground beneath my feet, usually so reliable, suddenly gave way. Instead of my regular, predictable pacing through the hours and minutes of my days, I was sent plummeting back three quarters of a century.

To be effective, a pit trap has to be big enough for its intended victim to fall into. You won't catch a mammoth if the hole you dig is only two feet deep and half that wide. I can place the watch on the palm of my hand and if I close my fingers I'll cover it completely. And yet for all its smallness, the watch constituted a deep rift in continuity; it acted like an incision in the flow of time that was big enough to pull me through it. Holding it, it seemed as if the ground beneath my moment-by-moment tread opened without warning. It was as if the normal chronology that carries me along, the steady incremental drift of seconds building reliably into minutes, hours, and days, was interrupted as I fell into the pit trap that lay hidden in the watch.

I know, of course, that all this was an illusion, a kind of trompe l'oeil. Time's flow cannot be paused or interrupted, let alone reversed. It carries us from our beginning to our end on an onward current that brooks no deviation in its flow. However much the watch made me feel as if my progression through the days had been derailed as I fell through its flimsy camouflage into the time-shaft that it hid, I know I was still rooted in my present, though it felt I'd been taken to a different age. I know that even as I was overwhelmed by the feeling of falling, I was still being carried along on my own usual life-stream, and that the seconds were ticking by in their customary way. Their passage is entirely unaffected by such imaginings. The duration that time offers us to live in is a fabric that can—will—be cut; but it's completely impervious to any effort to swim against the current of its weft.

As I fell into the watch's pit trap, Burian's picture came rushing back to mind—almost with the force of revelation—no doubt in large measure simply because it pictured a pit trap and that was precisely what I felt I'd fallen into—even though there were no fur-clad hunters waiting to dispatch me with clubs and boulders. I hope this explains why the watch came to be conjoined with so apparently incongruous an image. But in fact the mammoth itself was also appropriate, though this only became apparent later. I'm still unsure whether, somewhere in my mind, I realized this—and that it was a factor in retrieving Burian's picture—or if it's just an odd coincidence or an ex post facto maneuver rather than any evidence of deliberation in selecting the image that I did.

## V

There's surely something poignant about giving your child a *watch* before they go off to war. Clearly the timelines that bear us are made even more desperately precarious when conflict looms. Was the choice of gift an unspoken wish that his time be measured out routinely, safely, that it would continue to be nurtured by the dependable slow turn of the watch's hands, his minutes evenly ticking their way into the boon of more untroubled hours? I can't help thinking that—even if unconsciously—the watch was meant as a kind of talismanic pacemaker, almost a little supplemental heart, whose ticking would augment his own. Twinned with this mechanical doppelganger, Swiss-made for reliability, the pulse of my father's life would somehow be charmed and protected. When she held the watch, wound it, listened to its tick, was his mother reminded of the embryo whose germinal heart once stirred within her? How disconcerting it must have been—however much she may have felt a glow of pride in his going—to see the infant life she'd nurtured become adult, bear arms, stand poised to wage war across the sea.

I never met my paternal grandmother—she died before I was born—so I know her only from photographs and what others said about her. The paucity of the information I can draw on makes it seem more appropriate to ask questions than to try to picture an event I did not witness and never heard described—namely the moment in 1939 when she presented my father-to-be with the watch. Was it wrapped? Or did she press it into his hand just as it was? Had she wound it and set it to the right time, or was it my father who moved the hands and started it going? Was it a tearful moment with just the two of them, perhaps on the very brink of his departure from Ireland, first for basic training in England and Scotland, before being shipped out with his unit for combat in France and eventually North Africa? Or was the gifted watch bestowed some while before he left, perhaps at a family gathering where the mood was one of companionship—even celebration—rather than anxiety and incipient lament? Did the customary reserve and fortitude of their austere Ulster Presbyterianism prevent more than conventional expressions of emotion, or were the circumstances of a son's departure to fight in a war—the fact that his family might never see him again—enough to breach any dam of reserve with tears?

Though a watch seems an appropriate gift to give at such a juncture, a pocket watch seems an oddly impracticable choice. By 1939, wristwatches were far more common. In fact the growth in their popularity was, at least in part, related to another war. The artillery barrages that were such a feature of World War I required meticulous timing if the advancing troops were not to be wiped out by the friendly fire being laid down to try to clear a way for them. The military authorities in Britain issued wristwatches to combatants in the 1914–18 conflict precisely in order to make easier the synchronization necessary between artillery and infantry. The testing conditions of the battlefield also had an impact on design—watches needed to be easily readable, ideally with luminous hands and numerals, the glass over the face had to be toughened, the wrist-strap sufficiently strong to withstand the wear and tear of life in the trenches. Looking through old photographs, my father can be seen wearing a wristwatch in the 1920s. And in photos from the war he sometimes wears one too. I have no way of being sure, but my guess is that the pocket watch was intended to be special, something that—whilst functional—was yet meant to serve a different purpose from the quotidian timekeeping of his wristwatch. Of course it could be that my father left it at home to be kept wound up and ticking in his absence, a little surrogate heart awaiting his safe return. Or maybe it was a gift he never liked and simply abandoned. But the watch is dented, scratched, and worn. It has the air of something frequently used, well traveled; it has no hint about it of careful preservation or the newness that might come from neglect. My impression is that this was a token taken with him, something that served almost as an amulet as well as being a simple reminder of those who loved him. His reluctance to talk about it when I saw it on his desk all those years later, the way he quickly stowed it in his drawer of wartime tokens, suggests that it was an amulet which came to have attached to it memories he preferred not to recall.

## VI

I imagine the watch engraved "M to W 1939" kept safe in a uniform pocket, dutifully wound up every morning and ticking around the hours of every day as he fulfilled the duties of his new military calling. Was it with him, I wonder, when his timeline was so nearly ended? Or had he left it that day safely towel-wrapped in a kitbag beside his canvas camp bed? There are so many things about even the not-too-distant past that it's impossible to know—let alone the mysteries of what happened centuries before us. Finding the pocket watch has sparked a brace of questions I wish I'd been able to ask my father. I'm particularly curious to know if it was in his pocket when he was seriously injured by shrapnel from a German bomb. And, if it was, I wonder if the person who aimed and dropped that bomb was guided in so doing by instruments manufactured by the same company that made the watch.

Though they were sold in Britain under the brand name "Vertex," these watches were made by a Swiss company, Revue Thommen. Thommen had been making watches since 1853, when a Société d'Horlogerie was established in the town of Waldenburg in an effort to combat high unemployment there and the heavy stream of emigrants to America that had resulted. Gédéon Thommen and Louis Tschopp took over the Société in 1859. Ten years later, Thommen became the sole owner and the company was renamed accordingly. What I find particularly intriguing is that in the 1930s, the company began to turn its precision watch-making skills to the manufacture of aviation instruments. Thommen supplied these to both the German Luftwaffe and the British Royal Air Force. It's possible that the plane that dropped the bomb that came close to ending my father's life was guided by navigational instruments made by the same firm that made the watch given to him by his mother to mark his going off to war. Such coincidences flag up the dense network of interconnections, the mesh of interlinked causes and effects, that thread the tapestry on which our lives are woven.

When I retrieved the watch from the sarcophagus of its little oddment box, I had suddenly in my hand the same object that my father held, that my unmet grandmother held, the cold metal warming in their hands as it now warmed in mine. I guess because it measures time, the watch carried with it a kind of potency in that it seemed able to stimulate a sense of our different timelines/lifelines—where they intersected, ran together, parted. For a long while my father's time was empty of me. In 1939 he was thirty-four, single, childless, poised to go to war. It would be another ten years until he married, and six years after that till I was born. Our lifelines then ran closely together for thirty-two years, until his life-watch stopped in 1987 and I took the box of oddments from his desk. Finding the watch again now has awoken a whole raft of memories, tinged with a renewed sense of the briefness and fragility of our timelines—and how easily they're cut. It has made me wonder, too, how much of what ticks out, dictating what happens to us, is fixed, unchangeable, and how much of it consists of a flexible maze of contingencies that allow almost limitless variation as a welter of adjustments shift and reorder its themes. Imagine technicians working at fine instruments in a factory in Switzerland, imagine a pilot consulting the altimeter and compass in a cockpit, high above the African desert, imagine a watch ticking in a soldier's pocket. All of these instruments were designed to give precise readings, to record changes. Think of how my history—and no doubt that of many others—would have altered, or never happened, if any of the readings along so many lifelines had been changed by a second, a foot, or a fraction of a degree.

## VII

It felt somehow symbolic to find this stopped watch of my father's three quarters of a century after his mother gave it to him. Perhaps it symbolized nothing more complicated than the fact of his life's cessation, flagging up the nonnegotiable nature of loss, bringing me face to face again with the completeness of his absence. The watch stated with the mute eloquence that some objects possess an obvious yet easily skirted-over feature of our existence: namely its unstoppable transience. I suppose, too, that the shape and sound of pocket watches, the sense of focused energy they convey, is reminiscent of a heart, that pumping organic clock on whose timekeeping all of us depend. A stopped watch found in circumstances like this underscores the unpalatable truth that his time is over; that he has run out of the hours that provide being with the only fuel it can run on.

When I found it, the watch was stopped at 4:16. I suppose inevitably, this made me wonder what my father had been doing at the exact moment this happened. Not only that, I wondered what it would look like if a borehole was drilled through the time he occupied and a sample was retrieved that showed all the 4:16s he'd occupied, morning and afternoon, from when he was given the watch in 1939 to the moment of his death in 1987. For the early mornings, it's likely that most of these moments would have been occupied by sleep—except for those odd times when he might have been fishing, or traveling, or on duty. What dreams stirred in his mind at 4:16 a.m. across the years? Put together, what stories would they tell? For some of those early morning 4:16s the canvas of an army tent will have been all that was between him and the stars. Did he lie there wakeful and restless, fearful of what daylight would bring, his heart racing, almost keeping time with the watch's ticking? And at 4:16 p.m., if I could cut out that temporal contour from his life, take a core sample from this late afternoon time across all the years, what would he have been doing? I imagine different scenes at work, at home on weekends and on holidays, as a young man, and when he was retired. 4:16 is just one of multiple temporal locations at which a borehole could be drilled to take out a sample from a life of all that happened at that particular coordinate. At which time did my conception fall, at which time the moment when he first held me in his arms?

Knowing the right time was important to my father. There was an exactness to him, and a liking for routines. He was well organized, attentive to detail. He considered punctuality a virtue; lateness a vice. One of his daily rituals was checking his watch against the Greenwich time signal whose five electronic pips sounded on the radio at 8:00 a.m. and 6:00 p.m. (and on the hour at other hours as well, but these were the two he favored, though he'd also take in the 1:00 p.m. one on weekends). He would take off his wristwatch and hold it ready, listen carefully to the pips and make any necessary adjustments—this being in the days before digital watches brought routine reliability and rendered such checking redundant. He liked meals to be served on time so that we would be sitting down to breakfast or dinner—and at weekends lunch—when he checked his watch and then listened to the news headlines. He commuted between where we lived—in Lisburn—and Belfast, which was only eight miles away. He took the same train in to work and the same train back, giving a rhythm to his (and our) days. Knowing the time was essential to his working life.

In retirement, the need to be in a particular place at a particular time had vanished, and without the structure thus imposed he often seemed just to drift through his days. Listening to the Greenwich pips—once an iron routine—wavered and then petered out. Perhaps as time grew shorter, measuring it precisely made too bluntly evident the fact that it was running out. Or maybe he no longer saw any point in knowing the exact temporal coordinates of a moment; it was enough to know the natural approximations offered by the alternating gradations of the light and dark.

About two years before he died, he adopted a new locution: "Watch yourself." This was used whenever people left his presence—regardless of whether they were only going to the next room, or to Belfast shopping, or, in my case, back to where I lived in Edinburgh after a visit home. It was as if he was expressing a newfound realization that life was perilous and time uncertain. This frequent incantation struck me both as a routine bidding of farewell—his version of "cheerio" or "bye"—and a kind of benediction conferred on those leaving who, he realized, he might never see again. It was at once cautionary and valedictory. I can't help thinking that this frequent saying of "Watch yourself" was related to his increasing disregard for watch-time. His focus shifted away from worrying about the precise time of day to more fundamental issues. "Watch yourself" tapped more into the wakeful connotations of the word "watch" than its temporal ones—although of course the two are intimately interlinked. I think what he was saying was, in part, "Wake up!" "Watch out!," and I was reminded more than once of the birds in Aldous Huxley's novel *Island* that have been trained to sing out "Attention! Attention!" to keep people mindful of the realities of being. We have a strong propensity for slumber that extends far beyond our capacity for sleep.

## VIII

By the time of his "Watch yourself" urgings, my father was a shadow of the vigorous man he used to be. He was often, as local parlance gently put it, "not quite himself." It wouldn't have been right at this stage in his life, his mind frayed to threadbare, to trouble him with "big questions," curious though I was to know what his answers to them might be. I don't ever remember these being much addressed, even in his prime. Though we spent a lot of time in each other's company, I'm not sure what he thought about the meaning and purpose of human life, or if he thought there was one. From the little he said, I suspect he espoused a kind of happily-ever-after Christianity, an outlook of no great theological sophistication, but I think it brought him comfort.

As well as making me remember Burian's mammoth hunters, finding Dad's watch made me think again of William Paley's famous analogy about finding a watch "in crossing a heath" and inferring from it the existence of a watchmaker. The parallel Paley wishes to draw is that (as he puts in his 1802 work *Natural Theology*) "every indication of contrivance, every manifestation of design, which existed in the watch, exists in the works of nature." And this, he argues, allows us to infer the existence of a divine creator. My guess is that my father would have warmed to Paley's model and been readily persuaded by the move from watch to watchmaker, to world and world-maker. Despite the horrors he'd witnessed in the war, the idea of a benign creator seemed to be one of his articles of faith.

I'm more minded to take a skeptical view of Paley's analogy. It had, to my way of thinking, already received a fatal blow to its credibility several decades before Paley's formulation. This pre-Paley refutation came from David Hume's objections to the drawing of such comparisons. In particular, I'd agree with Hume that, even if it's justified to move from world to world-creator on the model of watch and watchmaker (and he argues convincingly that it's not), this would still not allow us to assume a creator who had the qualities usually attributed to deity in the traditional Christian view. After all, the "watch" of the world doesn't suggest much love. It mangles the innocent in its mechanisms. Built into its mainspring are parasites, hunger, war, the ravages of aging and disease. For me it is a watch that, far from suggesting the kind of goodness that was implied in the pictures of many of the books from childhood, points rather to the kind of world that Zdeněk Burian portrays—where violence, ferocity, want, and death close-shadow every second. Did Dad's "Watch yourself" mantra perhaps betray his suspicion that all was not as well-ordered as his naive theology suggested?

# IX

Susan Moeller is right, I think, when she says that images "have authority over the imagination." In her book *Compassion Fatigue* (1999) she provides a masterclass in visual literacy, robustly addressing ways in which, in an image-soaked culture such as ours, we can ensure that our seeing remains alert, our sensitivity vibrant. She recognizes that images inevitably simplify the world, but argues that what matters "is the *quality* of their simplicity." An image can be a picture— a painting, drawing, or photograph—or it can be the kind of word-picture Paley draws, offering as a point of focus something that the eye can readily grasp and wire into our remembrance. Part of the reason images have the influence on us that they do is because they are what Moeller calls "our most efficient mnemonic devices." Thus I can recall in detail the pictures Zdeněk Burian provided for *Prehistoric Man,* but I can remember next to nothing of the text that they were illustrating.

Whilst I agree with Moeller about the authority images have over our imagination, I'm not clear how that authority is wielded. In what ways have Burian's pictures influenced me? Would I have been changed if they had been eclipsed by some quite different visual stream? His images certainly seem to be weighted with a special significance; they feel as if they've had an impact. But could a map be drawn that would link their lineaments to the topography of the psyche in such a way as to show precisely how they've shaped its landscape? And why do individuals pick out and remember

the particular images that they do? Why are some simplifications—like Paley's watch—appealing to some of us but not
to others? These are far less obvious matters than the fact
that images constitute such potent mnemonic devices.

I grew up at a time of relative visual innocence. Certainly
compared to the insistent flood of images bombarding us
today, my pictorial heritage—my father's even more so—
might be regarded as slight, verging on the impoverished. The
index of images that left their mark would, I suspect, look
paltry beside that of someone who has grown up amidst the
clamor of images that pour from our screens today. And even
if we confine things to printed images, the pictorial dimension in children's reading has proliferated massively since the
time of my first forays into books. I'm not sure how our
personal portfolios of remembered pictures form and affect
us, but I'm glad not to have been witness at an early age to
many of the things that have become visually commonplace
for people growing up today. We each of us can draw on
a hoard of images that's unique to us. Once imprinted on
remembrance, do they lie invisible, inactive, only awakened
on those odd occasions when something calls them back to
mind? Or, for all their apparent inertness when we're not
thinking of them, do they constitute a kind of silent carbo-
rundum that hones the chambers of the psyche into shapes
that vary according to the types of images involved?

And I wonder, too, adapting Moeller's comment, if there
are objects, as well as images, that have authority over the
imagination. My father's old pocket watch sits on my desk
close at hand and seems capable of telling me far more than
just the time. It has an insistence about it that suggests it can
indeed command, as it whispers to me of wartime travels in
France and North Africa, not to mention its journey from
Switzerland to Ireland. It talks of love and longing, hints at
nostrums for fear and loss, carries with it a kind of peep-
hole into my father's history. One of the few things he talked
about from his time in the desert was the vicious sandstorms
that sometimes struck, powerful enough to peel the paint off

vehicles. He said the red sand dust got everywhere. Looking at some of the flecks that have gathered on the watch face, underneath the glass, I can't decide if they're traces of rust or tiny particles of sand dust. But whichever they turn out to be, the watch itself is part of the actual fabric of my father's world, offering tantalizing glimpses into it. It feels almost like a tiny buoy that has drifted from his waters into mine.

## X

When I found the watch, I wound it up and hoped that it would go. Disappointed when it didn't, I shook it a few times, sharply, in case the mechanism had seized up after all the time it had lain inactive in the box, the hands frozen at 4:16 for years. I thought the sudden lubrication of a jolt might set it off again. That too failed to work. As it sat on my desk while I wrote about it, the watch beckoned to my tactile susceptibilities. Every now and then I gave in and picked it up, warming the cold metal in my hand. On one of these pickings up I noticed that the second hand was moving. I don't know if it was my body heat that thawed it into action, or perhaps there was a delayed reaction to being shaken. Putting it to my ear I could hear steady ticking. So long as I remember to wind it the requisite twenty-one times every day, the watch now keeps reliably accurate time. I know that this will sound contrived—a compositional device rather than something that really happened. It even seems to hint at some vaguely sentimental happily-ever-after conclusion. But I can't help it if the truth seems improbable or invented. This is what happened and I'm glad it did.

Our ordinary talk seems often like a sea of words. Its tides erode experience, allowing us to walk unimpeded for miles along smooth sands. But sometimes the torque of written sentences can act quite differently, catching things in unexpected ways, and leaving us facing difficult gradients that our ordinary diction just ignores. And, cast in certain ways, words can themselves come to act like pit traps. In what I've written here, I've tried to move beyond an undemanding walk along the flat sands laid down by saying things like "I found my father's old pocket watch" and leaving it at that. Contained in the moment thus simplified there is so much more than meets the eye. Looking at it closely, what seems level ground tilts and ruptures into a series of sheer cliffs; the ground underfoot changes from sand to rock. Here and there along this more demanding way, there are pit traps, and in them traces of things vaster than any mammoth. Questions about time and memory, identity and absence, God and purpose get lodged in the shafts that words create. When I stumble on them, I wish I had the practical ferocity of a hunter so that I could dispatch them, skin them, butcher the meat to slake my hunger. But I know I can't.

In *The Fate of the Mammoth: Fossils, Myth and History* (2002), Claudine Cohen points out that although humans undoubtedly hunted mammoths, it's highly unlikely that any but the youngest, smallest animals would have succumbed to pit traps. Digging the frozen soil of the steppe to the depth required to trap an adult would have been a well-nigh impossible task given the rudimentary tools available. When I first discovered this I felt cheated—as if I'd been hoodwinked by the power of Burian's painting. Was it no more than invention—or, more brutally, just a visual lie? (Cohen accuses Burian by name of helping to perpetuate a myth.) There's still a vestigial sense of having been misled—or having been naive—but I've become reconciled to the questionable accuracy of Burian's picture and its continuing importance in my store of images. What he has depicted may never have happened, but it still provides me with the vocabulary to talk about things at greater depth than ordinary, workaday discourse would allow. Whether it's true or false makes little difference to its metaphorical richness. Without its help, the frozen steppe of language would not have yielded to my digging, allowed imagination to pepper sentences with pit traps of sufficient depth to catch at least some of what I seek.

I'm not sure if it belongs to the "thorny undertaking" Montaigne described, or if it's more a kind of ritual act that answers to a different logic, but instead of putting the pocket watch back in the box of oddments, I've placed it on my copy of Augusta and Burian's *Prehistoric Man*. Sitting on a table in my study, book and watch together have the air of some kind of shrine, though to whom, or what, or how I should approach it, I've no idea. But, looking at the invisible connections meshed between them, I have a sense of catching something almost like Paley's watch. In writing about it here I feel as if I've been lifting the boulders of sentences high above my head and smashing them down with a mingled sense of impotence and exhilaration. "Watch yourself" rings in my ears and, glimpsing something of the disparity in scale between language and what it tries to speak of, I'm reduced again to silence.

# DEATH AND THE MAIDEN

- Isn't it odd that, although we walked within a few inches of it, neither of us said anything?
- Or is such ignoring of the unpalatably obvious only to be expected?
- Was our inconsequential chatter preferable to what we might have said if we'd chosen to remark on what was there, so undeniably, staring us in the face?
- Were we trying to pretend it wasn't there, or even thinking that—somehow—it might be magicked away so long as we didn't openly acknowledge its existence?
- Was our silence a failure of nerve, a shying away from what we should have confronted, or just a commonsense evasion of something about which little can be said?

*I*'m not going to answer any of these questions; I'm not sure they can be answered. Instead, I want to try to put into words what I was thinking as—and after—we avoided talking about what surprised us with its unwelcome presence on that sunny Friday morning.

Let me start with what's straightforward and simply set the scene. It's a beautiful spring morning. I'm just leaving the café in the university library where a group of us regularly meet for coffee and amiable banter. I'm walking with a colleague—I'll call him Alan—and we're headed back across campus to our respective offices: he needs to prepare a lecture; I'm scheduled to discuss a failed essay with its student author. Around us there's a sense of life and youth and energy that's almost palpable. This is partly because it's such a sunny day and much warmer than it has been of late, partly because the birds are singing and the trees are newly into leaf, but mainly because the place is thronged with students. A few have books and laptops laid out on the rugs they've spread on the grass. Some look as if they're walking to or from classes. But it doesn't take much acuity in an observer to realize that they're much more interested in each other than in books or lectures. The overwhelming flavor of the atmosphere is closer to the erotic than the academic. The currents of attraction are everywhere. They're sufficiently numerous and potent as to be almost visible. It's easy to imagine the scene crisscrossed with their isobars, or to picture them flashing between people, like mini bolts of lightning, as the electricity of desire crackles silently around them. The shapely and the not-so-shapely have shed their winter coverings and are walking about in groups or singly, or lolling on the grass, scantily clad in brightly colored shorts and skirts and T-shirts. There's a pervasive sense of display, sometimes discreet, often not, occasionally peppered with a piece of flagrant flaunting. However demure or flamboyant, the common denominator is the bid to catch attention, to attract and feel attracted. Sex is in the air as obviously as the birdsong—and what is birdsong, after all, except avian sex-signaling?

Alan and I have just turned a corner and are walking up a cobbled street outside one of the university's oldest buildings. Facing us, at the top of the hill, is the Chaplaincy Centre. It's an anonymously modern building of no particular distinction. Outside it, a single parking space is marked on the cobbles. We know it has "Reserved for University Chaplain" painted in large white letters on the stones. But today the writing is hidden by the vehicle that occupies the spot. With the same lumbering air of polished excess that a stretch limo possesses, a hearse's long black bulk overfills the chaplain's modest parking space.

It's empty—no coffin, no sign of any driver. The high sheen of the black bodywork, the spotless glass of the windows and windscreen, the shiny silver runners on which a coffin would be placed, all mutely signal absence. Inside the Chaplaincy Centre we can see a few people milling around, their formal attire in contrast to what people outside are wearing.

The university has close to 30,000 students. As such, inevitably, there is the occasional instance of a life cut short before its time—either through accident, illness, or sometimes suicide. Such tragedies apart, death among students is rare. For the vast majority of them it won't happen until long after they've left these environs. Their quietus may be noted in the *Alumnus Chronicle* some five or six decades hence—with an obituary that gives details of marriage, children, career, travels, and date of graduation—but it's not something to think about now. There are of course some mature students, and some members of staff are quite elderly. But in the main the campus is a place of youth—which means it's not somewhere you expect to see a hearse. So, when one does appear, you'd expect it to excite comment, not to be ignored.

Alan and I work in different buildings. We part company just outside the campus shop. Thinking back, I can't recall what we were talking about. It was just the kind of casual interchange you engage in every day and don't remember. We certainly weren't talking about anything that might have claimed our attention so completely that it rendered us oblivious to the things around us. The only remarkable thing about our conversation was the fact that the hearse received no mention, even though we passed within a hand's breadth of it.

Yet, for all our studied avoidance, I kept colliding with the hearse all day. I don't mean literally, of course. But all morning, all afternoon, whatever I was doing, my thoughts were frequently interrupted as an image of it came to mind. Whenever I tried to concentrate, the task in hand was tripped up by its sleek polished presence. Even now, weeks later, it keeps intruding, silently, unexpectedly, parking its unwanted bulk across mental parking spaces I prefer to reserve for other thoughts.

I'd love to know what impact the hearse had on Alan. Is it possible that he really didn't notice it? I find that impossible to believe. But we don't know each other in the kind of way that would make it OK to ask. I can hear the awkwardness, picture the look he'd give me, if I were to speak what's in my mind.

Do you remember that hearse we both ignored?
Why do you think we did that?
Have you thought about it since?

And, truth be told, if he put such questions to me I'd be as likely to parry them with some flippancy as I would be to admit that I couldn't get the hearse out of my thoughts for the rest of the day and that even now it continues to haunt me. Admitting to that haunting in writing is less daunting than admitting to it in conversation. I suppose that's because writing leans more towards formality than speech does; its gradient of diction allows for a puzzling over things that, in conversation, would seem labored. The register of what I'm writing here allows for a level of reflection that, if it were spoken, could easily be thought too serious, or even morbid.

⚬

Though we've all probably fantasized about being telepathic, I think it's just as well we're not. As it happened, the student who'd booked in to see me because of her failed essay was distractingly attractive—and well aware of it. I'm fairly sure I know how she wanted me to view her, and I'm quite certain that she'd not have been pleased if she'd known that in the course of our tutorial I kept picturing her not remotely in that way but as the empty hearse's cargo. I'm relieved she couldn't read my thoughts.

I know it will sound macabre to think of a pretty girl as a corpse. It's certainly not something I normally do. It happened in this instance in part because I met her so soon after walking past the hearse, and in part because the girl—let's call her Julie for convenience—was at that point in her life where she was at the peak of her sexual attractiveness, thus offering a particularly striking contrast to a corpse. The sheer lissomness of her nubile presence, her air of effortlessly sensual warmth, the suspicion of a just contained blaze of ardor poised to ignite, her perfectly sculpted swells and curves, the sense of supple readiness for passion—all this demanded notice. Whatever the particularities of her personality, her outlook, her plans, whatever unique contours mapped her character and traced out her history and interests, this was a time in her life when Julie was also molded into a kind of beautiful organic master key that effortlessly unlocked desire. You could see it in the reactions of the people she walked past as she made her way to my office; I could feel it as soon as she sat down across the table from me.

That sex and death can each remind us of the other isn't as surprising as it may sound when stated bluntly. What's more natural than that our beginning and ending should be intimately interlinked such that each brings the other into mind? They are the two sides of the coin that buys us life. Even so, it's surely far from natural for a pretty girl to suggest that connection so directly that she appears in the mind's eye as a coffined corpse.

If it had been full when Alan and I walked past it, if a coffin had snugly filled the pod of its shiny black casing, I doubt if the hearse would have left as much impression as it did. Particularly if we'd known whose funeral it was, things would have slipped into a different declension of understanding and reaction. Funerals are a routine enough part of life, after all, even if unexpected on a university campus. I might have been momentarily saddened at the loss of whoever it was who had gone, but I don't think I'd have been prompted to try the hearse on for fit around myself and others as if it was a kind of Cinderella's shoe. It was the hearse's emptiness and the fact that we had no idea of the deceased's identity that gave it so much impact. Its emptiness beckoned to be filled; its anonymity demanded names. So it was that I pictured myself, and Alan, and Julie—any of the people I encountered for the rest of the day—as the body that the hearse had carried. The hearse's emptiness acted like a kind of mortal magnet, drawing into the vacuum of its absence the presence of named, tangible, flesh-and-blood bodies. Full, it would have been like a page on which a story was already written. Empty, it was like a blank page hungry for narrative. The easiest storylines to feed it were those that happened to be closest to hand.

❦

When I walked back to the library at lunchtime the hearse was gone and the small crowd that had been milling awkwardly in the foyer of the Chaplaincy Centre had vanished, their somber formality replaced by the usual mix of casually dressed students. Although things had so quickly returned to the appearance of normality, the hearse had left behind an invisible but persistent splinter. It pricked and nagged at my consciousness. Just as I'd put Julie in the frame it offered, just as I'd put myself and Alan there, so too with the students I saw later in the day. I imagined each of them coffined, hearsed, and mourned. Like a tongue returning repeatedly to explore a sensitive tooth—despite the pain its probings cause—my mind kept touching the memory's image of the hearse and the implications that it carried.

I know it's something obvious and entirely commonplace, yet I'm struck by the plain fact that the hearse exists right now, even as I write about it. It somehow seems strange that it should do so, that it's present somewhere in the city, that its tangible, particular substance accompanies my breathing at this very moment, that it is a cotenant of the time in which these words are being written. Whilst I'm talking to students, drinking coffee with friends, walking between the bus stop and the campus, eating, sleeping, the hearse exists. It's there somewhere, motionless or moving, bearing another coffin or standing empty again, waiting. As my thoughts kept returning to it I found myself wondering where it was garaged and who was responsible for keeping it so immaculately clean and polished. Did its driver, his day's work done, fold his uniform and go home, his mind emptied of the cargoes he'd ferried to and fro, the griefs he'd witnessed? Or, as he settles down to watch TV, eat his dinner, sit drinking in the pub with friends, as he talks with his wife and kids, is it impossible for him to banish from his mind completely an awareness of what lay boxed and embalmed just inches from the warmth of his living head?

How strange it must be to every day transport such explicit reminders of our mortality. For every corpse, whatever else it does, bears with it the message to the living that was a common inscription on old gravestones: "As you are now so once was I, as I am now so shall you be." Would the driver become deaf to this single note sounded so often and at such close proximity, or would he become desensitized to its insistence? Would such close daily contact with the dead make him savor life's fleeting transience as a connoisseur, aware of the rarity of its vintage and the privilege of drinking in its moments? Would he be braver or more cowardly in the face of death, or would it make no difference? Perhaps, like any job, however unsettling initially, its demands would soon shift and slow into something routine, expected, its sharp edges become rounded down by the erosion of repetition. Maybe, like most of us, he just navigates his path through the days allotted to him on the kind of autopilot that doesn't think too far ahead, that lulls us with the illusion of quotidian wellbeing.

⚘

There's a prayer in the Rig Veda, Hinduism's oldest scripture, that implores the gods to "let us die in order," the old before the young, so that parents will not have to endure the pain of mourning their children. I've always liked the tough practicality behind this Vedic prayer—not a fearful plea to live forever, to be let off dying, but simply that our inevitable end will happen in a way that's made more palatable by leaving behind, as yet unscathed, the next generation and their promise of continuance. The desired quietus of those ancient Indians was one in which they didn't have to bid goodbye to the future before they were swallowed into the past.

It was sentiments similar to those expressed in this prayer from thousands of years ago that made me hope the empty hearse had unloaded into the Chaplaincy Centre a coffin bearing the body of a recently deceased emeritus professor. If the life that had ended could be pictured as a long and fulfilled one, the sadness of its ending would be significantly diminished. So I tried to fill the hearse with this venerable classics scholar, a man in his nineties, whose death had been noted in an appreciative obituary on the university's website.

He was someone who had evidently inspired generations of students. He'd written brilliant books, married happily, sired children aplenty, traveled widely, had by all accounts been loved and admired. But this image failed to take—largely because I remembered a news story I'd read in the local paper a couple of days before Alan and I walked past the hearse. The story was about a student in her twenties who was hit by a van when she was cycling in for morning lectures. She died of her injuries in hospital.

Though I'd have preferred to think of the hearse transporting the professor's body, I know it's as likely to have been the body of this unfortunate young woman. Or it might have been someone quite unknown to me, whose death had happened without my hearing any mention of it. Perhaps I should have taken steps to find out whose funeral was happening on campus that fine Friday morning. But making such inquiries would have seemed a bit macabre—the intrusion of a ghoul. In any case, even if I'd discovered the exact details of the individual specifics, I'm not sure how much this would have softened the impact of the hearse. Seeing it empty meant that it had taken on the guise of a universal symbol. Stripping it of that potency might have required more than simply narrowing its reach by tying its presence on campus to a single set of personal circumstances. However securely I might have moored it at the quayside of one named person, I suspect the hearse would have kept drifting into the open waters in which all of us are voyagers.

☙

Whoever's funeral it was, the person my thoughts kept going back to was Julie. She became a kind of touchstone. In part, this was simply because she was the first person I encountered after Alan and I walked past the empty hearse. In part, it was because of the extremity of the contrast she presented—being filled so brimful with the promise of life.

Encountering so potent a manifestation of life's loveliness and potential in such close proximity to an encounter with the ritual regalia of death massively enhanced the impact of both. Her carnal bounty was given exaggerated emphasis by the disembodied absence suggested by the hearse and, in turn, her bounty made the hearse's emptiness seem more extreme in the loss it represented.

For a while, Julie became a kind of fulcrum around which my imagination turned. It wasn't just a case of being attracted to her myself. Of course I felt the power of her allure—it was as obvious as the fact that our different situations (old and young, staff and student, married and single) meant that it would never be acted upon. As I write this, I can hear the shrill voice of political correctness berating me for treating Julie as a sex object. Is my view of her not reprehensibly demeaning? I'm quite aware of her status as a whole person and her right to be treated as such. She's deserving of the same respect that any student should expect in the context of a tutorial about their writing, regardless of age, gender, race, religion, or attractiveness. She received that respect from me. But it would be a kind of dishonesty, a sly deception—or perhaps plain prudishness—not to acknowledge the animal voltage she exuded as strongly as a musky scent. Here was someone enwrapped in a powerful aura of sexuality. Why deny it? It exerted a gravitational pull that would undoubtedly attract meteor showers of prospective suitors. Though obviously they'd be expected to have the maturity and professional responsibility not to allow themselves to be pulled into her orbit, it would seem peculiar to suppose that her attractiveness wouldn't register on her teachers' notice. To pretend it wasn't there, to say nothing about it, might offer a kind of counterpoint to how Alan and I reacted to the hearse, but it would, I think, be a less excusable silence.

Encountering Julie's erotic charisma only minutes after passing the empty hearse occasioned a collision of electricities. The disruptive power as they crashed together was enough to derail the usual carriages into which the mind normally loads what meets it. Instead of seeing her as a pretty girl sitting across the desk from me, the pages of her failed essay spread out between us, I saw Julie not as she was at that moment but as a kind of kaleidoscope of images. Some of these were unashamedly sexual—but they had to do with procreation rather than pornography. I imagined her moments after her conception; as an embryo safe in the muscled fastness of her mother's womb; as a newborn infant; baby; little girl; young woman; falling pregnant; giving birth; mothering her own children; on the plateau of middle age; as an old woman surrounded by her grandchildren; as a corpse lying in a coffin, borne in a hearse and sparking a network of sorrow in the intimates she's left. And, who knows, as her hearse sits empty outside wherever her funeral will be held, perhaps two men in conversation will walk by and say nothing, acting as if it isn't there.

Imagining Julie like this makes her present form dissolve into what preceded it and what will come next. She becomes a process—a series of processes—rather than a singular person; a shifting collection of changes rather than a static body fixed at one fleeting point in its existence. And I'm powerfully reminded by this metamorphosis of the sixteenth-century ivory figurine of Death and the Maiden in the Bode Museum in Berlin. Viewed from the front, it shows a woman—young, full breasted, beautiful. Turn her around and the sculpture shows not her back but her skeleton. This ultra-literal depiction of how we're formed from life and death seems a suitable symbol for the impact the hearse had on my view of Julie. A skeleton's bones are on the obverse of every fleshy coin that's minted and time flips us repeatedly between the faces. The Bode Museum figurine offers a striking reminder of the polarities between which we navigate our way and out of whose creative tensions we are woven.

I know, of course, that Julie will drift away from the pin-
nacle of attractiveness she occupied so triumphantly when
I met her on that Friday morning. Her body will one day
be incinerated, the ashes scattered, blended with the air
and earth and water. Or, if she's buried, her body will be
embraced by all the intricate processes of decay and dissolution by which we are dismantled and slowly rendered
back to the earth, whose elements forge and feed and fell
us. There will come a point that will be the ten thousandth
anniversary of her death, as there already is a point in the
distant past that marked ten thousand years before her birth.
The contiguity of the mundane and the momentous sometimes makes it difficult for a sense of time on any human
scale to come into convincing focus. The way an afternoon
abuts with eons, how a minute is part of millennia, the fact
that we can be thinking one moment of what we plan to do
on the weekend ahead and the next moment be trying to
comprehend the thirteen billion years and more that the universe has existed makes every temporal calibration suspect.
There are similarly extreme contrasts everywhere—between,
for example, a university library, a hive of young brains ripe
with thought and promise, and a hearse driving past it bearing a cold brain in a polished wooden box. Once glimpsed,
such contrasts make it hard to accept any easy sense of
sense. Such violently disjunctive juxtapositions act like acid
on meaning—and yet we manage on most days to smooth
them into the guise of the ordinary.

꒰ꔷ꒱

As I walked home that Friday evening, the sun shone on the
waters of the estuary beside which the city clusters. Three
oystercatchers flew over the campus, piping their urgent
soulful chant as they made for the mudflats. Rush-hour traffic blared out its noise and movement. A plane made its final
approach to the riverside airport. Seagulls fought for scraps

of junk food in the streets where people jostled each other as they ran and queued for buses. In the university gardens a magnolia tree had just come into flower, unnoticed by anyone, keeping to its own timetable of living, in tune with a rhythm unaffected by all the surrounding bustle. And somewhere, not too far away, I knew the hearse must be garaged, out of sight again until the next time. I imagined the metal ticking as the engine cooled and pictured the driver sitting at a bar, his uniform neatly folded and put away at home, ready for another week. The body he transported to the Chaplaincy Centre is in ashes or in the dark of underground. The grief caused by its passing is slowly settling its weight upon the bereaved. Gradually it will edge towards becoming accustomed and routine and then, perhaps, forgotten. I put one word down and then another, stumble a way along the lines set out upon a page. The wind stirs a particle of ash, moving it from one cindered position to another. A carnivorous beetle hunts worms that have been drawn to harvest a body. The sun rises and sets. Students come and go, write essays, pass or fail, attract and are attracted.

As Julie passes through her life stages, an odyssey accelerated by my imagination, I picture the brevity of her individual existence connecting to the duration of the bloodline that gave rise to *Homo sapiens*. Her one life is measured in hours and days and years, a tiny part of a genealogy that runs back for millennia to the point when life first started. How can we reconcile a single person's experience, in all its minuscule particularity, with the wider picture that they're part of, bring into intelligible alignment our moments and the millions of years in which they're set, the paths we follow and the scale of the universe in which everything happens, our existence and our nonexistence? We chart our little routes—our birth, first steps, first kiss, marriage, children, education and career, our travel and achievements, and our death. We emerge from a plenitude of time, occupy a brief sliver of being and are gone again. Dwarfed by the darkness that's parked so massively at our beginning and our end, we say nothing.

> There is nothing to say.
> There is everything to say.

No wonder we fall back on ritual utterance and inconsequential chatter.

CRUX

## I

*A* large X traced out in stone, held within a circle and set into the ground, each line of the X almost six feet long, is a hard thing to miss. Yet, for years, that's precisely what I did, though I must have walked past it scores of times. Such a failure to see something so obviously intended as a marker might suggest that I'm spectacularly unobservant, or maybe willfully blind; in any case an unreliable witness to what's there before me open to plain sight. In fact I like to think of myself as more than averagely observant. Clearly if this self-image is to retain any credibility, I need to account for my failure to notice so arresting a symbol for so long.

What sounds, on first hearing, like something it would be impossible to miss, is actually quite easy to overlook. Failing to notice it illustrates not so much my fallibility as an observer as the way in which the world lays its visual presence upon us. This doesn't take the form of a straightforward one-for-one transference, so that every glance unfailingly records an exact imprint of what is there. Looking is more complicated than that; it's not the simple carbon copy we assume. Instead, it's angled, filtered, focused, and colored by a whole slew of factors—physiological, psychological, physical—that together imbue it with the character of our individual perspective. I'm reminded again of J. A. Baker's wise observation: "The hardest thing of all to see is what is really there."

Three factors combine to weave a kind of camouflage around the X. Together they render it effectively invisible, despite its size. Firstly, the X is marked out as a mosaic. It's inlaid in a patch of cobblestones in front of an arched entrance to the courtyard and garden of a large stone building. The circle around it, and the X itself, are themselves picked out in cobbles, albeit of a different, redder color than the ordinary grey of those surrounding them. But the hue is far from garish, all the stones are worn, and the design sits flush with the other cobbles. It's more understated than emphasized. For all the apparent flourish of X-ing the ground on this kind of scale, it doesn't really stand out much at all. Moreover, since this patch of cobbles is situated more towards the archway than the public pavement that runs past it, to actually walk over the X—which would surely result in noticing it—requires a detour off the obvious route. The pavement's regular, rectangular blocks adjoin the area of cobblestones, offering a smoother walking surface. Unless they're actually visiting the building into whose courtyard and garden the stone archway leads, almost everyone keeps to the pavement. And if, walking past, your glance did happen to be drawn in the direction of the archway, it's more likely to be led through it to the enticing glimpse of garden that it frames, rather than being directed downwards to a patch of faded stonework on the ground.

The second reason it's easy not to notice something that sounds so striking is because of what dominates the view here. It's not the large stone building, or the archway leading to its courtyard or garden, let alone the encircled X marked out amidst the cobblestones. All of these are easily eclipsed by the imposing ruins that are just across the road. These looming walls and towers of gaunt stonework are what rule the eye here, drawing it irresistibly to their massive bulk. Their presence so close at hand means that to look at the cobbled X would require a deliberate swimming against the powerful current that pulls the attention in one direction only. The visual imperative that governs here brooks no opposition; all eyes are drawn to the ruins.

If intrinsic understatedness and being overshadowed by something much more dramatic are not enough to obscure it, a third, less obvious, factor adds to the miasma of invisibility with which the cobbled X is shrouded. This has to do with the prevailing milieu of this place. It's one where history makes itself seem more evident than it does elsewhere, almost as if it was still in the process of unfolding. It sometimes feels as if the town's present denizens are living amidst the remnants of the hard cocoon that history left and that the ghosts of what hatched from it mingle surreptitiously among them. The stonework of the past is everywhere—ruins, archways, ancient buildings. Placed outside a modern glass-and-concrete tower block, an encircled X in cobbles would catch the eye immediately. Here, it fits right in; it's just an unremarkable component of the general atmosphere of ancientness. Absorbed into the steady background hum of the past, individual notes are hard to pick out. Merged with the many other traces of history that linger here, the X fades into self-effacing anonymity for all that it's meant to do exactly the reverse—for the reason that it's here is to commemorate a specific named individual and to protest at the manner of his death.

## II

By the time I'm walking past it with Anna and her friends, I've done my research, know the X is there and what it stands for, so I'm able to draw their attention to it. Standing in an untidy straggle on the pavement outside the arched entrance to the courtyard and garden, almost everyone in the group has stopped to look at the impressive ruins just across the road. Many are photographing them. They're puzzled to see me take a few steps in the opposite direction to the one in which they're expecting—wanting—to go. They watch bemused as I start to talk to Anna and the two others who have joined us about something on the ground just at our feet. A few of the main group come over and form a little cluster round the X, but for most the magnetism of the ruins prevails. It draws them across the road, phones and cameras held at the ready.

There are around thirty of us. I'm with a group of American students, most of whom are visiting Scotland for the first time. For some, it's their first trip to Europe; for a few, the first time they've left the States. They're on a study-abroad program, taking a month-long course on literature and landscape. I'm a minor stop on their busy itinerary. Unlike most of the writers they'll be considering, I'm neither dead nor famous. I'm happy to provide a point of contrast by giving a reading from some current work and talking to them about the impact of place on my writing. They're a cheerful, good-humored bunch with the verve and energy of youth. Their exuberance is catching; it's a pleasure to be with them.

"Anna" isn't her real name. It's a fig leaf of anonymity that I'm using to cover the naked truth of who she is. This may seem unnecessary. She clearly possesses considerable self-assurance, enough to suggest that she mightn't mind it if I used her real name. But the mask of "Anna" is as much for my sake as it is for hers. It allows me more freedom to say what I want to say than I'd feel I had if my words were directed at someone picked out and individualized with their actual name. To write about someone openly, with the arrow of attention aimed unambiguously at them, can seem more akin to attack than to inquiry or description. And trying to please, or just avoid giving offence, can push a writer into clumsy dissimulation. I prefer the honesty that pseudonyms help foster. Adopting one also allows me to use her not just as a single girl locked into the specifics that define her, but as a kind of archetype as well; a model who can try on and display some of the ideas that I'm interested in exploring. Draped in the gauze of relative anonymity, I feel able to say things I'd be more inhibited about saying if I was attributing them to a named person whose identity was revealed for everyone to see.

Anna has one of the brightest smiles yet most hurt-filled eyes that I've ever seen together in one face. This may sound as if her features pull in such opposing directions that they must result in the discord of a grimace. On the contrary, each part of this seeming contradiction acts to enhance the other: the smile is made more radiant because of the shadow in the eyes that fails to dim it; the shadow seems darker because she's clearly a cheerful person not given to the melancholic. Of course I'm curious about the shadow's cause. I'd like to know the reason for such hurt being written into the gaze of one so young. Her eyes convey a depth of suffering that suggests she's experienced considerable anguish, though of what variety—the pain of illness, disappointment, loss—it's impossible to tell. It would be impertinent of me to venture questions in this direction. We're at the stage— will never pass the stage—of pleasantries and small talk. The mystery of her life-story, its secret unfolding, the intimacies it contains, are not things I can decently ask about, however curious her conflicted expression makes me.

Of course someone who fails to notice for so long a large stone X marked out on the ground might not be considered a trustworthy reporter when it comes to noting the subtly shifting minutia of facial feature and expression. And in any case, even if I've recorded their presence accurately, how this striking pairing of brightness and shadow should be read is hard to say. Quite apart from any doubts about my prowess as an observer, there's a large measure of wisdom in Shakespeare's saying that "there's no art can find the mind's construction in the face." Maybe the smile was no more than the accomplished veneer of tutored politeness; the seeming hurt no more than tiredness from her long flight, or the heavy tread of a headache that will vanish overnight. All I can say in reply to such commonsense suppositions is that I was powerfully struck by the aura of dissonance on her face and that its quality seemed neither trivial nor temporary.

# III

We're in St Andrews, Scotland's ancient ecclesiastical capital. The ruins that catch everyone's attention are of its magnificent medieval cathedral, the original structure of which dates from the twelfth century. The encircled X in the cobbles is in front of the elegant archway that leads into the courtyard and garden of Dean's Court—once part of the cathedral complex, now a residence for postgraduate students attending the town's famous university, the oldest in Scotland, celebrating its six hundredth anniversary in the year that Anna and her friends are visiting.

On April 28, 1558, an execution was performed here. A fire was lit at the exact spot marked by the X. Tied to a stake at the center of the flames was an eighty-two-year-old man. His name was Walter Mylne.

Once a priest in the Catholic church, Mylne had been drawn to the new Protestant ideas that were starting to gain strength in Europe at this time. His growing disillusionment with Catholic ritual led to an accusation of heresy from the abbot of Arbroath, a small town some thirty miles' drive along the coast from St Andrews (or half that distance if you go by boat). Sensible of the peril in which such an accusation placed him, Mylne fled Scotland and settled in Germany. There, moving further from the strictures of Catholic orthodoxy and its demand for celibate clergy, he married, had children, further embraced the religious ideas that were fast gathering their history-changing momentum. Why Mylne returned to Scotland in 1556 isn't clear. Perhaps he was simply homesick, assailed by that powerful instinct that can call us back to wherever we've been raised. He lived quietly, but not quietly enough, in the environs of Dysart, a village not far from St Andrews. When the parish priest there discovered that Mylne had been giving religious instruction to a local widow and her family, he ordered his arrest.

Mylne (the records also give his name as Mill, Mille, and Milne) was taken to St Andrews, where the church hierarchy urged him to recant—with the promise of a monk's sinecure at Dunfermline Abbey if he did. He refused, offering instead a robustly spirited defense of his position. He was condemned to be burnt at the stake as a heretic. His courage and eloquence before his accusers so impressed the local populace that they refused to supply the ugly accoutrements needed for an auto-da-fé—rope, timber, tar. But the church authorities were determined and their will eventually prevailed. Mylne was burnt to death outside the cathedral in front of a crowd that included four of Scotland's bishops and other church dignitaries.

Writing about Mylne in the *Dictionary of National Biography*, Richard Greave reports:

> The townsfolk piled stones in Mylne's memory on the site of his burning, repeating their action after the stones were removed, only to have them taken away a second time. But the memory lingered in the popular imagination, and when John Knox preached in St Andrews in June 1559 on Christ's cleansing of the temple, a bonfire of images was made at the place where Mylne suffered.

This place of execution and remembrance is what's marked by the encircled X in the cobbles. It's an entirely appropriate symbol—in part because of its Christian connotations, which point to the role of sectarian intolerance in Mylne's death, but also because of the origins of this twenty-fourth letter of our alphabet. It's thought to have been derived from a Phoenician letter that meant "post" or "support"—so "stake" is already written into the DNA of its deep-structure. The way we've come to hang so much on two crossed lines shows our propensity for symbol-making. Those ancient Mediterranean minds that shaped X's precursor into its embryonic form would have been amazed at what their letter has been used to support over the centuries since they first wrote it—and no doubt dismayed to discover what it was used to represent in this cobbled cross outside Dean's Court.

Standing at the site of his immolation, I wonder if the woman Mylne wed—in order, so he said, to keep him from the sin of fornication and to be his helpmeet—bore any resemblance to Anna, her brow furrowed in distaste as she listens to me explain what's commemorated by the mosaic at our feet. History does not record the widow's story, beyond noting that she was alive at the time of the execution and for some years afterwards. I wonder what smiles passed between them as they lay together, this renegade priest and the chosen helpmeet he desired. What did they see in each other's eyes? Was her smile like Anna's? After her husband was taken from her, was her expression incised with the same look of familiarity with pain?

I'm not sure whether it was Mylne's fate, or Anna's conflicted expression, or the circumstance of someone coming from so far away to stand at the spot where he perished, but I was struck by a sense of the mystery attending the spaces between things—one person and another; one moment and the next; a feeling and its opposite. The gridiron of proximities that forms the tapestry on which our lives are woven seemed for a moment almost visible as we stood on those worn cobblestones outside Dean's Court in the shadow of St Andrews' majestic ruined cathedral. What might have been dismissed merely as ancient history, a barbaric act from long ago, seemed somehow nearer to us than it would have been had it been measured and contained by the conventional calibrations of duration. Perhaps it was the coincidence of place—our standing exactly at the spot where Mylne's stake had been—or perhaps it was the voltage of empathy raised to flashpoint by the cruelty of his fate, but something acted to make it seem as if, on the environing canvas of space-time, we were closer to him than the raw chronology of dates suggested.

## IV

When my daughters were younger, one of the games we sometimes played after breakfast at the weekend, when we were all still sitting companionably around the kitchen table, was putting things "disturbingly close" to one another. I'm not sure which of us invented the game, or its key phrase—or why any of us should have felt it was "disturbing" to have objects on the table pushed into such intimate proximity that it was hard to tell whether or not they were touching. We didn't think much about it. It was simply one of those idle games a family invents just for fun.

Thinking about it now, I wonder if the name and concept might have originated from my younger daughter's description of a classmate. He was afflicted with one of the myriad of behavioral malfunctions with which schools have to cope these days. This troubled—and troubling—individual had no sense of other people's personal space and routinely invaded it. He wasn't liked because he came "disturbingly close" to just about everyone—fellow pupils, teachers, catering staff, visitors to the school. He seemed unable to understand that this was something which caused other people disquiet. Blind to his own repeated trespassing, the subtleties of distance by which we plot a course through life were written in a script he didn't understand. Illiterate in the language of proximity, he was unable to fit in and, in consequence, was shunned.

Whatever the origin of our game—if so simple a pastime warrants game-status—putting things "disturbingly close" to each other involved exactly what the name implies. One of us would push the salt and pepper as close together as it was possible to place them without their actually touching. Then someone else would do the same thing with the table mats or mugs or glasses, edging one item closer, closer, closer to another until there was only an infinitesimal space between them. Usually we tired of it quite quickly and just pushed things together so that the game ended in laughter and the disqualification of collision. But occasionally we cooperated rather than competed and arranged every item on the table as disturbingly close to something else as we could manage.

The game was philosophically fertile in that it gave rise to speculation about what would happen if two items were placed so close to each other that they were within a breath of touching and left so arranged for eons. Would such an extreme degree of closeness, over an immense span of time, erode each object's discrete identity so that a drift of atoms might start to flow between one and the other? Perhaps the tiny space between them would gradually be bridged and blurred, sutured together by this invisible bleed of matter. We speculated about their original separateness being changed into new alignments and identities by a subtle melding, a gradual transfusion of substance, as once impermeable boundaries allowed hitherto forbidden ingress and egress. Are things as separate as we think? Might they not be gripped in a slow flux and drift of being that smudges the categories we rely on, making them less distinct? Or would every object remain totally separate forever, locked within the integrity of its own indissoluble borders; always—albeit minimally—apart from what stood next to it? It was one thing to deal in the simple, solid things sitting on our weekend breakfast table; to see them as impervious to the melding we imagined, immune to any drift into the other over time. But what of the disturbing closeness of less concrete things: intimacy and distance; greeting and farewell; attraction and indifference; the present, past, and future?

As we played the game we also wondered about what the greatest distance is—in time and space—by which two objects can be separated, and which two things in the entire universe are located at this maximal divide. What would happen if their relationship was suddenly reversed, or switched with that of whichever objects are deemed to occupy the opposite end of the closeness spectrum; things so minutely contiguous that their adjacence is hard to distinguish from unbroken singularity?

# V

I was reminded of our game of placing things disturbingly close to one another as I stood at Mylne's cross with Anna. In terms of the ordinary measures we apply, I know there are no connections between an eighty-two-year-old Scotsman martyred in 1558 and a twenty-something American girl with sad eyes and a bright smile who visited St Andrews four hundred and fifty-five years later. I know that her life and mine and his follow their separate contours and are linked only momentarily and tenuously by the circumstance of our standing here upon this selfsame spot, unique upon the earth. I know that distance can be mapped and measured in the units we use to calibrate the time and space around us. According to such routine gauges of proximity, Anna and I are separated from Mylne's agony by a safe cushioning of years. But the calculus of imagination and empathy gives a different reading.

As we stood at Mylne's X, I knew we lived in a world that, for all its stupidities and compromises, is a gentler, more enlightened place than the one regnant here four hundred years ago. I know a gulf of centuries separates now from then, that the attitudes and outcomes of a life in the 1500s are far removed from those attending our lives in the 2000s: Anna has before her all manner of possibilities that to a sixteenth-century woman of her age would have been inconceivable. What I know about the world would have struck Mylne and his contemporaries as miraculous (or perhaps satanic). Yet, for all the centuries spaced out between our now and Mylne's then, for all the conceptual distances that separate us, standing at that X outside Dean's Court gave rise to a nagging sense of contiguity—our shared occupancy of existence, consciousness; cotenancy of a common human element.

Time and place and circumstance enfold each of us in our own particular niche of being, wall us into our individual separateness. But it's often possible, with those we're close to, to feel a drift of substance moving from one life to another. Can imagination fused with knowledge facilitate a transfusion between lives we consider much more distant, so that a few rogue life-atoms become enabled and drift through larger spans of time—a kind of radioactive trickle, hot with the burden of the otherness they carry? What barriers are there, after all, between one passing second and the next, and what is time except the accumulation of such unfenced moments?

Difference does not mean distance. Being and not being, for example, loom disturbingly close together, both of them right beside us. A smile, a caress, an embrace; the quickening of two hearts, and a life is kindled. A few words exchanged, directions given, wood, ropes, and tar fetched together and lit, the scorching of flesh, the choking of lungs, and a life is extinguished. How should we separate what's past, what's present, and what still lies in the future, map the contiguities that time presents, arrayed on the artery of connections whose flow is history? In its blood race tenderness and savagery, ugliness and beauty, youth and age—and all the other pairings that peg us to the world, articulate our story. Our weaving of meaning's embroidery is done on a canvas whose stretch depends on the tensions drawn between opposites. What happens if they shift and slacken; if we lose faith in the spaces between them?

How do we bring into focus and map the relationships between what's been, what's now, what's yet to happen—

Mylne suckling at his mother's breast; on his knees in prayer; on his wedding night; bound to his stake; Mylne in Anna's thoughts, in mine, in yours now, and in the minds of those as yet unborn who'll visit St Andrews decades hence? With no more than our flimsy accumulations of seconds grown into years, we dam and irrigate time's flow. But can the ditches and sluice-work we impose—our todays, yesterdays, tomorrows, the numbered years—contain, still less control, the tidal surge of moments, time's saturating seepage? I have a sense of certainties dissolving, of what seemed clear-cut threatening to liquefy as time's tsunami sweeps over all that happens, and engulfs it in a scale that mocks our attempts at irrigation, all the little channels that we dig, our efforts to divide duration into separate categories, each labeled with the symbols we've X'd upon the world.

## VI

Anna and her friends stayed only for an afternoon. Enough time to take in some of the sights of St Andrews, listen to me give a reading, ask questions about the process of writing and the impact of place upon it, and get me to sign copies of my most recent book. I was just a brief detour on an itinerary that took in Shakespeare's Stratford and Globe Theatre, Jane Austen's Bath, Brontë country, the Lakes, and other well-known sites of literary interest. By now, most of them will have forgotten almost everything about their visit to Scotland's ancient ecclesiastical capital—except for a vague impression of a stone-built town with a violent religious history, impressive ruins, a cold east wind blowing in across the sea, and an obscure writer reading from his work in an unfamiliar accent. Particularly since—captivated by the cathedral ruins—so few of them stopped to look at the encircled X in the cobbles outside Dean's Court, I imagine almost none remember now anything to do with Walter Mylne. And perhaps that's as it should be. Even at the time, I wasn't sure if I should have burdened Anna with a knowledge of this ancient atrocity, about which she could do nothing but feel pity and disgust. Thinking of it now I'm even less sure about what we should try to X into our memories, incise upon our hearts from history's catalogue of happenings, carry with us from one moment to the next as we weave our paths between life's smiles and hurts.

I've been past Dean's Court scores of times since the day of Anna's visit and have become interested to note how routinely the X is overlooked. St Andrews is a popular tourist destination and for most of the summer the cathedral area is thronged with sightseers. It's rare, come June through August, to pass Mylne's cross without there being someone taking photos of the cathedral ruins that rise so impressively just across the road from it. But I've never seen someone stop to photograph the X itself.

On one occasion recently when I was walking past it, a family was dawdling along the pavement, enjoying the sun and the ice cream cones they were eating. Their son—a boy of maybe six—was riding a tricycle, one hand on the handlebars, the other tightly clasping a double cone of green-tinged ice cream, flecked with chocolate chips. He licked it with relish, steering erratically. As they came closer, he swerved his tricycle onto the patch of cobbles, rode bumpily across them—straight over the encircled X, through the archway, and into the courtyard of Dean's Court. He did a slow turn there and rode back out to rejoin his parents, crossing the X again. They had stopped, smiling, to watch this display of independence, as innocent of what had happened here half a dozen generations ago as Mylne, tied to his stake, would have been innocent of ice cream and tricycles and tourists enjoying the spectacle of the cathedral's ruins.

This exuberant toddler made me think of the martyr as a little boy absorbed in play, unaware of the fire that loomed ahead. I thought of him as a babe-in-arms, an embryo curled unborn in his mother's womb, the man he would grow up to be, the priest and lover, the father and martyr. And I wondered if Anna would have children, and how whatever life might quicken in her would unfold into the particularities of a unique biography. How would her child negotiate all the experiences that would define them? Where would the X of that postulated person's conception fall, the X of their birth, their infancy, their travels and trials, first falling in love, their marriage and children, their illness and death? What X would they leave upon the earth, testimony of their life's passing? Would they ever stand here, in St Andrews, at the same cobbled X where their mother once stood with me?

What links a tricycling toddler, his tongue and lips cold from ice cream, with an aged martyr, the taste of hot smoke in his mouth, flesh burning in the flames? What links the expression in Anna's eyes to those in the eyes of Mylne's widow, and to mine, and to those of every other person who has walked past this cobbled X in the last four and a half centuries? Thinking of the strange weave of a moment, how it seamlessly adjoins with what came before it and what will follow, the way in which the potential hovers around the actual, whispering of other possible unfoldings, I picture all the Xs that we leave, marking out our fingerprints of presence through the days, and I can't decide what measures I should use to fix and plot what happens, or to determine the relevance of one moment to another.

Considering Mylne as embryo and as boy, as priest and old man at the stake; considering Anna as child, young woman, mother; considering the tricycle-riding boy and whoever he will grow up to be, considering myself, and all the others who have passed—will pass—within an arm's length of where this cobbled X now marks the spot, I wonder what kind of hieroglyphics our varied passings leave upon time's fabric, what patterns they incise upon the area around the cobbled X. Can we read any meaning from them, beyond the bare fact of their occurrence? If some cartographer of our human spoor was able to join up all the Xs that we leave, trace out the isobars of human being, the agonies and ecstasies of living, what kind of routes, through what kind of landscapes, undertaken for what kind of reasons would be plotted on that map?

## VII

In algebra—in maths in general—"x" is used to symbolize an unknown quantity. Our calculations usually reveal what this unknown is; logic allows us to follow the requisite steps through an equation so that we can find a solution, identify what stands behind the x's mask of anonymity. The more I think about it, the more Mylne's X seems to represent a kind of nexus of unknowns—but I can't work out a way to calculate the burden of what it represents. Yes, in one sense I know quite well that there's nothing problematic about it—it's the most straightforward of equations: X = the place where Walter Mylne, at the age of eighty-two, was burnt at the stake for heresy. But close-shadowing such historical literalism, tripping up its simplistic equivalence of symbol and the event it symbolizes, a whole slew of complications gathers momentum. How does one life relate to others, one age to others, one act to others? What should our manifest of remembrance include; what should we retrieve from history, what consign to forgetfulness? How do temporal and physical closeness, degrees of proximity, translate onto a map of what should matter to us?

As well as standing for an unknown quantity, X can be used to represent an unnamed person. Sometimes it's used to symbolize a kiss or to indicate an error, or to stand in lieu of a signature, the mark of the illiterate upon a document. It records choice on a ballot paper, and acts as an abbreviation for Christ. I can hear echoes of all these senses in the cobbled mosaic outside Dean's Court. It represents the unfathomable nature of human cruelty; it stands for all the unnamed people in the crowd that gathered around Mylne's pyre, greedy for brutal spectacle. It stands for the incalculable number who have subsequently walked past this spot, knowing nothing of its history. The X can stand for the kisses that passed between Mylne and his chosen mate, or for the error of his supposed heresy, or for the lapse in humanity of the accusers who sentenced him, and those who carried out so terrible a punishment. It can stand as the ballot mark of those who would have voted to condemn him, or the mark of those who would readily have granted pardon. Its cruciform shape is embedded in the symbolism of Christian teaching. But all these nuances notwithstanding, the X has become something else for me.

I've come to see it not so much as any mathematical sign or religious mark, however much it may manifest aspects of each, but as a crux. I know that this is just the Latin word for cross, but in English its meanings possess a resonance that's hauntingly attuned to what I feel when I consider the cobbled symbol on the ground outside Dean's Court. "Crux" can be defined as "something that occasions difficulty or perplexity; that on which a decision turns; the essential point." All of those senses find some purchase on Mylne's mark, help draw it towards the light of understanding. But "crux" has two other meanings that make it yet more suited to my purposes—to the extent that the word seems like a kind of naturally occurring cobblestone found ready-cut and shaped to the dimensions needed to fit into the verbal mosaic I've been laying around Mylne's X, using all the letters of the alphabet to try to bring this single one to heel. The crux of the heart (*crux cordis*) is an area near where a narrow sulcus separates right and left ventricles. This can act as a reminder of the brutality of what was done here: Mylne roped to a stake and the frail heart of this old man straining and failing as it's immolated on a pyre of tar and timber. But I prefer to lay the stress on the less macabre sense that *crux cordis* brings—the suggestion that the cobbled crux marks some kind of heart of the matter, pointing to an area of deep and vital interiority whose pulse sounds out a tocsin gravid with a significance I struggle to decode. Crux is also the name of the cross-shaped constellation commonly known as the Southern Cross—which is used by navigators to plot a course through southern oceans, much as seafarers in the northern hemisphere use the Pole Star. For all the dullness of its cobbles, to me Mylne's cross has a kind of starlike quality, even if I'm at a loss to know where it will guide my vessel when I use it as a point of reference.

Sometimes, when I pass Dean's Court these days, I make a deliberate detour and stand for a moment at the epicenter of the X. This isn't done as a ritual of grim remembrance—though it does often make me think of Mylne's end—it's more a kind of contemplative sideways step off the evenly paved surface of routine preoccupations so that I can pause to wonder at the mysterious texture of life's moments and the way such different things are closely woven into the fabric of what happens. Standing there on the X, like a human arrow on one of history's bull's-eyes, I often think of Anna's smile and troubled eyes and wonder where she is and what she's doing now, at the precise same moment that my feet feel the rounded stones of this cobbled crux hard beneath their tread. Sometimes I see the X as a kind of pivot around which turns the trudge of human history in its complex circumambulations, locked into orbits of cruelty and kindness; sometimes it seems more like a question mark, heavy with the weight of the interrogations that it carries.

If I live to be the same age Mylne was when he was executed, Anna will, I guess, be somewhere in her early forties. When she reaches eighty-two, if she ever does, I'll long since have perished, my body burnt to the same residue of ash as Mylne's poor corpse was reduced to. Perhaps Anna's son or daughter, or their descendants, will visit St Andrews and stand here where we did, long after she and I have perished.

And however this may be, no doubt toddlers will still relish ice cream as they walk past with their parents; tourists will come to photograph the cathedral ruins; students will ponder the impact of landscape on the literatures they're studying. The world will continue to bear its load of pains and pleasures as, second by second, day by day, time continues. The moments that pass on this stone X will proliferate, repeat, and vary, as they do in every other place. And the crux of the matter, like the rumor of some undiscovered constellation in a distant galaxy, the *crux cordis* of existence, will continue to haunt and elude us.

# SHELLS

*T*wo photographs of my Uncle Tony are the obvious place to begin. One shows him in an open grave with another man. In the second, he's being embraced by a vampire. Even by themselves, unaccompanied by any pictures, these words conjure striking images. They do what a beginning is supposed to do: catch the reader's attention. The fact that the other man in the grave is Peter Cushing, and the vampire a youthful Christopher Lee, adds the spice of celebrity to the bait of the unusual.

I'll come back to Tony and the photographs later. Although it's tempting to focus at the outset on what—with no effort on my part—piques the curiosity, I want to begin with something less dramatic. It's not immediately intriguing in the way of vampires, open graves, and well-known faces; it makes more demands on a reader's patience—but it unfolds into something that I find more interesting than any hijinks with famous actors.

One of the best presents I was given as a child was a box of seashells, collected by my Auntie Daisy—Tony's wife—when she was stationed in Egypt during World War II. Daisy was the only one of my father's siblings to have left the close, confining clutches of life in Northern Ireland, where invisible walls of religious apartheid ran through every social structure. Dad's other sister and two brothers lived close enough to our family home near Belfast to make them accustomed figures of childhood. By contrast, Daisy always remained something of a stranger. For all the time I knew her, she lived in London.

She was the most adventurous member of her family. Intelligent, attractive, independent, with a wry sense of humor and a readiness to speak her mind, it surprised no one when she joined the Auxiliary Territorial Service (ATS)—the women's branch of the British Army—at the outbreak of war in 1939. Quickly promoted to the equivalent rank to captain, she was posted to the Middle East. There she met Tony, who was in the Army Film and Photographic Unit (AFPU).

When I say there are two hundred shells in Daisy's collection, it's likely this will give the wrong impression—unless I quickly add that most of them are so tiny they fit in a cigarette tin of a type that was common in her day. It would, I suppose, have held twenty cigarettes. There's a gold coat of arms on the tin's red lid and underneath it the legend: "By Appointment Tobacconist to His Majesty the King." Further down is written: "Benson and Hedges Super Virginia Cigarettes." The king was George VI, Britain's wartime monarch. Perhaps being in a cigarette tin added the allure of something adult and forbidden to the intrinsic appeal the shells already possessed. I imagined it sitting snug in the pocket of Daisy's smart ATS uniform and being brought out with a practiced flourish as she took a cigarette, offered one to friends.

Most of the shells are univalves, exotic variants of the periwinkles and whelks I was familiar with from British seashores. The toughness of the shells and their natural glaze—

together with the fact that they've been protected by their tin sarcophagus—means they're still in mint condition. Even after all this time, they have the look of something newly gathered. There are a few bivalves too—similar in shape to our native cockles, but with a delicacy of line and hue that immediately marks them out as alien. The vast majority of the shells are snail-shaped; a selection of miniature gastropods, most of them smaller than a pea.

I was given the shells when I was eight. They immediately became a prized possession. I loved their repeated perfection of form and color across a set of varied themes. They were as appealing as little gemstones. But the jewel in the crown of Daisy's collection—as different from its fellows as Daisy was from her siblings—was a *Mitra episcopalis* shell that was too large to fit in the tin.

The shell is about the length of my little finger, but nearly thumb-width at its thickest, before the spiral tapers to a point. It's covered with bright orange dots and splotches on a white background, the markings arranged in lines that are angled around, and help to accentuate, the spiral shape. It's as if a careful child had turned it slowly, daubing it with a paint-dipped fingertip. Then, wanting a more delicate effect, used a fine brush to echo the finger marks with a series of dots between them. At the shell's aperture, the opening where the visible part of the creature's soft body would have appeared, there are four ridged lines. These look like the tracks of some tiny railway, vanishing into the secret interiority of a once living tunnel.

The name *Mitra episcopalis*—bishop's miter—was bestowed for two reasons. First, the conical shell is reminiscent of the shape of a miter, the high hat worn by bishops and archbishops. Secondly, if these snails are threatened they exude a noxious liquid. This defensive emission is purple, the color traditionally associated with high ecclesiastical office.

Daisy's Egyptian shells are undoubtedly beautiful. But beauty alone doesn't account for their appeal. I think part of their spell lies in the way they have about them a sense of life frozen and preserved. Of course this is an illusion. The creatures that inhabited them don't partake of the seeming deathlessness of the shells. The shells are merely inert residue, an empty remnant, the rime left behind after the life that created them has gone. Yet, despite this, there's a sense in which they appear to stall the flow of time, let it pool for a while in the little receptacles they offer so that it seems to slow and still.

·ᴥ·

Until I started to write about them, I'd not thought of Daisy's Egyptian shells for years. What are regarded as treasures in childhood soon enough lose their luster. What gives them their magic fades over time. The shells never lost their appeal completely—I never wanted to throw them away—but for a long while they sat forgotten in a drawer. What made me think about them again was an unexpected visual prompt.

The prompt came when I was visiting the Bell Pettigrew Museum last summer. The museum is a Victorian natural history collection beautifully preserved and displayed at the University of St Andrews. As I was looking at a case featuring various gastropods, one of the shells made me start with the shock of recognition. It was a double of the orange splotched and dotted one that had pride of place in Daisy's collection. But now I had a name for it, courtesy of the Bell Pettigrew's captioning: *Mitra episcopalis*. As soon as I got home from the museum, I looked out my Egyptian shells again.

·ᴥ·

Coincidentally, at around this time I was reading *The Museum of Innocence,* by Nobel Prize winner Orhan Pamuk. The novel chronicles how Kemal Basmaci turns collector and curator of a vast number of ordinary objects that are invested with special significance because of their association with his inamorata, the beautiful but doomed Füsun. Some of the words Pamuk puts in the mouth of his increasingly obsessive protagonist resonated with how I felt when I handled Daisy's Egyptian shells again. Kemal recognizes that "the power of things inheres in the memories they gather up inside them." As he amasses the collection that forms his museum, he becomes "like a shaman who can see the souls of things" and "feel their stories flickering" so that even something as trivial as a cigarette end can yield rich harvests.

The memories gathered up in Daisy's Egyptian shells certainly invest their little cones and spirals with a kind of power, and trying to tap into its voltage feels not unlike some sort of shamanistic ritual. But whereas Kemal was interested in events in which he'd played a key role—and could therefore curate the objects he hoarded with the authority of direct involvement—I feel increasingly that the flickering stories held in the shells lead me into a tangle of other people's lives about which I know next to nothing. Behind the familiarity of a treasured gift given unexpectedly by my father's younger sister there's a kind of misty labyrinth into which the thread of every storyline soon disappears.

Even at the level set by the modest demands of telling in outline the story of Daisy's Egyptian shells, there's a great deal I can only guess at. The shells summon familiar images sure enough, but they arrive eviscerated. Look just below their surface and unanswered questions start to ring through them, emphasizing their hollowness. I don't know what Daisy's military duties were, or why they took her to Egypt. I'm not sure where—or why, or when—she collected the shells. I've no idea what they meant to her. After the war, in London, if she took the *Mitra episcopalis*, let it sit on her palm until it warmed to the same temperature as her blood, what memories and associations started to unfurl? And what made her decide to give the shells to me?

༄

There are a dozen or so wartime photographs of Daisy in one of my father's albums. Sometimes she's pictured alone, but usually in a group—soldiers, airmen, ATS, all in uniform. Often, the backdrop is the Nile, the Sphinx, or the pyramids. But there are two of her taken sitting indoors, in what's probably an officers' club. She looks pensive and beautiful, lost in her own world; oblivious to the presence of a camera. Tony features in several of the photos. In one he's flanked by Daisy and another smiling ATS officer. In another he's grinning broadly with Daisy in his arms, as if he's about to carry her across a threshold. Were the shells in Daisy's pocket in some of these photographs? Or were they stored among her things in a bedside locker in whatever quarters she was given? What did she dream of as she lay so far from home, with the noise of artillery rupturing the quiet of the desert night? Did she and Tony lie together, or was their union only consummated when they returned to Britain and got married? I wonder, too, how life unfolded for the other young ATS women in the photographs. Did they all survive? Or are some of their names among the ones inscribed on headstones in the military cemeteries in Alexandria, Suez, Heliopolis, and other sites in Egypt where those killed in combat were interred?

Thinking of the ATS women who lost their lives, I picture *Mitra episcopalis* moving in the warm Egyptian waters while above them battles rage and people die. As W. H. Auden puts it, suffering happens "while someone else is eating or opening a window or just walking dully along." Every day, whether in peacetime or war, people are injured and die, gather seashells, lay down memories that will stay with them for years—as others are walking dully by, oblivious to what's happening to anyone beyond the small circle of their acquaintance. The vast remainder of the world, what's apart from us, all the mass of things that crowd around us, contin-

ues without regard for the way our individual stories happen
to unfold.

᠕

When we were children we were told that we would "hear
the sea" if we held our ears close against the opening of large
conch shells. And, sure enough, whenever we tried this, placing their inviting pink-smooth apertures against our ears,
we could hear a kind of faint pelagic echoing. The more I
think about the Egyptian shells, the more it seems that, for
all their littleness, they each contain a tidal roar. The combined volume is overwhelming and defies my attempts at
transcription.

At the simplest level, the shells are tangible remnants—
mementos, souvenirs—from a time of war. They're things at
once caught up in, and completely independent of, the conflict that dominated human history from 1939 to 1945. To
hold one is to feel memory and imagination stir, populating
the mind with a ream of possible stories woven from the
few loose threads that have trailed into my life from the life
of my aunt. The shells possess the potency of objects that
have been there, occupying places talked about, but never
visited, where many of that generation went to fight. They
are like marker buoys that have drifted from their quadrant
of time's ocean into mine, carrying with them the authenticity of presence.

The life history of *Mitra episcopalis* may seem easy
enough to tell. The orange splotched snails are a predatory
species that feed nocturnally, mostly on worms. It begins as
an egg that hatches into a free-swimming larval stage. These
phases of its life cycle, the shell's growth, its markings, the
favored habitats, the physiology and anatomy of the adult,
the biochemistry that fires its metabolism, all submit with
little difficulty to a setting down of facts. But the shell that I
can so easily take in my hand and provide a rubric of infor-

mation about, soon points to what came before it—by which I don't just mean the parental duo responsible for its birth. It's rather as if the tiny tracks laid down in the aperture not only lead into the spiral tunnel of this one single shell and the intimacies of its life-processes, but into the vortex of the species' evolution; the creation of the whole bloodline of *Mitra episcopalis*. I feel myself pulled back through the eons, as if the shells opened a kind of trapdoor that leads back to their absolute beginning.

As well as making me think about their ancient origins and their journey through time to the moment Daisy found them, writing about the Egyptian shells has made me realize how little I know about Daisy and Tony. Their names are well-worn tokens from childhood, but such nominal familiarity is, itself, just a shell; beneath it lies much unknown territory. We only saw them infrequently. When we did, Tony in particular seemed to keep his distance—though perhaps it was us that did so, wary of what we read as his strangeness; his outsider's aura. The fact that he was a divorcee, worked in the film industry, visited foreign countries, mixed with celebrities, and was English caused a mixture of disapproval, interest, and envy in the local society of the time, with its strait-laced and often small-minded Ulster outlook. My impression is of a vigorous, impatient man with dramatically swept-back red hair. I suspect he found his visits as trying as we did.

჻

Uncle Tony was Anthony Nelson Keys. As children we were told he worked as a film producer. *Reach for the Sky*—a biopic of fighter pilot, double amputee, and war hero Douglas Bader, starring Kenneth More as Bader—was pointed to as an example of Tony's work. The film received a BAFTA award for Best British Film of 1956. It was filled with the kind of patriotism and bravery that our parents approved of. Fighting courageously against the odds, enduring adversity stoically, never giving up—these were seen as wholesome values to which children should be exposed. We were taken to see the film several times and made to sit till Tony's name appeared on the closing credits. The cinema was regarded with suspicion in the austere thought-world of Ulster Presbyterianism, but *Reach for the Sky* was considered an exception to the rule that films promulgated sin.

What I've only recently come to realize is that *Reach for the Sky* wasn't representative of Tony's oeuvre. In fact he was a prominent figure in Hammer House of Horror productions, the company that dominated films of this genre from the 1950s to the 1970s. Tony produced a whole ream of horror films—*Curse of Frankenstein, Quatermass 2, The Horror of Dracula, The Devil Rides Out*. In 1948 he was production manager for two films directed by David MacDonald. Major David MacDonald had commanded the Army Film and Photographic Unit's Number 1 Unit, stationed in North Africa. This thirty-two-man team, one of whom was Tony, covered the Allies' campaign against Rommel's Afrikakorps. It was their close-up footage of tank battles, bayonet charges, and artillery barrages that was used—together with captured German newsreel—to make the acclaimed documentary film *Desert Victory*, released in 1943. Of the thirty-two men in AFPU's Unit 1, four were killed, seven wounded, and six captured. Against such odds, Tony was lucky to have escaped unscathed—though who knows what impact his experience of filming war up close may have had. Perhaps working with made-up horrors provided solace for the real ones that continued to haunt him.

At the time when I was given the Egyptian shells, Tony was producing films like *The Pirates on Blood River, The Damned, The Gorgon*, and *The Brigand of Kandahar*—and having photographs of himself taken with some of the stars. Looking at him staring towards the camera from the open grave, a fat cigar in his hand, Peter Cushing beside him, or fooling around and striking a victim's pose, enveloped by Dracula's black cloak, with Christopher Lee smiling to reveal his fangs, I wonder what he thought about his wife's gifting of the Egyptian shells to her Irish nephew and what memories those shells held for him. I have a sense of someone's life known only fractionally and I'm saddened by this—not just by the fact that my knowledge of Daisy and Tony was built on such flimsy foundations, but by the wider realization that this brings. So many of the people I remember from childhood are likewise, once examined, little more than shadows; there's nothing of substance beneath the shell of name and appearance.

⚜

Our family holiday to London in 1963—my first visit to Britain's capital—left a cluster of deeply etched images. One of them is my memory of visiting Daisy and Tony and watching what they called a "ciné film" featuring their most recent trip to Africa.

They'd been staying at the famous Treetops Hotel in Kenya. After modest beginnings—it started as little more than a two-room tree house built in a massive fig tree—Treetops soon became a fully fledged hotel, attracting an international celebrity clientele. It was designed to afford guests the opportunity of watching wildlife in comfort and safety. Treetops came into the public eye because of a royal association. It was while staying there, as a guest of the owners, that the then princess Elizabeth received news of the death of her father, George VI, the king whose coat of arms adorned Daisy's cigarette tin.

In an age of sophisticated digital photography, it's common to see high-quality footage in a private context. But our visit to Daisy and Tony was at a time long predating such technology. In 1963, watching a moving film at someone's home was rare. Given his professional expertise, it's not surprising that Tony's holiday film was so good. The animals were impressive, yes, as was the unique structure that is Treetops, but what struck me most about the film wasn't the elephants and giraffes, it wasn't the pride of lions or the alert-looking cheetah, instead it was the way the waiters at the hotel cleared the tables. I was amazed at how they pulled the white tablecloths off the set tables. With a deft tug they whisked the cloths away, leaving all the cutlery and plates and glasses still arranged on the tables, exactly as they'd been before. I'd heard the expression "having the rug pulled out from under your feet." Here was something similar but more exciting—removing the ground on which a whole array of things was standing, without knocking any of them over.

I can still picture that clip of film, hear the whir of the projector as it turned the reels, and Daisy's raised voice telling us to watch out for what the waiters were about to do. What I can't understand now is *why* it was done. Surely it would have been just as easy to clear a table first and then take the tablecloths away. And if the tables were already set, why would you then want to remove the tablecloths? But such questions didn't occur to me at the time. I was simply captivated by the waiters' legerdemain, their expertly confident whipping of the cloths away without disturbing any of the things that had been standing on them. It seemed like a kind of magic.

This image of whisking a cloth away, but leaving all the things that were standing on it undisturbed, has come back as a powerful memory from that time. I think again of Orhan Pamuk's comment: "The power of things inheres in the memories they gather up inside them." It's as if those Treetops tablecloths were folded into tight bundles and stored inside Daisy's Egyptian shells. But it's not just as a memory of vanished times that they've come back. They also offer an image that says something about the nature of remembering. I have a sense of leaving the intricately set tables of Daisy's and Tony's lives untouched, undisturbed—essentially undiscovered. All I have in my hand is a kind of white cloth underlay that remembrance, for whatever reason, has pulled away. It's marked here and there with a ghostly tracery of imprints—from where the few things that made an impression on me left their mark. But in the main the cloth is white, unblemished—signaling that almost everything about them has been lost.

꙳

In *Sand: A Journey Through Science and the Imagination* (2009), Michael Welland explains how, in many places in the world, beaches are made from broken pieces of shell, coral, and other hard parts of marine creatures. Such sand is termed "biogenic." It seems likely that some of the sand on the beaches Daisy walked on in Egypt will have contained millions of tiny particulate remnants from ancient human and animal bones, from shells hatched at the time of the pyramids and slowly ground down over the centuries. Perhaps the dust of pharaohs too was present in the sand beneath her tread. Whatever its provenance, each grain is pregnant with a story.

When I looked at them closely, I noticed that several of Daisy's Egyptian shells have their apertures filled—with fragments of sand, quartz-like pebbles, and other even littler shells. Using a magnifying glass to look at these smaller shells, like Russian dolls within their larger hosts, it's just possible to make out that *their* apertures too are clogged with particles.

And it strikes me that each of these particles represents the trajectory of a story through time. If we choose one and follow its course, it might take us to two men standing in an open grave; follow another and it would lead to a young woman taking a cigarette from a tin, the sounds of war raging around her; another has incised on it the moment when a snail with a striking orange shell emerged from the sand and started its slow nighttime hunt. One grain has followed a course that would take in Kenya and Treetops Hotel; another Northern Ireland; another the Bell Pettigrew Museum; another a young boy's delight at an unexpected present; and another's course would twist and turn over miles and years and lead to the words of this essay and the eyes that are currently reading this sentence. Every grain, even the tiniest, is charged with the electricity of history. If we could really become "like a shaman who can see the souls of things" and "feel their stories flickering," that flicker would quickly change to flame and furnace as story links to story in a conflagration that's beyond the grasp of any narrative.

# THE ARCHAEOLOGY OF DAYS

## I

*I*t has become my custom to start the day with two small rituals, unimportant to anyone but me. First, I write a paragraph about what happened the day before. This takes the form of a brief entry handwritten in a notebook, turned by this usage into a diary—albeit an improvised, amateur one without any official details of public holidays, religious festivals, phases of the moon, and such like. Secondly, I consult my *Chambers Book of Days* and read the entry for the day ahead.

So, for today—Friday, September 28—the date on which I began to write down these reflections, I turned first to my personal notebook of the days and wrote about what I'd done on September 27, that is, the preceding day (nothing of much interest). Then I read the Chambers entry for the day ahead. This begins by noting the death of Pope John Paul I on September 28 in 1978.

These rituals perform a hybrid mix of overlapping functions. Together, I think of them as a kind of faithful mongrel that pads along beside me at the start of every day. Our walks together offer a cross between cutting a series of handholds into time, erecting scaffolding against the passing days, and drawing a map on which some of the routes I've taken can be marked, showing how they meander from past to present and on into the future.

Keeping this kind of record of my own relatively uneventful days, and seeing what has happened on the same day, more dramatically, for other people elsewhere and else-when in the world, provides a spectral feeling of kinship with humanity's scattered tribe—my temporal compatriots, our brief lives dotted through the centuries. It also gives a sense of orientation and reminds me of time's passing. This helps steel my will and pace my energies so that I can address the tasks I wish to undertake.

Without the braking devices that are offered by these little rituals, the pauses for reflection they provide, I picture myself plummeting through the days in a kind of mindless free fall through time. The absence of deliberation in such an uncharted descent might not be thought to matter much. Whereas I'd tend to see it now as a deficiency, the missing out of a vital ingredient without which I'd soon become directionless and lost, I know this view would not be widely shared. Far from being seen as something necessary, still less desirable, such daily annotations would be regarded by many as I would once have regarded them myself: stale intrusions, heavy with the encumbrances of history; spurs to a kind of artificial nostalgia that keeps on looking back, clogging the flow of time with what has gone and should simply be let go of; pointless backward glances that get in the way of the spontaneity of living. How differently we view our days— and reflection on them—at different times in our lives. What might seem folly at twenty can, by fifty, have taken on the appearance of something close to essential.

## II

I've kept a diary, sometimes more an occasional journal, on and off for years. In part, this is just a writer's tool—or a writer's compulsion. It's obedient to that insistent, irresistible urge that's harbored in the blood to record, to catch in words, to store, preserve, reflect on, not to let things get away—to *write*. Not only does it then provide a bank of raw material on which to draw when I'm composing a deliberate, considered piece of prose, it is itself—albeit in a rough-and-ready fashion—an act of writing. It affords daily practice—keeps the muscles trim—in the always challenging business of putting thoughts and feelings into words.

Whereas keeping a diary of some sort is, for me, a long-established practice, consulting *Chambers Book of Days* is something new. In fact it was an entirely accidental addition to my daily routine. Prior to a year or two ago, I didn't even know that such a book existed (though I should have guessed as much from the "Now and Then" or "On This Day" columns that appear in newspapers). Then, when I was browsing in a bookshop, I spotted the Chambers volume. Its full title describes its nature more fully than I've done so far:

*Chambers Book of Days*: A Miscellany of Popular Antiquities in Connection with the Calendar, including Anecdote, Biography & History, Curiosities of Literature and Oddities of Human Life and Character.

The original *Chambers Book of Days* appeared in two volumes in 1864, brainchild of Scottish writer and publisher Robert Chambers (1802–1871). Chambers devoted so much time and energy to compiling this mammoth compendium that his health suffered. In fact, his labor of love on this eccentric almanac of days is supposed to have cut short the number of *his* days.

My copy is a radically revised one-volume edition, brought up-to-date and published in 2004. It's a cornucopia of eye-catching snippets. From it I've discovered, for example, that the guillotine was last used as a means of execution in France on September 10, 1977; that the screw-top bottle was patented in 1889—on May 10—by one Dan Rylands of the

Hope Glass Works in Barnsley; that the term "tuxedo," used for a dinner jacket in America, stems from tobacco tycoon Griswold Lorillard's first wearing one at Tuxedo Country Club on October 10, 1886. I was surprised to learn that the famous Lascaux cave paintings were found during World War II (on September 12, 1940); that Chaim Herzog, president of Israel, was born in Ireland (on September 17, 1918); and that the prime minister of Ceylon (now Sri Lanka), S. W. R. D. Bandaranaike, was assassinated—on September 26, 1959—by that most unlikely of assailants, a Buddhist monk.

## III

I find such nuggets of information interesting, sometimes entertaining, occasionally educative, but they're not the main reason that I've come to value *Chambers Book of Days*. For me, its major worth lies in the way in which, every now and then, it throws up an item which intersects with my life—when its days and mine seem to collide, become entangled, as if some kind of temporal bolas had been thrown from its pages, so that I stumble and fall back through the years to see with new vividness a vanished moment that I've scarcely thought about since it happened.

I don't mean by this just the accidental sharing of one date which happened to bear on it the same thing for others as it did for me—like the fact that my birthday (February 6) happens also to be that of, among others, Christopher Marlowe (1564); Babe Ruth (1895); Ronald Reagan (1911); François Truffaut (1932); and Bob Marley (1945). The odd concatenation of birthday confrères does give pause for thought, and prompts speculation about how big the tribe would be and who'd be in it if *everyone* born on February 6, since humans first existed, could be assembled, named, and detailed. How many million would belong to this time-clan, marked by the totem of its date? And of course, given our mortal symmetries, such imaginings soon move one to wonder about the clan of those who *died* on February 6—amongst whom, according to the *Book of Days,* can be numbered Thurston, Archbishop of York (1140); King Charles II (1685); landscape gardener "Capability" Brown (1783); King George VI (1952); and Austrian-born British biochemist and Nobel Prize winner Max Perutz (2002). I sometimes wonder idly who I'll share a death-date with and whether—whenever a final tally can be made—more people will have come into the world on February 6 or gone out of it. And—as a kind of footnote—how many will both be born and die on February 6. I was struck when reading the entry for August 29 to find that this was Ingrid Bergman's day of birth (1915) and death (1982).

Nor am I referring—when I talk about the way in which I value the *Book of Days* because of intersections between what it details and days in my own life—to the way in which some event that long predated my appearance on the scene came to have an impact on me. For instance, I visited the flourishing Marian shrine at Knock, in Ireland's County Mayo, in the early 1990s. What struck me most was the sheer mundanity that seemed attached to the running of this unlikely place of faith. The tackiness of the religious gew-gaws on sale, for example, and the fact that "holy water" was, quite literally, on tap made a far stronger impression than any spiritual dimension. There was more of a sense of the marketplace, of matter-of-fact supply and demand, than of anything even remotely numinous. I found Knock curi-ous in the extreme. I'm still not sure exactly what it illus-trates about the persistent religiousness of our species. Given my fascination with the place, I was therefore predisposed to make a connection when I came to the page in the *Book of Days* for August 21 and found that it was on this day in 1879 that "an apparition of Mary, Joseph and St John the Evangelist" was allegedly seen by fifteen people at Knock. The vision that they claimed seems a bewilderingly far cry from what developed as a result of it.

Like shared birthdays, the way in which a line can be drawn between past events and something in my present—between what people thought they saw at Knock over a century ago and what can be seen at the shrine today—brings time into sharper focus, suggests long nerves of cause and effect, of inference and influence, development and distortion, stretching through the centuries. But so far as I'm concerned, the *Book of Days* has its greatest impact not when it sparks this kind of connection, but when it details something that takes me back—with considerable force and potency—to what was happening in my life at the same moment it occurred.

## IV

The most famous example of this kind of phenomenon—hearing about an event and being prompted by it to remember whatever coordinates pinpointed your whereabouts and what you were doing at that exact selfsame moment—used to be the assassination of President John F. Kennedy on November 22, 1963. According to the *Chambers Book of Days*:

> It is said that everybody can remember exactly where they were and what they were doing when they heard about the assassination, a phenomenon that was subsequently studied by psychologists and termed "flashbulb memory."

At only eight years old when I heard the news that Kennedy had been killed, my flashbulb memory of that moment is dim. It has the same blurry quality that's possessed by those fragments of dreams that stick indelibly in mind but are only vaguely remembered. They seem ingrained with a haunting, if indistinct, imagery that's resistant to all but the most minimal degree of verbal explication. Such things feel as if they're branded on the very walls of some deep chamber of the psyche, equally beyond the reach of forgetting and description. All I can say about the "flashbulb memory" of hearing the news of Kennedy's death is that I was in the hall of our family home in Ireland. I can see a white-painted door into a room ahead of me that's standing half-opened. I have a whispered sense of my parents, silenced, in the room. The TV is on. Then my mother comes out, sees me, and tells me something terrible has happened. But even this flimsiest of accounts risks damaging with the fingers of specifics the bright, but blurred, butterfly wing that delicately, persistently flutters out with iron elusiveness its version of the moment.

Each generation will have its own triangulation points of tragedy which insistently pinpoint where they were and what they were doing when these events occurred. For most people today, September 11, 2001, will be a far stronger impetus for recall than the Kennedy assassination. I can certainly remember with a depth of detail and completeness that doesn't attend November 22, 1963, exactly where I was, with whom, what doing when I heard the news about the Twin Towers. A local counterpoint of discord also sounds for me, as it does for many Ulster folk, alongside internationally recognized outrages. January 5, for instance, makes me remember the moment when I heard the news that day in 1976 of the Kingsmills massacre. A minibus, carrying workmen traveling home from the textile factory that employed them, was stopped by the IRA. A Catholic was told to flee the scene. The remaining eleven men, all Protestants, were shot, the bodies left on the roadside. Only one survived. Hearing the news of what happened left an indelible impression on the mind.

Although I'm affected by such terrible events as much as anyone in terms of the "flashbulb memories" they can command, although their impact always jolts me when I come to the relevant page in my *Chambers Book of Days* and find them noted there as part of the cargo of whatever date they sullied, it is in fact a far less prominent event than the Kennedy assassination, or the Twin Towers, and one lacking any of the Troubles' local savagery, that affected me most strongly.

## V

The entry for September 28 in the *Chambers Book of Days* made such an impression because of the way the headline for this date—"Pope John Paul I died on this day in 1978"—acted as a tripwire. Reading this simple statement of record made me fall back through the years.

I'm twenty-three again, sitting beside my father in his car. We're driving along a quiet road that meanders through the countryside between Ballynahinch, where an aunt and uncle live, with whom we've just had dinner, and Lisburn, which is home. It's a journey of only a few miles through two of Ireland's northern counties—Down and Antrim. My father's driving slowly. He's said nothing, but I'm almost certain that he's thinking about my mother, currently in a Belfast hospital awaiting surgery on a small facial tumor that has the medics worried. He slows down further as the radio news comes on and the death of Pope John Paul I is announced. We're not Catholics, but the news seems to affect him. It's not so much this death itself—I don't think he knew anything about Albino Luciani, the laborer's son elected Pope that August. It's more the possibility of unexpected death, represented by this news, which touches him. This is something already weighing on his mind. The bulletin on the radio makes the weight increase. Also, as a civil servant whose professional life has been devoted to ensuring the smooth running of things, he knows how disruptive the new Pope's sudden demise will be. For someone elected to high office to die only thirty-three days later sparks sympathy in him for the administrators of the systems who will have to put all their procedures into operation again so unexpectedly soon after they thought things had been concluded. Dad's expression of regret, even condolence, is addressed more to the bureaucrats who will be affected than to the family and friends of Albino Luciani.

Nineteen seventy-eight, a year filled with all manner of event and occurrence, the new Pope's death just one infinitesimal part of the story. And all of the year is gone now, its cargo lost in the silt of time. All that remains are the odd fragments of remembrance carried in the memories of those who lived through it. Each one of its 365 days could be catalogued, set in the context of the days that preceded it, days stretching back and back through history, and beyond history, each one loaded with the events that make up our lives. Looking daily at a book of days underscores the twin facts of simultaneity and loss: that as I read, as I write, as I go about any of my days and fill them in whatever manner I do, others will be being conceived and born, dying, getting married, making discoveries, fighting, grieving—embroiled in the diverse tangle of actions and circumstances that define our humanness. And all of these diverse expressions of what happens will vanish; extinction awaits them, and us, as surely as it did the dodo.

Of course it's simplistic to say that a year has vanished except for our memories of it. What happens in its days is not imprisoned in them as if each twenty-four-hour span was a cell into which events were permanently locked in solitary confinement. Things are not held incommunicado behind the barrier of the specific moment in which they occur. Rather, time is permeable—allowing a constant seepage from past through present into future. What happens at any moment is part of the complex mesh of cause and effect, the interconnections of which sprawl untidily through the days. For instance, in September 1978 I'd just completed my MA at the University of Edinburgh. There would be a specific date, if I could be bothered to look it up, on which I was awarded that degree. But the consequences of studying, the opportunities opened up by having that qualification, stretch their filaments of consequence far beyond any single date. The impact of my four years as an undergraduate in Edinburgh reach long after them, one thing influencing another, and another after that, and another still beyond it. It's no exaggeration to say the MA affected the rest of my life. It wouldn't be hard to find things in the days I now occupy that can trace at least part of their genealogy back to the lecture classes and libraries and pubs and parties in that Athens of the North nearly forty years ago.

## VI

In 1978 Ulster was in the midst of its Troubles. On that September evening, driving between Ballynahinch and Lisburn, we had to pass through two road-checks. These makeshift, impromptu roadblocks could happen anywhere. They were set up by the security forces so that vehicles could be stopped and searched, their occupants questioned. Such road-checks were a common feature of life in Ulster then. They were an odd mixture of being routine and disturbing. Common enough for anyone who traveled around the province in those turbulent times to have got used to, yet they possessed a frisson of danger. Terrorists had mimicked them, flagging down vehicles and then opening fire; and there had been cases where, due to some misadventure (or, who knows, maliciousness), personnel at legitimate road-checks had opened fire on innocent citizens. The road-checks were manned either by the British Army, the police (at that point the Royal Ulster Constabulary, or RUC), or a local security force, the UDR (Ulster Defence Regiment), which had been recruited because of the Troubles and worked in conjunction with army and police. The most dramatic road-check I was ever stopped at happened when a helicopter flew in low a few hundred yards ahead of me as I was driving out of the ferry port at Larne. A detachment of troops leapt out of it as it hovered and in seconds had set up a road-check, complete with "stinger" (a spiked chain which could be pulled across the road to puncture the tires of any vehicle that didn't stop).

The first road-check on the evening of September 28, 1978, was an army one, just outside Ballynahinch. The soldier who waved us down, gun held at the ready, looks younger than I was then. He asks my father for some identification in an English regional accent that's so thick—so foreign-sounding—it's hard for us to understand him (I think its geordie—from Tyneside in the northeast of England). My father, who fought in the desert in World War II and sees himself as unambiguously British, a comrade-in-arms to this boy soldier, jokingly offers to show him an old army ID card. The boy soldier looks at him uncomprehendingly and with suspicion. Perhaps he finds our native accent as hard to understand as we find his. "Driver's license!" he barks out, with no attempt to reciprocate my father's friendliness. He raises his gun slightly. To him, we're indistinguishable from those of our fellow Ulstermen who would gladly put a bullet in his head. The license is produced, scrutinized, then after a few brusque questions about where we're going, where we've come from, we're waved through, the gun still trained on us.

The next checkpoint, on the outskirts of Lisburn, is a police one. An RUC sergeant, machine gun slung around his torso, is fluent in all the subtle signals the boy-soldier couldn't read. I can't remember what was said—it can only have been a few words—but from my father's accent and demeanor, as much as from anything he said, the sergeant soon placed us in terms of class, religion, political affiliation. We were on the same side as he was. No identification was needed. He saluted as we drove through.

I think two bastions of my father's secure and ordered world were shaken on that day. The new Pope's unexpected demise made him realize keenly something that of course he knew already, but like most of us didn't dwell on. Namely, that death doesn't come to order; it's independent of all our plans and wishes, all our structures—it can strike seemingly at random and unexpectedly. There was no guarantee that my mother (his junior by twelve years) would outlive him.

At seventy-three, his wife in hospital awaiting surgery, the outcome uncertain, I think he was fully recognizing, perhaps for the first time, the possibility of being left alone after all their years together. And in his failure to make any connection with the English boy-soldier, the way he was treated not as a compatriot or ally, but as a potential terrorist, his feeling of Britishness—integral to his sense of identity—had been undermined.

In the contrast between how he was regarded at the army and police checkpoints that evening, I think my father received a masterclass in miniature in the way the Troubles were changing traditional Protestant values and allegiances. If he wasn't recognized as British by the British, what was his place in what he saw as decent, civil society? His self-image as a law-abiding citizen who respected, was part of, the establishment, had been rudely jarred. Yet the sergeant saw him at once in the way in which he wanted to be seen. Might it be time for him and others of his clan to take on some kind of Ulster/Northern Irish identity? Also—though of this I'm less sure—I wonder if his evident sadness at the unexpected death of the Pope suggested some nascent sense of sympathetic connection with Ulster's Catholics, that other tribe we viewed so warily and about whom knew as little as they knew of us.

## VII

Sometimes I use my own book (or rather books) of days—the notebooks made into diaries by my daily handwritten entries—to take a sounding back through time. So, after looking at what I wrote for September 28, I might leaf back through the pages to August 28, July 28, June 28, May 28, and so on, as far back as the pages record, looking at what happened on the 28th of every month, this year, last year, the year before. I think of this as taking a kind of core sample of time, sinking a shaft through the surface of the present moment and drilling down through this particular point in my days. In one sense, of course, the drill bit can only reach so far—I didn't start to keep diaries or journals seriously until I was in my teens, so the written record is soon exhausted. But that doesn't stop the imaginative deepening of the shaft, the drill reaching down and further down—soon my childhood, infancy, embryonic phases are cut through and this taking of a sounding leads on into the stupendously immense strata of deep time with which every second is underlain—geological time, planetary time, the time it takes for a species to emerge, evolve and become extinct again, the time galaxies take to form and disintegrate. Such measures of duration make a diary or a book of days seem ludicrously tiny—like incising rows of miniature alphabetic symbols on one grain of sand that's part of a strand that stretches further than the eye can see. Even the work of the great diarists and journal writers—Amiel, Bashkirtseff, Pepys—is quickly reduced to microscopic endeavor; even the most dramatic events recorded in *Chambers Book of Days* fade as they're overtaken by what follows and are slowly buried in the deluge of new days.

I realize, too, that my core sample is just one of billions that could be drilled. Choose another day, another person—*any* day, *any* person—and a different temporal sample would result—albeit one that would share the same sediments of deep time, whatever happens to occur at its surface. If, for instance, Brian Russell had taken a core sample on September 27, 1978, he'd little have guessed the chilling contiguity of that day to the last he'd spend on earth. Looking back he'd find echoes of childhood, schooling, youth, employment, marriage, the birth of his now two-year-old son, the moment, perhaps, when his unborn second child was conceived—all the usual markers we attend to when we look back on a life, milestones that eclipse in their personal importance even the most momentous public event listed in a *Book of Days*. But no one can take a core sample of the future, even if it's just a single day ahead. Little did this thirty-one-year-old know that the next day, when Pope John Paul I would die, as we were driving between Ballynahinch and Lisburn, listening to the news, he too would meet his end. He was shot in the head by the IRA and died two hours later in Londonderry's Altnagelvin Hospital. He was one of the Troubles' accidental victims. The gunman had been aiming at members of a military police patrol, beside whom Brian Russell had the misfortune to be walking. I wonder, too, about the boy-soldier at the checkpoint just outside Ballynahinch. What would a core sample through his September 28 have yielded? What lay ahead for him? Did he survive his tour of duty in Ulster? Did he go on to serve in Iraq, Afghanistan? Is he still alive today? And how does his life, my life, any life relate to the fossils and the planets that threaten to crush all our days, pulverizing them into insignificance with the weight of eons that they carry?

## VIII

We are all time travelers. Not in the way science fiction depicts this, where we can move backwards and forwards into past and future at will, but in the sense that time is the medium in which we exist—where, as that well-worn expression has it, we live and move and have our being. Time surrounds us like air. Helpless to swim against its onward current, the strong pull of the future, each day takes us closer to our dissolution. If we dig down through the sand of the everyday that seems to ground our lives so securely in the commonplace, we'll soon come to water that has the flavor of our minuteness. It tastes of daunting vistas of duration that dwarf us into insignificance. The continuum of time stretches out all around us. Beyond our minuscule territory of occupancy—before we appeared; after we disappear—the fabric of duration stretches out its enormous, daunting presence.

Perhaps because the *Chambers Book of Days* is a *book*, the unoriginal but fertile metaphor of time as a kind of book often occurs to me. But it's a book whose pages aren't pruned to fit neatly between two covers. Instead, they proliferate into an effectively endless surface and what's written on them seems without any clear point of origin or end, let alone a plotline we can understand. Our brief individual lives are no more than part of a single word, a fraction of a letter lost amidst countless lines on countless pages. Is it possible to glean any meaning from the centuries that generate and then annihilate us?

Using the *Book of Days* inevitably involves looking back. But often when I read the entries for a date, particularly if they long predate my life, I find there's a kind of boomerang effect and I imagine the same period into the future as what I'm reading about is in the past. On this day in 1066, for example, William the Conqueror invaded England. That was some 950 years ago. What will be recorded for September 28, 2966? If a picture could be taken then of the quiet country road between Ballynahinch and Lisburn that my father and I were driving along in 1978, would it show anything we could recognize as familiar, or by 2966 will the world have changed so utterly that roads and Ireland no longer exist?

In a review of the *Chambers Book of Days*, published in *The Guardian* on Saturday, December 4, 2004, Ian Sansom neatly catches something of the book's appeal—and the blade that lies within it, giving it its edge of interest:

> If the *Chambers Book of Days* does nothing else, it helps to make the everyday vivid and surprising, reminding us that whether we like it or not we have eternity with us all the time. Cardinal Newman wrote, "I wonder what day I shall die on— / One passes year by year over one's death day, / As one might pass over one's grave." Like all great and sacred books, the sound you hear between the pages of the *Book of Days* is the crunch, crunch, crunch of human bones.

Sometimes now when I perform the two small rituals that mark the start of every day, it feels as if I should incorporate a third, based on a practice of mathematician Clifford Pickover. He once calculated that he had 10,000 days left to live—an assessment based on his age and life expectancy. He drew up a grid that showed 10,000 little squares. Every morning, Pickover crossed one out. I'm not sure, though, if I need—or want—to x things in this way, as if with tiny headstones, emphasizing the fact that (in Philip Larkin's words) "unresting death" is "a whole day nearer now." Already it feels as though the paper that I write on in my notebook, and the paper I read from in the *Book of Days,* is made of thin slivers cut from the skeleton of yesterday, to whose bones the flesh of today momentarily clings as it dances its brief quotient of time away. I know that my own dance will soon enough be done, my steps will falter, my little rituals cease, and that the handholds they used to offer on time's sheer wall (or the illusion of handholds) will disappear, as I fall into the abyss of what once was but now no longer is.

# PUTTING TWO AND TWO
# TOGETHER

## I

- Two men chatting in a County Down farmyard
- Two brothers in a passing car
- Two boys sitting in a room, bored and restless
- Two parents sipping tea and wondering how soon they can go home
- Two elderly ladies, white haired, their faces deeply lined, lamenting bygone days

Five apparently ordinary pairings—there's nothing exciting or alluring about them. They'd be easily dismissed as trivial, if not boring. Yet, for me, they constitute a mini-constellation in the inner sky of memory that keeps catching my attention. Their relative positions trace out a kind of pentagram. It glimmers with the promise of meaning's elusive magic; something that might illuminate what passes and mark out a navigable route through time.

I can't think of any straightforward label to describe what I'm writing here, nor can I explain why one side effect of writing it has been a tendency to think in twos. So I've started simply by listing five of the pairs I've found—or into which my musings have cleaved things. As so often, it's difficult to tell for sure what's there independently of our scrutiny and what owes its shape to the touch of our perceptions upon it.

Other larger-scale pairings underlie and inform my mini-constellation—now and then; here and there; youth and age—but to begin with at least I want to stick to specifics. The rough texture of the particular gives a firmer grip on things, I think, than any smoothing over that generalization can offer.

"Meditation," "Memoir," "Narrative," "History," all fall variously short. "Essay" is such a generously capacious term that it might fit well enough, though within its roomy, ill-defined territory there's ample room for misapprehension. If "Putting Two and Two Together" is seen as an essay, the original resonance of that term must be emphasized, with a nod to Montaigne, stressing the sense in which "essai" indicates an attempt, an experiment, a try (and let's not forget that an important characteristic of tries is that they often fail).

What am I trying to weave, then, in this piece of prose, already jutting with pairs and pentagrams and hesitations? I want to bring two moments into alignment so that I can see more clearly the context in which they're embedded and through which, perhaps, they'll point a way to a better understanding of the nature of part and whole and the linkages that suture them together.

I'm not sure why the two moments in question presented themselves so forcefully as needing to be brought into a more precise and considered focus than that in which they, like countless others, are normally held—in recollection's rough-and-ready patchwork of blurred approximations. Neither moment was particularly important. I'd have much more readily understood the insistence with which they prompted this piece of writing had they been in some way life-changing. For some reason that I can't yet fathom, they've acted together in a way that neither, taken singly, would have done. It's as if, put side by side, they've become reciprocal catalysts. Once charged with each other's energy, they exert a kind of magnetism that pulls to them all kinds of thoughts and feelings, reminiscences and reflections.

The two men chatting in a farmyard are standing just outside the looming cavern of an open-sided barn. It seems likely they were taking shelter there from the heavy rain that only stopped its clamorous downpour a minute or so ago. Water makes the road's black surface sheen and glare. All around, there are so many drips still running off the rain-washed leaves, glinting in the sudden sunshine, that beneath the trees and hedges it would seem as if the cloudburst hadn't yet shed all its load.

The men stare at the car that's moving at a snail's pace past the entrance to the farm. The concrete surfaced yard is separated from the road by a vertically barred black metal gate that's been left wide open, tied back to its gatepost with a coil of orange cord. Their expression as they watch the car is one of surprise, suspicion, curiosity, fear, and hostility. In part, this is no doubt due to the infrequency of traffic on this very minor rural road. It's as much a lane or track, really, as it is a public thoroughfare, so it would be easy to see passing strangers as trespassers. In part their expression is also sparked by the fact that the car's occupants are showing such intense interest in the pebble-dashed farmhouse that faces the road and backs onto the barn. Not only have they slowed their vehicle to stare, but the man sitting beside the driver has opened his window. He points a camera out and starts to take pictures.

This moment that I've just sketched out happened in the Country Down countryside a few miles from the village of Moira, a name probably derived from the Irish "Maigh Rath," which is open to two interpretations: "Plain of the ring forts," or "Plain of the wheels." It's June 2013 and things are mostly peaceful in Northern Ireland, but memories of the Troubles run deep. An unknown car slowing, its window opening, can still conjure grim scenarios of sectarian attack. Such brutalities apart, in so quiet, countrified a place as this it's surely an impertinent intrusion for someone to photograph its denizens or their dwelling places without a by-your-leave.

## II

- Two accidentally taken photographs
- Places in childhood and adulthood
- Leaving and returning home
- Ireland and out of Ireland
- Ulster and "across the water"

As I try to bring things into focus, arrange them in a way that makes more sense than any rawly chronological listing of their occurrence would do, I'm struck by the way the pattern of recall throws up pairs. It's difficult to assess the significance of this, or to determine if I'm acting in response to a fundamental quality in this seam of experience—some elemental yin and yang, an archetypal positive and negative—or if, obedient to the urge to replicate patterns, the mind is merely parsing into twos what could as readily be arranged in some altogether different order.

I hadn't meant to photograph the men. When my brother, driving, slowed the car, I was simply trying to get a few images of the farmhouse. There was nowhere to stop and in any case we were already late for an engagement several miles away on the other side of Moira. My camerawork was, by necessity, hasty. I'd been vaguely aware of the men—an impression, almost subliminal, of them breaking off their conversation to turn and stare at our suspect vehicle. But their facial semiotics and body language would have been impossible to decode in any detail given the distance between us and the short time that elapsed as we drove past. It wasn't until I was going through the pictures at home on the computer a week later than I even realized they were included in two of the frames I'd taken as we inched our way along the road beside the house. Looking at their faces and their posture as they're revealed on a large screen makes clear the mix of feelings. Surprise, suspicion, curiosity, fear, and hostility are all expressed with silent eloquence by these two unknown figures.

What draws us back to where we've been before—I mean when we have no particular, practical reason to revisit, no necessity to be there? What makes us want to return to places we once knew, the haunts of childhood, long deserted? Why do we feel periodically impelled to retrace our steps? I've grown curious about the instinct—if such an intermittent, unpredictable thing can be so called—to take ourselves again to those locales in which we were born and brought up. And, as a corollary to this, I wonder too about the different senses of the world, the different senses of belonging and feeling cut adrift, the different senses of self and nation that must be etched into the hearts of those who stay forever settled in one place and those who, whether through choice or force of circumstance, move far away from home.

It doesn't take much grasp of things to recognize the presence of a large lacuna snaking through Ireland's history. This is the country's open vein, its diaspora, a yawning conduit hemorrhaging people. Its periodic clotting and unclotting is powered by different factors at different times—famine, poverty, employment, discrimination, education—but whatever the particular motivation, it impels a common action: leaving. For our generation of migrants, the Troubles were a potent factor in many people's decision to quit the place and go elsewhere. My brother and I both left Ireland ostensibly to go to university, but our decision to leave was strongly influenced by the sectarian violence whose atavistic poison was leaching out and disfiguring life in the North when we were in our teens and twenties. I went to Scotland, my brother to England. Jobs and marriages subsequently conspired to anchor in a permanent mooring a leaving that, initially, had only been provisional; a temporary berthing underlain by the unspoken intention of coming home. Soon enough we were settled "across the water," as many folk in Ulster refer to the rest of the UK.

Are some people immune to the homing instinct? Perhaps if the home you leave is somehow hateful it short-circuits any desire to return. And of course, for many, distance, work and family commitments, or simple lack of funds combine to make return impracticable, however strongly the desire to return is felt. I know my brother and I both felt—continue to feel—drawn to Ireland, and that every now and then we make the trip back to where we still feel in our blood that we belong. When these periodic returns were made to visit parents, family, friends, our motivation was clear enough. There's no need to seek reasons beyond the pull that loved ones exert upon the heart. But when, as now, parents and other key family members are dead and friends are almost all "across the water," what is it that powers this urge to revisit? Why go back to places that are emptied of the people that gave them their significance?

I sometimes think it's a kind of searching for yourself, part of an ongoing effort to shepherd together the disparate bits of a life—the different times, the different places that you've occupied—and to see them in a way that affords the possibility of a more coherent, more comprehensive perspective than the day-to-day passing of existence normally allows. Going back to places you've been as a child and walking those same haunts again, but this time with the weight of adult years and all their accumulated experience close-woven in your tread, means that you can overlay or shadow your earlier traces with a step that sinks deeper, allowing the weight of time to secure new angles of vision from which to reexamine origins and the outcomes that they lead to. This kind of walking with your earlier self allows the opportunity for dialogue between now and then; the person you once were and the person you've become.

Sometimes the homing instinct accrues enough force to send me on the long journey back to Ireland. But I remain uncertain of what moves this tide that surges its waves over me every now and then, or why a few of them are strong enough to carry me with them. Perhaps, rather than any quest for identity or understanding, or the longer, wider view, the walking in my own footsteps that's entailed in these returns is more a response to a kind of territorial imperative—a pacing of home ground again to (re)claim it, to leave upon it the spoor of my passing, to return after long absence and mark it indelibly as mine. Or maybe, far from having anything to do with self or territory, it's just a kind of curiosity to see how things have changed, to match for fit the contours held in memory against whatever shapes now meet the eye. Or, simpler than any of these suggestions, maybe we just feel affection for familiar places in the same way that we do for people; responding to the curve of a country road, the shape of a hillside, the way the light touches a lakeside forest, just as we respond to the particular alignments of a body's features. Can a country lay its presence on us so that it touches the heart and kindles love?

# III

- Two migrants going "across the water" to study in Scotland and England
- Two origins of the name "Hunters Hall"
- Two lurchers that would "bite you as soon as look at you"
- An orchard tended and abandoned
- Being single and being married

Another little constellation picked out in my sky, its pentagram of pinprick pairs suggesting ways in which we can rule lines between events and instances, attempt to draw from what's around us patterns in which things may be arranged, named, ordered, understood. They are underlain by a shifting play of larger factors, more encompassing relationships, things whose torque suggests ways in which life's quotidian scattering of stars might be aligned according to the deeper waters around them: Ireland's diaspora; education's impact; the couplings that sustain us; cultivation and neglect.

Hunters Hall is one of the places my brother and I are drawn back to. It's the name of the farmhouse we drove past at a snail's pace, much to the consternation of the two men by the barn (nor is it the first time we've returned there). The origin of the name is contested. One view says that it's derived from the fact that a local foxhunt used to gather here before setting off in pursuit of its quarry through the adjoining fields and lanes. Others are impatient with this explanation, dismissing it as historically flawed. Their view is that the foxhunt was a recent occurrence, long predated by an individual called Hunter—his first name is forgotten— who built the house and farmed its sixty acres of land in the early 1800s. The name is written without an apostrophe, so there's no grammatical clue to whether it was Hunter the man or hunters in the plural that led to the house being so called. "Hall" seems inappropriately grand for what appears to be a fairly ordinary, albeit large, farmhouse. Perhaps it reflects the nature of some earlier building, or the relative size of the house compared to others in the vicinity, or maybe it's merely a wish to claim grandeur on a scale the actual bricks and mortar can't deliver.

Whatever the reason for the name, my mother knew the place as a working farm in her childhood and often talked about her visits there. It was owned by her maternal uncle, Johnnie McCullough. He lived there with his wife, Tessie, and unmarried older sister, Ellie. For me and my brother, Hunters Hall was a kind of ghost farm. By the time we appeared on the scene, Johnnie was long dead and the place was occupied only by our two elderly great-aunts. The farmyard, with its barn and outbuildings, its pigsties and chicken coops, was tidy and deserted, emptied of the bustle of laborers and livestock. The orchards and garden were overgrown and untended, the sixty acres of prime arable land had been rented out for grazing to the shadowy figure of a local cattle dealer. We never met him, but it was clear that Aunt Ellie disapproved of this cattle dealer—despite allowing him tenancy of her land. That she regarded him as her inferior was unsurprising. Her hauteur was pretty much all-encompassing. Certainly no one in the neighborhood was regarded by her as of remotely equal, let alone superior, status. But it was as if Ellie thought the man had a whiff of brimstone about him, so negative was the picture she painted. If she was to be believed, the cattle dealer drank and gambled, was often seen in the company of "fast women," his "subnormal" son (Ellie's description) had been killed in a tractor accident she claimed was suspicious ("Accident my foot!"). His house was "a disgrace," though in what sense I don't recall her specifying and in any case I wondered how she'd ever seen inside it given her warning that his two lurcher dogs "would bite you as soon as look at you." Though of course it didn't strike me at the time, I've wondered since if the man had made a pass at her—or maybe her overtures to him had been hurtfully rebuffed. The fact that the cattle dealer was always referred to in the second person and not by any name had an unintended effect; to my childish ears Ellie's talk of "He" and "His" conferred an authority and importance on her unmet tenant that a proper name would have lessened. It seemed to me that these anonymities were spoken with capital letters, a distinction that lent the cattle dealer a kind of godlike aura.

One of the regular occurrences of childhood, part of the catechism of our days, was Sunday afternoon visits to Hunters Hall, which was only about half an hour's drive from where we lived in Lisburn, County Antrim. The visits didn't happen every week. My mother shared with her two sisters the obligation of keeping in touch with her aunts, so our turn for duty—and it was a duty, not a pleasure—came round every three weeks or so in an irregular rhythm of obligation whose exact beat was determined by the shifting patterns of people's engagements. But the visits were frequent enough, and their impact on me strong enough, to leave sufficient residue such that whenever I think of childhood Sundays now, it's often Hunters Hall that comes to mind.

On rare occasions, if the weather was fine and my brother and I were allowed to roam unsupervised, visits to Hunters Hall could be enjoyable. Outside, there were all kinds of opportunities for pleasure. I have a picture of us sitting ensconced in the branches of a plum tree in a neglected orchard where no one had picked fruit for years. We gorged on the sun-warmed plums and were utterly content. I remember finding a cache of old farmyard implements stored in one of the outhouses, as entrancing, almost, as a collection of swords and bayonets. Among them was a curved whip, perhaps eight or ten feet long. The flexible wood of its tapered cane core was sheathed in a kind of linen latticework. It belonged, so my mother told us, to the pony and trap she remembered being driven in by her Uncle Johnnie. Best of all were those very few occasions when we investigated the expressly forbidden well in the garden beside the house. Dragging the heavy concrete cover open by the two iron rings embedded in it—it took both of us to shift it— made an enticing, hollow-sounding noise. It grated with the promise of hidden depths below it. Looking in, we could see our reflections—tiny pale faces far below on the surface of the deep, dark water. The sound of occasional drips gave out a kind of cavernous resonance. Sometimes we glimpsed a swimming frog. The temptation to drop stones in and count the time before they splashed was irresistible.

But fruit-gorging, implement-finding, and well-exploring were the exceptions. As a rule, we had to sit with our parents in an airless front room as they talked to Auntie Ellie and Auntie Tessie—or, more usually, listened while Ellie held the floor. Tessie was a gentle, quiet person who always smiled at us and gave the impression that she liked our being there. The sadness of her life was that she was widowed early and never had any children of her own. But it was Ellie who ruled the house and dominated every conversation. She was a fierce, domineering presence, strongly opinionated, intolerant of dissent, disapproving of others. She was not given to making allowances for anyone, least for all for children. We were supposed to sit there quietly, not fidget, respond politely—and briefly—to the occasional question she put to us. Those Sunday afternoons could bring on agonies of boredom as we sat there and endured the drone of adult talk. To our ears it was like the tired buzzing of bluebottles lumbering with hopeless persistence around and around a room they'd got trapped in, windows tightly closed, air stale. To complete our sense of entombment, the heavy velvet curtains were often pulled halfway closed to protect the mahogany furniture from sunlight, giving the room a semidarkened tint and somehow adding to its musty atmosphere.

There was an old harmonium—or pedal organ—against one wall, all polished wood and alluring rows of shiny keys and stops that could be pulled and turned. Two large pedals worked a kind of bellows system that pumped air through the pipes. We were forbidden to touch it, naturally, and mostly resisted the temptation—though once or twice we dared Ellie's censure and played a few soft, wheezy notes when she went into the kitchen to make tea. The presence of the instrument gave the room an air of churchiness that recalled another locus of intense childhood boredom, where time also seemed to move so slowly that it became almost tangible and you could sense it heaving its massive bulk past you inch by endless inch like a suffocating behemoth, breath laboring as it floundered in the stagnant air of some interminable sermon.

Yet, for all the stifling, sepulchral atmosphere, those Sunday afternoon purgatories of adult conversation at Hunters Hall also contained heavy swells and currents that rippled under the polite restraint, like tumors ripe with their own dark vigor. Even a bored child could sometimes catch a glimpse of gigantic whalebacks of resentment, disappointment, anger, frustration surfacing for a moment before they vanished again beneath the surface of the slickly oiled waters of small talk about the weather or ailments or the failings of tradesmen and neighbors.

## IV

- Our past and future selves
- Looking out and looking in the same window
- Two doors in a room
- The badger and the egg
- Individual lifelines and the human hieroglyphic

Another pentagram of pairs to reiterate the cleavage that driving past Hunters Hall seemed to spark, as if we'd driven over a trigger as we slowed the car and that it set off a slow quake of combining and recombining potency that shivered its way across a whole landscape of recollection, dividing and joining as it went, leaving me with a series of things sutured together, twinned in the mind, and acting to retrieve further pairings from the sea of memory.

Ellie and Tessie were long dead by the time my brother and I drove past Hunters Hall in 2013 to the consternation of the two men in the farmyard. My great aunts' bodies were laid to rest in Moira churchyard over forty years ago. I suppose their mortal remains by now would be reduced to no more than an assemblage of discolored bones. Our parents, too, have gone, their ashes scattered. My brother and I are the last survivors of those vanished Sunday afternoons that were played out in this place for years. As we drove past we reminisced of course—remembering the feel of the chairs' harsh upholstery prickling our legs—and we wondered at the strangeness of being here again, outside the same room we'd sat in all those years ago, innocent of the fact that our older selves, with decades of life behind them, would venture back, slow down, look in, think about the boys we used to be. I felt my life pincered between two moments, held for examination in the forceps of now and then.

"Lifeline" has another sense, I know. But often now I think of it as the line drawn by our progress through the years, the path we take, the route we follow, the pattern we leave upon the earth. Whatever shape my lifeline makes, it will contain many loopings back as I revisit old haunts, go again to places like Hunters Hall that were significant parts of childhood. I'm not sure if I can read any meaning out of my meanderings, let alone from the human hieroglyphic that's constituted by all our lifelines put together. It's possible, of course, to trace out a segment of the story, perhaps even call it "Irish history," list some of the occurrences within one small territory and plot lines of cause and effect within it. But is it possible to discern any sense in the composite intricacies of all the lines that are drawn as our species blooms its way through time, laden with billions of transient individuals, their sheer number reducing everyone to seeming insignificance? Considering so many lifelines together presents a crisscrossing of enough complexity to cancel out and suggest meaning in riotous abundance. Looking at the smaller scale of nations, periods, individuals may seem to bring things more within the ambit of a manageable scale, of graspable meanings, but even the most modest and minuscule beginnings soon spiral into burgeoning complication as one thing links with another. Our attempts to plot and measure and explain seem to have affixed to them tokens of their own superficiality; we seem held in a kind of double helix where whatever is bounded and familiar is close-shackled to an unnerving sense of fathomless strangeness.

When I looked at the photographs I'd taken as my brother and I drove past Hunters Hall that June day in 2013, our childhood visits there seemed to condense and coalesce into a kind of distillation of themselves, a single moment heavy with the concentrated taste of their accumulated flavor. Those many moments become a single one to set beside the moment that happened years later as we drove past at a snail's pace, the farmhouse emptied of anything to do with our family and those two men staring at us from the yard, strangers confronting strangers. It was these two segments of my lifeline that, unaccountably, made me wonder about what lay on either side of them, how they connected and interconnected, what they amounted to, whether, put together, they led anywhere that might be illuminated by a glow of meaning different from those jarring starbursts of contingency that seem to punctuate our lives, lighting existence with the flicker of chance and accident.

Looking at the window in that front room as we drove past, looking at the photograph of it later, remembering the window from my childhood, looking out through the same glass as a bored boy on a vanished Sunday afternoon, I imagined all the lifelines leading to that room and leading out of it again; our entrances and exits; our footsteps through the years; the way our lifelines tangle and untangle, touch with others, generate new lives, begin and end. There are so many stories—such a daunting plethora of individuals—even if we just cut from the immensity of the human fabric a single room, in one farmhouse, in one of Ireland's counties and consider what's been played out here across a tiny span of time.

The front room we sat in had one door leading into the hallway that in turn led to the front door. This was how visitors came in and out. A second door, curtained, easily missed at first, led to the kitchen and to the secretive "back stairs," a narrow wooden flight leading from the kitchen to what had once been a maid's bedroom. At the top of those dark and creaking stairs, on a narrow landing, was one of the two things inside the house that fascinated me: a stuffed badger. It was one that Uncle Johnnie had shot. The taxidermist had portrayed it snarling viciously. The teeth and long claws and rough pelt over the broad muscular body drew me like a magnet.

The second object in the house that held a similar appeal was a large onyx egg kept on the hearth in the other front room—where we never sat and that seemed to be even more formal and hedged with prohibitions than the rest of the house. Occasionally, we managed to creep in and explore unobserved. The weight and coolness of the onyx egg impressed us. This heavy polished stone, of uncertain provenance or use, sits beside me now as I write this reflection, a mute orb, witness to times past and distant places. Holding it brings a sense of proximity that I know is illusory—yet, in spite of that sure knowledge, it still seems somehow charged, as if it's thickly imbued with the concentrate of Hunters Hall's sluggish currents.

## V

- Ellie and her doomed love
- Fudge and seedcake
- Two ancestral photographs
- Crabbit old woman and desirable girl
- Being remembered and being forgotten

However insistently they impinge, as I reflect on the moment we drove past Hunters Hall and recall those Sunday afternoons of boredom sitting there as a boy, I suspect the pairings that I've listed are provisional, expedient—no more than a stratagem of recollection, pegs to hang things on, a net to fish with. Each pentagram may possess the twinkle of a constellation in my skies, but none of their components are fixed points in any firmament. Rather, they are like dice that, shaken again, would show another value, fall in a different sequence. I could as well rethink things in fours or ones or threes. Like so many of the patterns we incise upon the world and read our meanings from, there's no immutable, intrinsic authority in these pairings. They don't trace out the only map that's possible but are merely a selection of individual isobars by which to chart one reckoning of a segment of life's weather. Just like the larger pairings of national history that are wielded hereabouts—Catholic and Protestant; nationalist and loyalist; Irish and British; six counties and thirty-two counties; Derry and Londonderry—they offer only approximate groupings, rough-and-ready sketches. The texture of what actually transpires eludes our attempts to catch more than fragments of it, even when we fine-tune the mesh in our word-nets so as it seems virtually impermeable.

In our eyes, Ellie was just a "crabbit old woman" ("crabbit" was a word in common parlance when I was growing up; the *Concise Ulster Dictionary* gives its spread of meaning as "short-tempered, grumpy, twisted"). It was only years after our visits to Hunters Hall that it properly occurred to me that she had her own life, her own story, her own needs and passions, and that our Sunday afternoon duty calls were perhaps as tediously irksome to her as they were to us. On the way home, after one particularly ill-favored occasion, when the whalebacks of resentment and frustration had broken the conversational waters more often than usual, I remember my mother saying, "She might have been a different person if she'd married her chemist." It turned out that Ellie had been "sweet on" a young man who had worked in a pharmacy in Moira village. Romance had ignited—but, before it had a proper chance to blaze, he'd died quite unexpectedly. He was only in his twenties. Ellie was deeply affected by the loss of her sweetheart. When I knew her, her life seemed soured and she seemed bitter. The only sweetness at Hunters Hall was in the fudge and seedcake she made and offered to visitors. Even children were allowed some. I can remember with the precision that sometimes accompanies a memory woven into taste or smell the exact texture and flavor of the fudge; the somehow coolly mysterious aroma of caraway seeds that stole into the room as soon as the cake tin was opened.

Going through some old photographs at a cousin's house on my 2013 visit to Ireland, I found a picture of the person I assume must have been her chemist friend, a large-nosed serious-looking young man with sensual lips, hair neatly combed. He's pictured in a slightly profiled stance and his gaze seems fixed on something distant, far beyond the camera. No one now remembers his name, or anything much about him, other than that he was a chemist, that Ellie was "sweet on him," and that he died before his time. The figure in the sepia-tinted photo gives no clues about specifics. Clad in a smart suit for the occasion, the photo is deliberate, posed—completely unlike the accidental shots I took of the two men standing in the Hunters Hall farmyard. On the back of the photo, in now faded ink, he's written: "To Ellie with Love 10/12/08." Just before Christmas one hundred and five years ago. Had they planned to get engaged, to marry? Had he sat in the same front room with her where we sat, years later, when the girl he'd desired had become the crabbit old woman whose company we chafed at? Was this where he gave her the photo? Had they kissed? Talked about a future together? Whatever happened in that room was witnessed by forbidding images of Ellie's parents, my maternal great-grandparents. Their large portrait photographs looked down from the walls like tutelary spirits of Victorian respectability. I can still picture their severe-looking faces frozen within heavily ornate gold frames. Sometimes I think my sentences catch as little of what passes as those portraits caught of the people pictured, their stiff poses remote from the individuals who once animated their somber, unsmiling features.

Putting two and two together is a synonym for something that should be child's play, something utterly straightforward. Only a fool would fail to see the answer. "Four!" shouts out and stares you in the face, impossible to miss as it stands on the podium of obviousness atop its two paired steps of simple addition. But the more I think about it the less certain I am about which twos I should put together, or what should, in fact, be joined. Why not sunder all the apparent links in my five sets of pentagrams, throw the dice again, recalibrate my recollections? I think of all the in-breaths and out-breaths that have been taken in that room where we sat in Hunters Hall, all the systolic and diastolic drumbeats, the two-stroke rhythms of every heart that's beaten there, each eye that's blinked open and shut, each egg and sperm carried unseen within the bodies that bore them to this place, each leg that's walked in and then walked out again, taking the individual on whatever life-contour they're following. We all negotiate our way between a host of pairings that flank us, spinning our lifelines, alone, together, through the days and nights allotted to us.

The photo given to Ellie with love in 1908 was no doubt treasured by her before it ended up bundled together with miscellaneous papers in a large brown envelope, the hoarded residue of her possessions that no one really wanted, but didn't feel quite able just to throw away, even after her death. As I look at it, think of Ellie's life, remember our Sunday visits to Hunters Hall and our slow drive past the farmhouse in 2013, an image comes to mind forged from the elements of recollection and reflection. Moonlight glints off the glass eye of a stuffed snarling badger standing at the top of the back stairs at Hunters Hall. Downstairs, Ellie looks up from the book she's been reading. Tessie sits slumped in the chair beside her, gently snoring and dreaming of giving children boxes of fudge and seedcake. Twenty miles away, across the dark fields in a house in Lisburn, I'm curled in my mother's womb, a six-month-old embryo. Elsewhere in Ulster, the two men who'll be startled by my camera in half a century, as my brother and I drive past the farmyard where they'll be standing, are not yet conceived, their individuality is still waiting to be born, though the human script that has us all enmeshed within its lifelines has the raw potential already encoded from which their uniqueness, like ours, like everyone's, will be quarried. We all traverse our particular trajectories, orbit around the constellations that define us— gender, nationality, age, health, disposition—moving towards moments of encounter and separation as the planet spins and turns, laden with fossils and their progeny and buzzing with the lather of processes—photosynthesis, respiration, circulation, digestion, reproduction—that keep life happening amidst the great binaries of being and not being.

How do we add up the tally of our days, let alone compute the wider sums: Irish history, European history, global history? We forge our numbers, fetter what happens with our word-patterns, draw faces on the surfaces we encounter. But underneath the sieve of words, the sluice-work of language, all the earthworks of what's familiar, the watery tonnage of the real mocks our frail devices. Bound with the fetters of imagination, these few fragments lashed together two by two make a crude raft of intelligibility on which to float precariously across the surface of a miles-deep complexity. For within every quotidian specific—the two men in the farmyard, the two brothers in the car, the front room at Hunters Hall—the twined chasms of time and space beckon. In the crucible of their pairing is it possible to find a thread that might make sense of things—my story, my brother's, Ellie's, Tessie's, the cattle dealer's, the badger's, a piece of fudge, a furtive note sounded on a harmonium, a frog glimpsed in a well, Ireland and all her scattered sons and daughters?

Looking again at the faces of the two men I accidentally photographed, I almost feel I owe them an apology, or at least some explanation of why we were driving past so slowly, staring at the farmhouse. Perhaps the next time I'm passing I should stop, knock on the door, and tell them who I am. But I fear that whatever words I could summon might sound close to incoherent. Perhaps I should simply make a copy of these pages and mail them to Hunters Hall. But that, I imagine, would cause as much consternation as any intrusive camera. Best just to lay the notebook in which they're written beside the onyx egg, another unlikely pairing, two flints to knap and strike as I try to kindle the warmth and shape of meaning.

# SKIMMING

*L*ike swimming or riding a bicycle, skimming—in the US skipping, in parts of Ireland skiffing—a stone is a skill that, once learned, is never forgotten. Somehow, selecting the best size and shape of stone, knowing how to grip it, understanding the angle and thrust needed for a successful throw, seems to get laid down in the deep fabric of the nerves and muscles. From there it can be recalled, word perfect, even after years of desuetude. It's as if the knowledge beds into the flesh and sleeps there unnoticed, as ready to awaken when it's summoned as it is to resume its slumbers. I suspect a decade would have passed, maybe close to two, between skimming stones that morning on a remote beach on the west coast of Scotland and the last time I'd cast stones across water in this way. Yet the skill came back to me as readily as if it had been only yesterday that I'd called it into action.

Some places invite skimming more than others. On sandy beaches, stones are often so scarce that the possibility rarely presents itself. On some shingle beaches the stones, though plentiful, are either the wrong size or, if they do fit the grip, the wrong shape—rotund as eggs instead of flat as discs. Sometimes the waves are too choppy to provide a smooth enough surface. Boats, swimmers, and people fishing can create obstacles whose presence issues a prohibition, whether on the grounds of safety, courtesy, or self-consciousness. But sometimes conditions are perfect—the sea glassy calm, no one in sight, and a beach strewn with an abundant supply of flat, rounded stones that fit the hand so snugly and skitter across the water so well that they seem to have been designed precisely for this purpose. The Scottish beach I walked to recently provided all of these ideal conditions.

Why skim? The most obvious answer, and I think the right one, is simply that it's fun. The urge to skim stones is similar in kind to the desire to kick a ball or sit on a swing and swing. It's one of those uncomplicated physical activities that beckon to us with the promise of immediate satisfaction. Walking along a quiet beach where there are many good stones and no waves to speak of, I'd find it hard *not* to skim; it seems an entirely natural thing to do, no more needing of an explanation than beachcombing. Like kicking a ball or swinging, it requires no great skill. Anyone can learn to do it and when they do, it is its own small reward— an intrinsically pleasing activity that achieves nothing more than the admirable goal of passing time agreeably.

As well as simply being fun, part of the appeal of skimming lies in its appearance of doing the impossible. A thrown stone sinks in water immediately. So, to witness one skating across the surface, displaying an unlikely buoyancy as it takes a series of bouncing jumps, seems like the defiance of a natural law. Of course it isn't really. The stone will sink eventually, as soon as the momentum of the skim peters out and there's nothing left to power the continuance of that linked series of little leaps that slice across the surface like a flotilla of miniature miracles. But for the duration of its improbably graceful progress, it's as if the iron imperative of sinking has been suspended.

In addition to the lure of performing a kind of alchemy and making a stone glide across the surface instead of being swallowed by the water, transmuting the lead of its dense grounded heaviness into the gold of flight, there's the compelling nudge of an intrinsic, low-key competitiveness. Every skim competes with the one before and beckons for another try as the thrower attempts to best the number of jumps the skimmed stone takes and the distance that it travels from the shore. For reasons that I don't think I could easily explain, getting a stone to bounce seven times is far more satisfying than only achieving three bounces. Likewise a twenty-meter throw is far more rewarding than one that covers only half that distance. Could it be that such skills are a vestigial echo of the hunting prowess that allowed our species to flourish? Perhaps when we perform them well it stirs some ancient sense of aboriginal satisfaction. Certainly the pleasure of skimming seems to tap into something deeper than the activity itself can easily account for.

꒰ꕀ꒱

When I first saw my father skimming, I was entranced. My picture of that moment is of a little boy—seven at most—watching spellbound as stone after stone was made to dance across the water. Suspended in the slicing line of temporary incisions that perforated the surface, their spinning momentum let them clip the water and continue on. They commanded the gaze to follow their trajectories, as unlikely on first encounter as seeing someone walking on the water. The skite and splash of each stone as it made its journey from my father's hand to the moment when it sank acted like punctuation marks written on the blank page of the sea. They gave the impression that between them, not yet visible, there was the thread of some narrative whose sentences the skimming stones would pull out and quickly arrange into sense. I watched as carefully as I attended to the unfolding of a

story and, thinking about it now, I can see a definite conso-
nance between my father as stone-skimmer and my father
as the storyteller who lulled me to sleep at bedtime with
impromptu made-up tales that skittered their unlikely plot-
lines across the still waters of my tired child's mind every
night before sinking with me into the dream-laced deep. I'm
not sure why, but the fact that no story ever did emerge to
join the dots of dad's skimmed stones left more of a tantaliz
ing sense of something imminent, just beneath the surface,
still to come, rather than disappointment that the sea's blank
page remained inscrutable, marked only by the ripples the
stones left in their wake.

My picture of myself as a little boy watching my father
skimming puts us in Rathmullan, a village in Donegal on
the shores of Lough Swilly, on Ireland's beautiful northwest
coast. We holidayed there for two weeks every summer for
years, enjoying the contrast that this seaside haven offered to
the workaday urban world of the town near Belfast where
we lived. But memories of so long ago are suspect. Remembering bears little resemblance to the process by which a
kinesthetic skill like skimming is inscribed upon the flesh
and held there, pitch-perfect, for years. My picture of my
childhood self standing on that Donegal beach enraptured
by his father's skimming can't boast anything like the degree
of exactitude that the recall of the action itself possesses.
Such images are vulnerable to a whole series of glitches in
the genetics of their remembering. It's easy to confuse similar
times and places—maybe that first witnessing of skimming
happened not in Rathmullan but in Dunfanaghy, another
Donegal seaside village where we stayed. Perhaps I was ten,
not seven. As we look back on them, the years have a tendency to merge and blur, rather than each maintaining the
strict integrity of its twelvemonth duration. And it's hard—
perhaps impossible—to ensure that the past is preserved
intact, brought back exactly as it was, rather than being
overwritten with what happened later, or angled according

to the imperatives of the present. I suspect most memories approximate more closely to palimpsests than the original manuscripts we too often take them for.

⚜

Watching my father skimming and learning how to skim myself—through that mix of imitation and instruction by which so much passes from one generation to the next—these are memories from half a century ago. What made me think of them again was one of those occasions when the present places its steps into old footprints, reawakening them as it presses down the weight of its occurrence and leaves its own tread amidst what's already there. Nearly all the paths we follow are densely marked with the spoor of the generations before us. We add our own tracks, which will in turn be covered by whoever walks here next. Skimming stones on that deserted Scottish beach, about the same age as I remember my father being in Rathmullan when I learnt the skill from him, I'm being watched by my daughter. Like me all those years ago, she's intrigued at the way a stone can be made to do what seems impossible and is eager to learn for herself how to conjure its strange skipping progress across the water.

Together we search through the shingle for possible skimmers, selecting and discarding until we have a small heap of close-to-perfect stones. We stand side by side at the water's edge and throw, refining each attempt according to the success or failure of the one before. She alternates between observer and practitioner, between listening to advice on how to do it, watching how it's done, and attempting it herself. Gradually the blueprint is transferred, so that what became my knowledge all those years ago becomes her knowledge too. And as this happens an old truth of teaching reasserts itself—namely that the teacher also learns from what they do, so that my own skimming improved as I showed her how it's done.

Thinking about the invisible transference of what's written into my nerves and muscles to what's written into my daughter's, I wonder about the history of this process of transmission. How did it begin? Someone, somewhere must have been the world's first skimmer; an individual who discovered it independently of watching any precursor. I wonder if there was a single point of beginning, one innovative stone-thrower, a singular moment of ignition, which sparked our knowledge, a fons et origo from which all subsequent skimming was derived. It's just as likely, though, to have been a skill discovered independently, at different times and in different places, by a whole range of different hands. But whether there was just one point of genesis, or a cluster of pioneers, each sparking their own lineages of learning, the skill spread through the human tribe like rings of water moving outwards from a stone's point of impact when it's dropped into a pool. There are expressions for skimming in almost every language—their different intonations stand testament to how the skill's ripple effect has been caught and further transmitted through a score of different vocabularies. It's interesting how often the words chosen to describe a stone's jumping over water are frog-related. In languages as diverse as Bengali and Bulgarian, in regions as far apart as Eastern Europe and southern India, skimming is referred to as "frog jumps," "making frogs," or just "frogs." Ducks are another frequent point of reference—in Britain skimming is sometimes referred to as "ducks and drakes," in Polish as "letting the ducks out." The Hungarian for "skimming" means "making a stone waddle like a duck." The words we use are like little linguistic stones aping the skimming that they name as they spin their meanings from one mind to another.

I imagine some Paleolithic hunter throwing stones at ducks or geese swimming on a glassy-surfaced lake. One stone happens to catch the water at just the right angle to buoy it along a series of leaps before it sinks. Intrigued, the hunter tries again, works on the skill and slowly masters it. Or perhaps it was discovered by children playing, or by someone beachcombing who idly tossed a few stones into the sea and one of them happened not to sink immediately. Whatever its ultimate historical point—or points—of beginning, I know I learned skimming from my father in the same way that he learnt it from his. I know I taught my daughter. Based on such modest tracings back from the current endpoints of skimming's family tree, it's easy to imagine something of this skill's bloodline as it stretches back through the generations. But beyond this single thread of transmission, of which only a fragment is visible, there must be a vast capillary network of daunting complexity, a maze of multiple interconnections. Skimming's ancestry soon sees the roots of any simple family tree vanish into the mists of uncertainty as supposition and guesswork render its links increasingly tentative. In the absence of an exhaustive genealogy, knowing with certainly only a minuscule segment of its bloodline, I picture skimming as an ancient filament that's wired through the labyrinth of human being like an intricate spider's web, stretching back as far as some distant ancestor's densely haired strong arm. Or—who knows?—perhaps this skill predates the dawning of our species and has its origins in a thrower who was closer to being ape than being human.

ᴸᵞ

Thinking of the first hand to release the first skimmed stone prompts me to wonder also about the last hand that will ever be thus employed. How many more generations will the skill of skimming pass through? Of course it's as impossible to identify the last skimmer as it would be to identify the first, or to plot the where and when of such unconsciously epochal moments. But sometimes, looking at human history, looking at the present we've created, considering the damage we've inflicted on the land and sea and air around us, *Homo sapiens* seems not unlike a skimmed stone nearing the end of its momentum, a species that's petering out, victim of its own proliferation. I hope at least that my daughter will have the opportunity to pass on skimming to her children and they to theirs and the generation following. If wisdom could be passed on like skimming, wired as securely to the blood as the knowledge of how to choose and throw stones across water, perhaps the outlook for us would be better, but this hard-to-acquire accomplishment seems even harder to communicate from one generation to another.

 ⁂

When I was a boy, I liked to throw things, so—unsurprisingly—I took to skimming like a proverbial duck to water. It appealed on some visceral level that required no reflection. Doing it was unaccompanied by any thought beyond choosing the best stone, aiming the throw, counting the leaps, and assessing the distance covered so that the next skim could do better than the one before. Skimming offered mild satisfaction when it worked, mild frustration when it didn't. It was as uncomplicated, as unselfconscious an action as running or kicking a ball. But when I skimmed stones with my daughter across that Scottish bay, although the same visceral pleasure was there, it was overwritten by thoughts my boyhood self would never have entertained. They brought to skimming a more reflective turn of mind than the one that accompanied his happy-go-lucky chucking of stones across water.

I don't mean by this that I've adopted the kind of outlook that makes skimming into something serious, almost professional—more systematic, regulated, and competitive than the casual settings that, for me, have always characterized it. I know that world stone-skimming championships have been held annually since 1997 on Easdale, the smallest inhabited island of Scotland's Inner Hebrides. Competitors are judged in terms of the distance skimming takes a stone—the only stipulation being that it must bounce for a minimum of three times before sinking. A disused quarry offers a large pool of undisturbed water that's ideal for this event, as are the pieces of Easdale slate that were once taken from it. There's also a North American Stone Skipping Association (NASSA) which likewise holds competitive events, though their ranking is based on the number of skips a stone makes on the surface of the water rather than just the distance that it travels. According to *The Guinness Book of Records,* an astonishing eighty-eight skips were achieved by a skimmed stone flung by one Kurt Steiner at Red Bridge in Allegheny National Forest. Such things spark slight, wry interest, but they were far from my thoughts as I sent stones skimming across that Scottish bay.

Neither do I mean—when I say this most recent skimming prompted a more reflective turn of mind—that I focused on the physics of the process, how a skimmed stone obeys the conservation of momentum principle, acting like a kind of flying saucer that generates enough lift to skitter across the surface, its angle and thrust pressing down on the water, the gyroscopic effect of its spin setting up enough rotational velocity to cut a channel of smooth transit between air and water, an invisible flight path along which a stone rides, cushioned, until the moment when it sinks. I know that scientists have studied the process and provided detailed explanations, looked at how changes of speed, angle, and rotation affect it, offered calculations and equations to explain how skimming happens and to show its obedience to mathematical and natural laws. But I'm not any more interested in the theoretical underpinnings than I am in the competitions or the records.

Skimming stones that day with my daughter I was struck by the way in which what we were doing bore with it a symbolic significance that pointed far beyond the simple process of casting stones across water in this way. Of course it's easy to dismiss skimming as something ineluctably shallow, a mere skittering over surfaces, an action that intrinsically lacks depth. But it can also tap into other resonances of metaphor and meaning beyond these usual tropes of superficiality. As I watched the flat stones my daughter and I skimmed across the water, it struck me that our lives are skimmed across the fabric of space-time. Each individual in essence follows the same trajectory, whatever individual variations we might embroider on its underlying theme. We find ourselves thrown across an unknown number of years and only notice our whereabouts when life has already skipped some way along its span. We skitter our way precariously across our moments of existence and then vanish, sinking beneath the water of being as surely as a skimmed stone sinks once the lift of its momentum has been spent. Looking at the way in which my stones and my daughter's clipped their way across the water's surface, I had a sense—a hope—of hers continuing far beyond the point at which mine will disappear, and her offspring's throws subsequently reaching out still further, beyond whatever lifespan she'll enjoy. We skim life on from one generation to the next. Our throws, contained within the channels of embrace, follow moves wired into us as indelibly as the carnal blueprints that tell us how to walk or cry. The shudder and spurt of sperm, like shoals of skimmed stones in miniature, patter their trajectories across those secret inner seas whose tides sculpt and resculpt our flesh, our bodily forms arising from and vanishing into the waters of mortality that are streaked and pitted with our presence and our absence.

꜠

I'm not sure why skimming—once so matter-of-fact and of the moment—became that day something more symbolic. As I stood with my daughter on the shore it felt almost sacramental; as if we were engaged in a ritual that points beyond its own simple form to something far less ordinary. Perhaps it was just an upshot of the heightened sense of life's brevity and end that comes with age. For whatever reason, the innate superficiality of skimming came into different focus and the stones took on new resonances of meaning. For all the sophistication of our knowledge and technology, fundamentally there remains a sense in which we don't know who we are, or why we're here, what we should do with our time, or what happens to us when it ends. Such imponderables, life's "big questions," glazed skimming with a reflective surface so that it became a kind of metaphysical mirror reflecting the essentials of our situation. In it I could see my life skittering briefly across the surface of existence, speeding its way over incomprehensible depths until the moment when it vanishes into them, joining on a hard-to-grasp seabed of extinction the billions of other life-stones whose spin is stilled, whose flight has ended. It is a bleak enough picture. But finding such a likeness embedded in something as straightforward as skimming is also strangely satisfying. It's as if its simple fluency has caught precisely, almost without trying, the likeness of a fleeting feature in a difficult piece of portraiture.

Where, at this moment, is the first stone that was ever skimmed? Does it still exist as an identifiable whole, or has it been so eroded over the millennia that all that remains is a disparate cloud, a dust of dispersed particles? Perhaps, buried in the soft encasing mud at the bottom of an African lake, it retains its form. I imagine some great cataclysm of the earth releasing it from there, a violent hatching from its protective chrysalis, an upheaval followed by such storms and currents that it's brought at last to some distant shore, there to be picked up and flung again by the hand that casts the last skimmed stone ever to be thrown by our species. Such an unlikely closing of the loop is of course pure fantasy. The probability of such a dotting and crossing of apocalyptic "i"s and "t"s must be so close to zero as to be indistinguishable from it. I was minded to imagine this grim fantasia of the future because of a much less unlikely scenario from the past. The Scottish bay where I taught my daughter how to skim is overlooked by the ruins of an Iron Age fort. That made me wonder if its occupants had ever skimmed stones as they walked along the same beach where we searched for our stones. If so—which is surely close to certain—might the tides over the years have shuffled and returned them, so that some of those same stones were heaped in the shingle and among those chosen by us to skim again that day?

I like the thought of skimming again a stone that had been skimmed centuries ago by an unknown figure standing where I stand today. The possibility seems to kindle a sense of tribal solidarity, a feeling of connection, continuity and continuance forged by a common communion, our all taking part in a familiar human action that has remained essentially unchanged across all the changing generations. To hold in my hand a skimmer selected and thrown by a hand several thousand years ago turns an ordinary stone into a kind of talisman of the extraordinary. Under its impact I can feel my veins and arteries breaking out of their imprisonment in the individual circuitry of my body to entangle and connect with the blood that, for a moment, centuries ago, warmed this same stone that now sits in my palm. I would clutch such an artifact close, keep it with me, savor the mystery it's imbued with, a mystery in which all of us are implicated.

It seems odd that as my life draws to an end, as the skimmed stone of my being slows and falters, I'll remember the skill of how to skim a stone across water far better than I'll remember so many other things I value more. The ABC of skimming will be securely stored in the vaults that flesh and blood provide. They'll contain it, keep it safe, until they are themselves dissolved. Even if I become so feeble that I can no longer throw, even if I no longer remember my name, or recognize my children, I've every confidence that my nerves and muscles will still have laid down in their repertoire, even if I can't perform it, every step and move of skimming. The script will still be there, written into the bones, readable even if I've become blind to books and faces. And I wonder when and where my own last skimmed stone will sink and if it might in time find its way into another skimmer's hand. It's comforting to think it might, as it is to imagine that, whatever travails may await me in the years ahead, there will be others elsewhere, entirely unconcerned, idly skimming stones across water, counting the leaps, measuring the distance, trying again, deriving simple pleasure from this simple act that humans have played with for so many millennia.

# HITTING THE RIGHT NOTE

## I

*T*he choir at the boarding school I went to in Belfast had a well-deserved reputation for excellence. Among the boys, the teacher who ran it also had a reputation. Having an older brother at the school meant that, on arrival, far from being a starry-eyed ingénue, I was already in possession of sufficient local knowledge to be wary. As a result, I always gave the man as wide a berth as possible. Getting to the high standard the choristers invariably displayed involved a lot of hard work. There were benefits too—giving recitals at a local girls' school, going on tour to foreign countries, sometimes missing games or classes for singing practice. But the view among the streetwise boys was that choir was something best avoided. Only two things could save you from it: lack of musicality, or someone tipping you the wink about the proficiency test that all new boys were required to undergo.

The test involved an individual appointment in the music teacher's classroom—missed on pain of heavy punishment. He sat at the piano. You were perched, exposed and uncomfortable, on a high wooden stool pulled close beside him. He played a note and asked you to sing it, paused and played another, again asking you to match it, all the time subjecting you to intense scrutiny. He'd do this for maybe half a dozen notes, some close together on the scale, others separated by an octave. Next, he'd ask you to hold a note for as long as you were able. The ordeal culminated in having to sing along—in excruciatingly embarrassing *la-la-las*—to a simple melody he picked out on the keys.

Not wanting to be press-ganged, I hit the wrong note every time, let my voice break and quaver between discords for the held note; made my reluctant *la-la-las* falter and then meander tunelessly at varying distances from the simple path laid down by the music teacher's playing. Listening to each of my voice-shots whistling past his ears, whapping unerringly into the bull's-eye of the covert target I was aiming for, made him arch his brows and frown. At the end, he looked at me with a mixture of suspicion and contempt. I was gruffly dismissed and told to summon the next nervous candidate from the line of boys standing fidgeting in the corridor outside his classroom.

## II

There are two ironies in my deliberate botching of the test. In the way of ironies, I only became aware of their existence years later. First, I love music. Despite the music teacher's reputation as a hard taskmaster and worse, I'd probably have enjoyed singing in the choir. The main thing I hit in aiming so wide of all the prescribed marks was my own foot. Secondly, as things have turned out, I've spent a large part of my life since leaving school trying to hit the right note—albeit with words rather than music.

Botching the choir proficiency test was unexpectedly hard. It required considerable concentration to sing strategically off-target. I had to fight against a strong instinctive pull to let my voice take the directions that were indicated. In contrast, when it comes to writing, my errors are unforced; they occur quite naturally, without any effort on my part needed to produce them. The difficulty here is not making sure to shoot wide of the mark, but getting my words to fall even on the outermost rings of the targets I want to hit, let alone the bull's-eye. Often I miss by a margin of which my younger, choir-dodging self would have been proud. I can only dream of the fluency that would result if my inarticulacy was just a disguise, another deliberate deception, something I could lay aside at will and let the right words come as naturally as the right notes would have done if I'd not taken such pains to suppress them all those years ago.

# III

I was reminded of my botched choir test when I started to think about why I write. For most of my life I've just written, without thinking much about it. It's simply something that I do; part of who I am. Until now, I've not felt any great need to explain it. But I guess there comes a point at which you've spent so many hours in this way that the sheer accumulated weight of time-spent-writing acts like a forgotten batch of stocks and shares. After years of holding them they suddenly yield an unexpected dividend—paltry, nonnegotiable—in the form of a question about why you've made—and keep making—such a heavy investment in this particular sector of the market.

Trying to figure out why I write, the choir proficiency test came to mind as a kind of inverted point of reference. With writing, the world sounds its notes and I attempt to match them, try to trace out in words a faithful echo of what I hear. Where once a boy sat uncomfortably on a high wooden stool trying deliberately to pitch his voice anywhere except where it was meant to go, as a writer I try hard to ensure that what I write corresponds as exactly as possible to the siren music of existence whose notes repeatedly catch my attention.

"Let not a hair's breadth separate your mind from what you write." That comment—from Japan's great haiku poet Matsuo Basho—keeps coming back to mind. Sometimes it feels that I've spent a large portion of my life pushing against that stubborn gap, trying to close the hair's breadth, trying to secure a closer, flusher fit between what I put down on the page and whatever notes of the world's music are at that moment caught in my mind and heart, demanding that I give them voice.

I've used two vast and perhaps ridiculous-sounding generalities to get to here—"the music of existence" and "the world's music." It's time to jettison them—like those first-stage rockets whose unsubtle whoosh provides the surge of liftoff but is unsuitable for finer maneuvering. Left unqualified, the thrust of such all-encompassing locutions might be taken to imply that there's just one gigantic score and that exactly the same music falls identically on everyone's ears. To some extent, of course, that's true enough. We all feel the sun's heat on our skin; night lays its darkness upon everyone with an even hand; there's a repertoire of emotions and experiences with which all of us are familiar. We're all actors in the human drama; we know our lines, recognize the cues the other players give us, as they recognize ours in their turn. But despite such shared notes we are differently attuned—the diversities of our individuality, the varieties of our experience, mean that we hear different music. There are countless variations on the common themes.

What I feel impelled to write about reflects this ingrained mix of similarity and difference, the intertwining of what's shared with what's unique. For all that others will be able to recognize the pitch and tone of my particular notes, they neither hear them, nor could they play them, identically to me. In *The Art of Description* (2010), Mark Doty suggests that poetry is "a kind of perceptual signature, a record of an individual way of seeing." I think the same thing holds with much prose writing too. Certainly an essay can be viewed as "a vessel of individuation, a distillation of the way one person experiences the world."

# IV

What motivates one writer may be alien to another, however much they're engaged in the same basic business of arranging words into intelligible sentences. I've no wish to try to explain why others feel impelled to put pen to paper / keystroke to screen, or how they understand their craft. For my part, I know that writing involves responding to some of the music played to me and upon me. My response is spurred by a kind of instinctual prompt—some notes, the ones I want to write about, carry with them the imperative to come up with words that answer them, that provide a kind of echo on the page; something that reflects them, celebrates them, puzzles over them, encapsulates them—rather than just letting them pass by unremarked.

Presenting things thus, heavily reliant on metaphor, is quite deliberate. I do it to introduce an important theme. Like many writers, I'm drawn to making metaphors. The reason for this perhaps becomes apparent if we pause to consider what they really are. It's easy to see metaphors only in their spectral guise—ghosts of themselves denied their vividly embodied form by the dulling, toned-down definitions they're too often shackled to at school. To see a metaphor merely as a "figure of speech" is to eviscerate it and leave behind a neutered husk that drifts vaguely through the understanding, trailing unconvincing examples behind it, unanchored by the tough hawsers and weights of its vital function. In fact, as George Steiner points out (in *After Babel*), metaphors offer "new mappings of the world." They can help "organize our habitation of reality." Metaphors suggest fresh perspectives; they create different angles of alignment at which to place ourselves in relation to existence so that experience falls upon us in ways we'd not anticipated.

It's indicative of how central metaphor is to the way we think about and act in the world that George Lakoff and Mark Johnson entitled their magnum opus *Metaphors We Live By* (1980). Their title sums up the enormous conceptual, ethical, and political significance that metaphor holds. As they put it, "Metaphors are capable of giving us new understandings of our experiences." It's no wonder, then, that writers devote so much time to minting them.

But even the best metaphors lose their power with use. The traction they initially provided, in terms of getting a conceptual grip on things, wears thin and smooth and soon they spool emptily into the clichés of run-of-the-mill language, eventually falling like so much verbal drizzle. The new mappings they once offered become threadbare, commonplace; their potential to "organize our habitation of reality" gets so faded it just blends with what's routine. Sometimes I see my writing as a kind of weaving and reweaving of the fabric of language, forming it into containers made of metaphors that can hold a few embers from the fire of experience so that we can savor their warmth, examine their glow. Once the containers are incinerated—and none of them lasts long—I have to start again, weaving my word-baskets anew.

## V

Writing about Anna Akhmatova, Joseph Brodsky talks about how in her poems she tried "to make the monotone of the infinite more audible." That phrase has stuck in mind since I read Brodsky's essay "The Keening Muse" (included in his collection *Less Than One*) ten or more years ago. I don't want to comment on the way he uses it in his analysis of his countrywoman's verse, still less do I want to compare myself to a poet of Akhmatova's stature. Rather, like a magpie of words—and which writer is not?—I want to purloin this little gem of Brodsky's and use it for my own purposes.

"The monotone of the infinite" is the note I most often want to write about. Thinking about it brings back to mind again the choir proficiency test at my old school in Belfast and the music teacher asking me to hold a note for as long as I was able to. Even supposing I'd complied and honestly attempted this, I know I couldn't have sung any note beyond a minute or so at most. Picture our surprise if, after my best effort petered out, we'd both become aware of a low base note continuing, far outpacing any reasonable expectation of duration. I imagine this monotone of the infinite to be a kind of constant hum sounding behind things. We're only intermittently conscious of it. It's so much there, so much an integral part of our experience, it's easily overlooked. It wears that most effective of disguises: the camouflage of what we're used to. "Estranging the familiar"—one of the functions of art and literature—allows us to penetrate the disguise of the ordinary and not only hear this normally unnoticed note but also see how utterly extraordinary it is.

Brodsky's phrase makes me think of an unwavering note of something elemental woven invisibly into our mundane experience. The fact that it's a monotone emphasizes its sameness, the way in which, with unchanging constancy, all of our moments are underlain by the same motif of transience set amidst durations of such massive scale they do indeed seem infinite. However hard it is to remember in the midst of our daily preoccupations, we are ephemeral creatures; our presence in the world is only momentary. The vast reach of the centuries mostly contains our absence. "The infinite" reminds us that we're waifs in time and space—that however well we learn to sing the tunes of our age, however much we feel at home in our environs, we're part of a swarm of entrances into and exits out of being that dwarf us with their number and point inexorably toward vistas of a daunting scale: the eons that yawn their chasms between the birth and death of planets; the light-years that separate galaxies.

Alongside this monotone our individual notes are minuscule. Can the mystery of their brief specificity sound any sense in the echo chamber of the infinite? Can a person claim any depth of meaning for their life, or is it rather crafted and cut by mere contingency?

Another gleaming phrase that caught my magpie eye the first time I saw it, and that's now hoarded in the nest of memory alongside Brodsky's "the monotone of the infinite," is one of Alexander Smith's remarks about essay writing. In his intriguing book *Dreamthorp* (1863) Smith observes that "the world is everywhere whispering essays and one need only be the world's amanuensis." I like that "whispering"— it suggests that you've got to cock your ear to hear—and the way that "everywhere" conveys the same perpetual, but potentially invisible, constancy as Brodsky's monotone. A whispering that happens everywhere, all the time, isn't easy to detect. Being an amanuensis—scribe—suggests that there's a strong element of transcription involved in the creative process, catching the way in which writing at once echoes and responds, records and embroiders.

# VI

Trying to catch the monotone of the infinite in words, attempting to transcribe the world's whispered essays faithfully on the page, is far from easy. Somewhere in mind there's an image of what's needed, but tracing out its lineaments, matching word and image, often makes language seem like a clumsy large-meshed net employed to try to catch tiny butterflies of dazzling color, speed, and agility.

I was poised to say that I sometimes fantasize about a perfect piece of writing—one that offers flawless transcription and that sounds its words pitch-perfect with the elusive monotone that Akhmatova tried to make more audible. But "fantasize" is the wrong word. That would suggest I thought such a thing was possible to achieve, and I know it's not. A

fantasist is able, if only temporarily, to swap illusion for reality, and that's not a substitution I've ever been able to accom-
plish—at least not in the realm of writing. "Daydream"
might be better than "fantasize," but it lacks sharp edges; the
word seems swathed in billowy clouds that drift aimlessly
across one's inner skies. I'll settle for saying that I sometimes
"muse" about a perfect piece of writing. I know such a thing
is impossible to achieve. To imagine you'd found it—worse,
to imagine you'd created it—would be to settle for second
best and to hoodwink yourself about the nature of the written word and those who deal in it. Sometimes in my musing I toy with the idea of starting with something small and
utterly simple—a pebble from the beach, perhaps—and writing the perfect description of it. But I know that would soon
proliferate into numerous variations around an uncatchable
theme as the object shrugs off every attempt to pin it down
in words. Quite apart from the ordinary difficulties of finding the right words to fit what's there, to imagine that something's "utterly simple" is to start off on the wrong foot. The
pebble might sit comfortably on my palm, but the apparently
straightforward scale suggested by the ease with which it can
be picked up, held, examined, belies what it contains. Anyone foolish enough to think that they could easily transcribe
in words the essays that a pebble whispers would do well to
read Jan Zalasiewicz's book *The Planet in a Pebble* (2012), a
lyrical journey into Earth's deep history via the portals contained in an ordinary grey slate pebble found on a beach in
Wales. Zalasiewicz shows how such an object, closely examined, contains far more than we could ever say.

# VII

Musing about language that fits its subject perfectly, I'm
reminded of Rudolf Otto's speculations (in *The Idea of the
Holy*) about what he termed "original numinous sounds."
Otto noted how the Sanskrit word "ascarya"—used in the

Upanishads to try to describe moments of intense mystical experience—simply means "that in whose presence we must exclaim 'aaah!'" Otto wondered if certain types of religious experience reduce—or elevate—those undergoing them to the utterance not of perfectly fitting words, but of noises that sound in flawless synchrony with whatever sparked them. He points to the holy syllable "Om" in Hinduism and suggests that it is "a sort of growl or groan, sounding up from within as a quasi-reflex expression of profound emotion." Such utterance, he says, serves "to relieve consciousness of a felt burden," namely the pressure upon it of something rawly numinous. Otto raises the intriguing possibility that "the innumerable names of gods and demons and perhaps also the various designations for ghost, soul and spirit" may have their origins in the same kind of outbursts—sounds wrenched from us in the face of profound experiences; states of mind or being that are inexpressible beyond these visceral noises.

The kind of correspondence between experience and utterance that Otto points to might suggest a situation of seamless unity, where the noises we make contour our experience so precisely that no daylight glint of loose fit shows between them. But it is surely in that crack of daylight, the hair's breadth that Basho urges us to close (but knows we never can completely), that the miracle of language happens. Yes, we need to push for a closer and closer fit between word and world; good writing demands that. But were we able to close the gap completely, the result would be more like the kind of primal screams that Otto alludes to than anything we'd consider literate. Such closure would be no more useful than the kind of one-to-one maps ridiculed by Lewis Carroll, Josiah Royce, and Jorge Luis Borges—absurd point-for-point equivalents that merely replicate the landscape instead of mapping it.

The thing is, words never fit perfectly what we attach them to—and if they did they'd lose their power. They'd no longer be able to celebrate, explore, analyze, describe, explain, point to, and question. Instead, they'd just become a kind of howl of recognition; like echoing like. Otto's speculations on original numinous sounds show what would happen if utterance was somehow made to match actuality exactly, one fitting the other so well that they sit completely flush—no gaps, no overlaps or creases, not even the slightest wrinkle of approximation to iron out. In such circumstances, expression would be reduced to no more than a kind of ejaculation—emotionally satisfying perhaps, but bereft of all the intellectual and lyrical potential that abounds in words.

# VIII

One of the choral highlights of the year at my old school in Belfast was the carol service, just before Christmas. It began with the choristers processing through the candlelit main hall to reach the choir stalls in the chapel, singing "Once in Royal David's City" as they walked. The hall was packed with boys and their parents. There was a relaxed, end-of-term feel to the service, taken by the school's chaplain. The congregation enjoyed joining in with singing well-known carols and listening to the choir being put through its paces in some more challenging seasonal pieces.

Each November and December, the music teacher rehearsed the choir with even more then his customary rigor. We could hear them practicing their festive repertoire for weeks in advance. As the day approached, choir members were routinely taken out of class and games to go over the pieces yet again in additional rehearsals. He also took a session with the whole school. About a week before the service we were summoned to the main hall for a special practice assembly—to ensure that everyone would join in properly with the carol singing. One year, inevitably, when it came to "When shepherds watched their flocks by night," a few boys substituted the "washed their socks" version. The accompanying organ fell silent immediately, mid-verse. The music teacher rose from where he'd been sitting playing at the keyboard and strode to the front of the hall. He was in a fury. We held our corporate breath, waiting for the explosion to happen. His anger wasn't about the childish disrespect involved in substituting "washed their socks" for "watched their flocks" in what is, for all its familiarity, a religious composition. What had incensed him was what he took to be the slur cast by the miscreants on his musical abilities. "I can listen to an organ playing," he roared at us, "and identify which of its several thousand pipes isn't precisely attuned." He stared at the section of the hall from where the sock-washing version had emerged. "I've worked with full-size national orchestras and can tell when any player deviates from the score even by a fraction." He fell silent for a moment as he glared at us. "What makes you think that in a group of only two hundred boys I won't be able to pick out ANY ONE OF YOU BY NAME"—his voice had risen to a shout—"who isn't singing, or who chooses to sing his own silly version? Be warned," he looked around the hall admonishingly, "on the next run-through I'll have any boy who's not singing properly out at the front to sing it by himself. And if anyone puts in the wrong words at the carol service I'll give the names of those involved to the headmaster." I'm not sure if this was bluff, or if his hearing did possess the acuity he claimed, but what he said carried the ring of authenticity and had the impact he desired. Everyone sang properly.

As a writer, I hope I've developed a sense of when my sentences, or individual words within them, aren't properly attuned, or when, in effect, they're singing some version of their own rather than the lines I want to craft. I'm not sure if my ear is as good as the choirmaster claimed his was, but I like to think that I can spot at least most of the verbal miscreants in my prose and weed them out. And though his insistence on sheer hard work and repeated, meticulous rehearsal made no appeal to me back then, I hope these are qualities I now possess myself. Because I know with the certainty of repeated practice that it's only by drafting and redrafting that I can hope to reach that point of completion where there's a proper appreciation of the inevitability—and the desirability—of approximation; where Basho's hair's breadth has been vigorously pushed against and minimized as far as possible, but not to the extent that there's no space left for the daylight of misfit and metaphor to stream through, bright with its promise of meaning.

# Thirty-Six Ways of Looking at an Essay

*C*onsidering the essay through these multiple lenses will, I hope, help to promote a more enlightened view of the possibilities offered by this form of writing. Too often, essays are confused either with academic assignments or a form of belles-lettres whose day is done. It's a great shame that what Robert Atwan described twenty years ago as "our most dynamic literary form" (in his foreword to *The Best American Essays* 1997) continues to be dogged by these powerful misconceptions. They've resulted in too many people dismissing the essay as something of little interest, a relic occupying a literary dead-end, or a chore that belongs in the academic backwaters of student assessment. As I hope *Hummingbirds Between the Pages* shows, essays have a great deal more potential than such negative stereotypes suggest. The following thirty-six views are a parting shot—or fusillade—against these commonly encountered misperceptions of the genre.

1. An essay richly complicates the commonplace, revealing mazes of meaning coiled within the mundane.

2. An essay is a net for catching butterfly moments as they fly past us; it allows us to examine them more closely.

3. An essay remains true to its etymological springs—*essai, essayer, assay* (attempt, experiment, weigh up, test, investigate)—even though its waters have flowed far beyond them.

4. An essay is a listening device that allows us to hear extracts from the music playing in another person's head.

5. An essay is a way of carving out with words some semblance of the things that have caught the essayist's attention.

6. An essay picks out threads of meaning from the fabric of existence.

7. An essay is a borehole in the dry dirt of the ordinary. When it works, it floods us with unexpected artesian water.

8. An essay seeks its quarry from the herds of ideas wandering the mind's savannahs.

9. An essay interrupts the silence with an individual's voice speaking briefly, intimately about what it's seen.

10. An essay is a verbal lens ground and polished to the focal length of a particular personality's outlook.

11. An essay is a report from the crow's nest of the self; it tells us about the view and the viewer.

12. An essay attempts in words what a mind attempts in thoughts.

13. An essay records a beachcomber's finds as s/he wanders a particular stretch of time's shoreline.

14. An essay constructs permeable enclosures through whose word-walls momentarily captive ideas can freely pass and intermix.

15. An essay is a short prose track that simultaneously leads into the mind of the essayist and whatever aspect of the world that mind is engaged with.

16. An essay is as far removed from a scholarly article as a sonnet is from a butcher's cleaver.

17. An essay is poetic prose tuned to follow the gradients of the essayist's experience, close-shadowing the twists and turns of thought and feeling. It is a contour map of consciousness in words.

18. An essay is a considered composition that applies the high polish of fluency to the raw inarticulacy of immediate impressions.

19. An essay does in words what music does in notes.

20. An essay is an extended signature spelling out the essayist's name and identity.

21. An essay arranges words with one eye on sense, one eye on style, and a third eye on wisdom.

22. An essay is a literary electrocardiogram that traces out in words the pulse of thoughts.

23. An essay knocks the flints of words together over the tinder of experience and blows on the sparks.

24. An essay's short filaments of prose shine the light of reflection into overlooked places.

25. An essay eavesdrops on consciousness.

26. An essay leaves a fractional record of one individual's fleeting moments of being.

27. An essay is a distillation of one voice; it offers at a higher proof than the liquor of ordinary diction what might be said in conversation between friends.

28. An essay is a carefully worked prose map whose lines and shadings show aspects both of the landscape under scrutiny and of the scrutinizing cartographer.

29. An essay casts word-bait on the mind's waters and sometimes gets a bite.

30. An essay pulls into the light of attention commonplace things that are generally consigned to the dusk of being scarcely noticed.

31. An essay is a path, usually meandering, to a false summit from which higher peaks can always be seen.

32. An essay is a fragment of prose infused with ideas and individuality.

33. An essay isn't amenable to definition or summary, doesn't follow a blueprint of progression, and may not arrive at any clear conclusions; it leans more toward heresy than orthodoxy, prefers meanders to straight lines, favors digression, eccentricity—and yet is lucid, focused, and well planned.

34. An essay tries to lure verbal coherence out of the chaos of experience.

35. An essay opens veins in the body of meaning and writes with what bleeds from them before the clots of convention form.

36. An essay is a witness statement that testifies to what it's like to be alive.

꒦

I like the fact that Hokusai's famous *Thirty-Six Views of Mount Fuji* in fact contains forty-six prints. It's likewise pleasing that, far from thinking he'd completed his take on Japan's sacred mountain with this series, he went on to create *One Hundred Views of Mount Fuji* (a magnificent work which contains 102 depictions). These repeated attempts to catch the same subject underscore the fact that it's impossible to exhaust its potential; there are an uncountable number of ways in which Mount Fuji might be pictured. In the same way, it would be foolish to think that we'd seen everything there is to see about the essay in the views of it I've suggested here. The essence of the genre—if it has an essence—can't be captured in thirty-six views, still less in any single definition. This is a richly protean literary form; by nature it's resistant to attempts at systematization or regulation. Even if my thirty-six views were multiplied tenfold, it still wouldn't give a perfect 360-degree perspective that ringed the essay round, containing it within a stockade of complete control and circumscription. Such multiple efforts, like the thirty-six I've offered, would simply lay down more paths of meandering circumambulation. These might reveal further nuances, angles, aspects, currents, emphases, features, trends, and tendencies—but they could never completely contain or encapsulate the essay. It will always remain possible to create another view. The more views we can formulate and consider, the better chance we have of deepening our appreciation of this mercurial mode of writing. But to take any of them as offering the last word on the matter would be to misunderstand its nature completely; it would be as misguided as supposing that, after Hokusai, there is no view that could be drawn that would enhance the way we see Mount Fuji, or believing that there are only thirteen ways of looking at a blackbird—or a hummingbird.

# ACKNOWLEDGMENTS

"*A*nyone who can look attentively, think freely, and write clearly can be an essayist; no other qualifications are needed." The words are Graham Good's—one of the key modern authorities on the genre—and for me they identify much of the appeal of this form of writing.

I'd like to thank the many people who have helped me to hone my looking, thinking, and writing into a form that might at least approximate to the demanding ideals Good lays down. Friends, family, teachers, students, unmet correspondents, and of course a whole legion of books have been helpful in this regard over the years.

Versions of many of the essays in *Hummingbirds Between the Pages* have been published singly. Thank you to the *Dundee University Review of the Arts, Earthlines, Green Mountains Review, Hippocampus, Hotel Amerika, New Hibernia Review, Southwest Review, Tahoma Literary Review, The Dalhousie Review, The Literary Review,* and *World Literature Today.* I'm grateful to the editors of these journals not only for allowing me to reprint the essays here but also for providing valuable encouragement along the way.

Any contemporary essayist owes a debt of gratitude to Robert Atwan for his stalwart support of the form over so many years. As series editor of *The Best American Essays* he has produced an ongoing showcase of fine writing which has done much to kindle, maintain, and develop public interest in the genre. He has also been generously supportive of my writing. Thank you, Bob, for all your encouragement.

*Hummingbirds Between the Pages* was largely written during the time I was a Royal Literary Fund Fellow, first at the University of Dundee and then at Queen Margaret University, Edinburgh. Not only has the RLF Fellowship provided the kind of financial security writers rarely enjoy, but the way in which the scheme is operated does much to bolster a writer's sense of literary self-worth. Under the deft but light-touch leadership of Steve Cook and David Swinburne, the Fellowship offers a wonderfully supportive milieu in which to work. Steve and David have, I suspect, played a significant role in moving many books toward publication. I'm grateful for the part they've played in doing so with this one.

Without the good offices of Kristen Elias Rowley and her staff at The Ohio State University Press, *Hummingbirds Between the Pages* would never have seen the light of day. I'm grateful for all the care, patience, and professionalism they've brought to the making of this book. I likewise appreciate the input of David Lazar and Patrick Madden, both for initiating "21st Century Essays" and for accepting this book into the series.

Writing claims time in abundance and requires extensive periods of quiet and solitude. I'm grateful to Jane, Lucy, and Laura for putting up with the demands my books make on them and for good-humoredly accommodating into the routines of family life the not always easy presence of an essayist. Their support is invaluable. I hope I never take it for granted.

"At the heart of the essay," says Graham Good, "is the voice of the individual." If that voice speaks only after looking attentively, thinking freely, and writing clearly, what it says should be worth listening to. But of course Good's essayistic virtues are easier to state than put into practice. If my looking sometimes seems lazy, my thinking imprisoned in assumption, or my writing lacking in clarity, these and any other failings are the sole responsibility of the individual voice speaking in these pages.

## 21ST CENTURY ESSAYS
David Lazar and Patrick Madden, Series Editors

This series from Mad Creek Books is a vehicle to discover, publish, and promote some of the most daring, ingenious, and artistic nonfiction. This is the first and only major series that announces its focus on the essay—a genre whose plasticity, timelessness, popularity, and centrality to nonfiction writing make it especially important in the field of nonfiction literature. In addition to publishing the most interesting and innovative books of essays by American writers, the series publishes extraordinary international essayists and reprint works by neglected or forgotten essayists, voices that deserve to be heard, revived, and reprised. The series is a major addition to the possibilities of contemporary literary nonfiction, focusing on that central, frequently chimerical, and invariably supple form: The Essay.